The Ultimate Tower Air Fryer Cookbook

....

365 Healthy and Affordable Air Fryer Recipes for Beginners and Advanced Users, with Tips & Tricks.

Rosemary West

Copyright © 2023 by   All rights reserved.

The content contained within this book may not be reproduced, duplicated, or transmitted without direct written permission from the author or the publisher. Under no circumstances will any blame or legal responsibility be held against the publisher, or author, for any damages, reparation, or monetary loss due to the information contained within this book, either directly or indirectly.

Legal Notice: This book is copyright protected. It is only for personal use. You cannot amend, distribute, sell, use, quote or paraphrase any part, or the content within this book, without the consent of the author or publisher.

Disclaimer Notice: Please note the information contained within this document is for educational and entertainment purposes only. All effort has been executed to present accurate, up to date, reliable, complete information. No warranties of any kind are declared or implied. Readers acknowledge that the author is not engaged in the rendering of legal, financial, medical, or professional advice. The content within this book has been derived from various sources. Please consult a licensed professional before attempting any techniques outlined in this book. By reading this document, the reader agrees that under no circumstances is the author responsible for any losses, direct or indirect, that are incurred as a result of the use of the information contained within this document, including, but not limited to, errors, omissions, or inaccuracies.

Table of Contents

Table of Contents 3

Chapter 1: Introduction 7
Tower Air Frying vs. Deep Frying: 7
Benefits of Tower Air Frying: 7
Functions of a Tower Air Fryer: 7
Tips on How to Use a Tower Air Fryer: 8
Cleaning and Maintenance of a Tower Air Fryer: 8

Chapter 2: Measurement Conversions 9
BASIC KITCHEN CONVERSIONS & EQUIVALENTS 9

Chapter 3: Bread And Breakfast Recipes 10
Classic Cinnamon Rolls 11
Banana-pecan French Toast 11
Chicken Saltimbocca Sandwiches 11
Cajun Breakfast Potatoes 11
Parsley Egg Scramble With Cottage Cheese ... 12
Shakshuka-style Pepper Cups 12
Salmon And Brown Rice Frittata 12
Sweet Potato & Mushroom Hash 12
Cranberry Beignets 12
Apricot-cheese Mini Pies 13
Mashed Potato Taquitos With Hot Sauce 13
Awesome Everything Bagels 13
Apple-cinnamon-walnut Muffins 13
Soufflé 14
Chorizo Sausage & Cheese Balls 14
Buttery Scallops 14
Smoked Fried Tofu 14
Cheddar Tater Tot With Sausage 15
Creamy Cinnamon Rolls 15
Bacon Puff Pastry Pinwheels 15
Baked Eggs With Bacon-tomato Sauce 15
Viking Toast 16
Sweet-hot Pepperoni Pizza 16
Blueberry Pannenkoek (dutch Pancake) 16
Egg & Bacon Toasts 17
Banana-strawberry Cakecups 17
Cream Cheese Danish 17
Cinnamon Rolls 17
Egg & Bacon Pockets 17
Crispy Fish Sticks 18
Southwest Cornbread 18
Strawberry Pastry 18
Green Onion Pancakes 19
Mushroom And Asparagus Frittata 19
Avocado Quesadillas 19

Chapter 4: Appetizers And Snacks Recipes 20
Root Vegetable Crisps 21
Garlic Mushroom Bites 21
Tortilla Chips 21
Air Fried Pot Stickers 21
Plantain Chips 21
Parmesan Cabbage Chips 22
Chinese-style Potstickers 22
Home-style Taro Chips 22
Baked Ricotta 22
Panko-breaded Onion Rings 22
Crab-stuffed Mushrooms 23
Stuffed Mushrooms With Bacon 23
Bbq Cocktail Sausage 23
Bacon-wrapped Onion Rings 23
Roasted Nut Mixture 23
Crunchy Spicy Chickpeas 24
Crispy Old Bay Chicken Wings 24
Cheesy Jalapeño Poppers 24
Cheesy Tortellini Bites 24
Honey-mustard Chicken Wings 24
Roasted Red Salsa 25
String Bean Fries 25
Veggie Salmon Nachos 25
Bacon-wrapped Jalapeño Poppers 25
Veggie Chips 25
Bacon-wrapped Goat Cheese Poppers 26
Crunchy Zucchini Fries With Parmesan 26
Tomato & Halloumi Bruschetta 26
Jalapeño Cheese Balls 26
Deviled Eggs With Ricotta 27
Garlic Edamame 27
Rumaki 27
Easy Crispy Prawns 27
Parmesan Breaded Zucchini Chips 27
Cheesy Green Dip 28
Potato Skin Bites 28
Corn With Coriander And Parmesan Cheese 28
Crispy Bacon Strips 28
Spicy Turkey Meatballs 29
Spicy Chickpeas With Paprika 29
Pesto Bruschetta 29
Buffalo French Fries 29
Air Fried Pork With Fennel 29
Classic Chicken Wings 29
Avocado Egg Rolls 30
Grilled Cheese Sandwich Deluxe 30

The Ultimate Tower Air Fryer Cookbook

Cauliflower Wings With Buffalo Sauce 30
Antipasto-stuffed Cherry Tomatoes 30
Fried Cheese Ravioli With Marinara Sauce 31
Air Fry Bacon 31
Buffalo Cauliflower Snacks 31

Chives Meatballs 31
Savory Eggplant Fries 31
Greek Street Tacos 32
Garlic Parmesan Kale Chips 32

Chapter 5: Fish And Seafood Recipes 33

Very Easy Lime-garlic Shrimps 34
French Grouper Nicoise 34
Chili-lime Shrimp 34
Horseradish-crusted Salmon Fillets 34
Cilantro Sea Bass 34
Peppery Tilapia Roulade 34
Coriander Cod And Green Beans 35
Stevia Cod 35
Bang Bang Shrimp 35
Snapper Fillets With Thai Sauce 35
Halibut Soy Treat With Rice 35
Chinese Firecracker Shrimp 36
Cornmeal Shrimp Po'boy 36
Cajun Lobster Tails 36
Oyster Shrimp With Fried Rice 36
Almond-crusted Fish 37
Salmon On Bed Of Fennel And Carrot 37
Zesty Garlic Scallops 37
Pasta Shrimp 37
Kid´s Flounder Fingers 37
Honey Pecan Shrimp 38
King Prawns Al Ajillo 38
Shrimp Al Pesto 38
Garlic Salmon Patties 38
Bean Burritos With Cheddar Cheese 38
Snow Crab Legs 39
Yummy Salmon Burgers With Salsa Rosa 39
Air Fried Calamari 39

Mojo Sea Bass 39
Garlic-lemon Scallops 39
Speedy Shrimp Paella 40
Coconut Shrimp 40
Delicious Grouper Filets 40
Crab Cakes On A Budget 40
Simple Salmon 41
Trimmed Mackerel With Spring Onions 41
Korean-style Fried Calamari 41
Almond Topped Trout 41
Flavor Moroccan Harissa Shrimp 41
Zesty Mahi Mahi 42
Fried Catfish Fillets 42
Autenthic Greek Fish Pitas 42
Crispy Fish Tacos 42
Catfish Fillets With Tortilla Chips 43
Fish-in-chips 43
Pecan-crusted Tilapia 43
Lemon Jumbo Scallops 43
Cajun Fish Cakes 44
Snapper Scampi 44
Baltimore Crab Cakes 44
Five Spice Red Snapper With Green Onions And Orange
Salsa 44
Basil Crab Cakes With Fresh Salad 45
Country Shrimp "boil" 45
Maple Balsamic Glazed Salmon 45
Southwestern Prawns With Asparagus 45

Chapter 6: Poultry Recipes 46

Cheddar Chicken Stuffed Mushrooms 47
Marjoram Butter Chicken 47
Chicken Breast Burgers 47
Buffalo Egg Rolls 47
Rosemary Partridge 48
Spinach And Feta Stuffed Chicken Breasts 48
Chicken Pesto Pizzas 48
Maewoon Chicken Legs 48
Turkey And Cranberry Quesadillas 49
Simple Grilled Chicken 49
Herb-buttermilk Chicken Breast 49
Popcorn Chicken Tenders With Vegetables 49
Chicken Tenderloins With Parmesan Cheese 49
Healthy Chicken With Veggies 50
Chipotle Drumsticks 50
Chicken Burgers With Ham And Cheese 50
Easy Turkey Meatballs 50
Sweet Marinated Chicken Wings 51
Chicken Cordon Bleu 51
Simple & Delicious Chicken Wings 51
Jerk Chicken Kebabs 51
Garlic-roasted Chicken With Creamer Potatoes 52

Lemon Herb Whole Cornish Hen 52
Gluten-free Nutty Chicken Fingers 52
Ham And Cheese Stuffed Chicken Burgers 52
Israeli Chicken Schnitzel 53
Nacho Chicken Fries 53
Flavorful Chicken With Bacon 53
Betty's Baked Chicken 54
Herbs Chicken Drumsticks With Tamari Sauce 54
Fiesta Chicken Plate 54
Seasoned Chicken Thighs With Italian Herbs 54
Ginger Turmeric Chicken Thighs 54
Mediterranean Fried Chicken 55
French Mustard Chicken Thighs 55
Grilled Chicken Legs With Coconut Cream 55
Crispy Cordon Bleu 55
Tandoori Chicken 56
Chicago-style Turkey Meatballs 56
Windsor´s Chicken Salad 56
Glazed Chicken Thighs 56
Parmesan Chicken Fingers 56
Cajun Chicken Drumsticks 57
Homemade Chicken Sliders 57

Flavorful Spiced Chicken Pieces 57	Family Chicken Fingers 59
Paprika Chicken Drumettes 57	Jerk Turkey Meatballs 59
Mumbai Chicken Nuggets 58	Rosemary Chicken With Sweet Potatoes 59
The Ultimate Chicken Bulgogi 58	Buffalo Chicken Meatballs 59
Turkey Stuffed Bell Peppers 58	Chicken Burgers With Blue Cheese Sauce 60
Daadi Chicken Salad 58	

Chapter 7: Beef, pork & Lamb Recipes **61**

Mozzarella-stuffed Meatloaf 62	Horseradish Mustard Pork Chops 69
Rice And Meatball Stuffed Bell Peppers 62	Pepperoni Pockets 70
Pork And Pinto Bean Gorditas 62	Lollipop Lamb Chops 70
Mustard Pork Tenderloin With Ground Walnuts 63	Meat Loaves 70
Roasted Pork Tenderloin 63	Marinated Flank Steak 70
Pork & Beef Egg Rolls 63	Roast Beef 71
Flank Steaks With Capers 63	Marinated Pork Tenderloin 71
Pork Sausage Bacon Rolls 64	Avocado Buttered Flank Steak 71
Tamari-seasoned Pork Strips 64	Mini Meatloaves With Pancetta 71
Beef Cheeseburger Egg Rolls 64	Sage Pork With Potatoes 71
Kale And Beef Omelet 64	Balsamic London Broil 72
Meatloaf With Tangy Tomato Glaze 65	Hungarian Pork Burgers 72
Cheeseburger Sliders With Pickle Sauce 65	Beef Brazilian Empanadas 72
Flavorsome Onion And Sausage Balls 65	Polish Beef Sausage With Worcestershire Sauce 72
Honey-sriracha Pork Ribs 65	Best Damn Pork Chops 72
Roast Beef With Herbs 66	Paprika Pork Chops 73
Blackberry Bbq Glazed Country-style Ribs 66	Maple'n Soy Marinated Beef 73
Balsamic Beef & Veggie Skewers 66	French-style Steak Salad 73
Easy Tex-mex Chimichangas 66	Homemade Steak 73
Delicious Pork Shoulder With Molasses Sauce 67	Pork Chops 73
Tender Country Ribs 67	Garlic Lamb Rack 74
Spiced Rib Eye Steak 67	Classic Salisbury Steak Burgers 74
Parmesan Sausage Meatballs 67	Tonkatsu 74
Better-than-chinese-take-out Sesame Beef 68	Stuffed Cabbage Rolls 74
Fried Spam 68	Pepperoni And Bell Pepper Pockets 75
Spicy Hoisin Bbq Pork Chops 69	Cheese Ground Pork 75
Greek-style Pork Stuffed Jalapeño Poppers 69	Carne Asada Tacos 75
Marinated Beef And Vegetable Stir Fry 69	

Chapter 8: Vegetarians Recipes **76**

Pizza Eggplant Rounds 77	Powerful Jackfruit Fritters 80
Caramelized Brussels Sprout 77	Stuffed Mushrooms 80
Chili Tofu & Quinoa Bowls 77	Skewered Corn In Air Fryer 80
Tropical Salsa 77	Vegetarian Eggplant "pizzas" 80
Pizza Margherita With Spinach 77	Italian Stuffed Bell Peppers 81
Easy Zucchini Lasagna Roll-ups 78	Roasted Green Beans 81
Cauliflower Steaks Gratin 78	Roasted Vegetable, Brown Rice
General Tso's Cauliflower 78	And Black Bean Burrito 81
Vegan Buddha Bowls(2) 78	Crustless Spinach And Cheese Frittata 81
Cauliflower Rice–stuffed Peppers 79	Home-style Cinnamon Rolls 81
Cheese Ravioli 79	Chive Potato Pierogi 82
Asparagus, Mushroom And Cheese Soufflés 79	Spaghetti Squash And Kale Fritters With Pomodoro
Thyme Lentil Patties 79	Sauce 82
Garlic Okra Chips 80	

Chapter 9: Vegetable Side Dishes Recipes **83**

Saltine Wax Beans 84	Gorgonzola Mushrooms With Horseradish Mayo 85
Beef Stuffed Bell Peppers 84	Chili Fingerling Potatoes 85
Roasted Lemony Broccoli 84	Balsamic Stuffed Mushrooms 85
Beef Stuffed Bell Pepper 84	Rutabaga Fries 85
Crispy Tofu With Soy Sauce 84	Simple Green Bake 85

The Ultimate Tower Air Fryer Cookbook

Cauliflower Fried Rice 86
Cheesy Cauliflower Tots 86
Basmati Risotto 86
Green Beans 86
Sweet Potato Curly Fries 86
Truffle Vegetable Croquettes 87
Fried Green Tomatoes With Sriracha Mayo 87
Cheese Broccoli With Basil 87
Broccoli With Paprika 88
Cheesy Cauliflower Tart 88
Smashed Fried Baby Potatoes 88
Potato And Broccoli With Tofu Scramble 88
Garlic Asparagus With Provolone 88
Fried Green Tomatoes 89
Turmeric Tofu Cubes 89
Chili-oiled Brussels Sprouts 89
Citrusy Brussels Sprouts 89
Mexican-style Roasted Corn 89
Roasted Yellow Squash And Onions 90
Tomato Salad 90
Creamy And Cheesy Spinach 90
Kale And Brussels Sprouts 90
Awesome Mushroom Tots 90
Polenta 91
Stuffed Avocados 91
Quick Air Fried Potatoes 91
Vegetable Fried Rice 91
Zucchini Tots With Mozzarella 91
Brussels Sprouts 91
Creole Seasoned Okra 92
Creamy Corn Casserole 92
Famous Potato Au Gratin 92
Chinese Cabbage With Bacon 92
Healthy Caprese Salad 92
Panzanella Salad With Crispy Croutons 93
Marinara Pepperoni Mushroom Pizza 93
Breadcrumb Crusted Agnolotti 93
Air Fried Bell Peppers With Onion 93
Pork Tenderloin Salad 93
Cheese & Bacon Pasta Bake 94
Provence French Fries 94
Fried Pickles With Mayo Sauce 94
Tamari Green Beans 94
Home Fries 94
Southwest-style Corn Cobs 95

Chapter 10: Desserts And Sweets Recipes 96

Nutty Fudge Muffins 97
Fudgy Brownie Cake 97
Black Forest Pies 97
Chocolate Rum Brownies 97
Vanilla Banana Puffs 98
Fluffy Orange Cake 98
Banana Chips With Chocolate Glaze 98
Creamy Pudding 98
Donuts With Cardamom 98
Thumbprint Sugar Cookies 99
Brownies For Two 99
Pumpkin Almond Flour Muffins 99
Merengues 99
Apple-cinnamon Hand Pies 99
Banana Bread Cake 100
Keto Butter Balls 100
Enticing Cappuccino Muffins 100
Vanilla Cookies 101
Coconut Cheese Muffins 101
Brownies With White Chocolate 101
Peanut Cookies 101
Air-fried Beignets 101
Chocolate Bars 102
Spiced Fruit Skewers 102
Puff Pastry Apples 102
Applesauce And Chocolate Brownies 102
Banana-lemon Bars 103
Oatmeal And Carrot Cookie Cups 103
Cauliflower Rice Plum Pudding 103
Cinnamon And Pecan Pie 103

Recipes Index 104

Chapter 1: Introduction

In the world of modern kitchen appliances, Tower has established itself as a prominent brand known for innovation, quality, and efficiency. One of its standout offerings in the realm of cooking technology is the Tower Air Fryer. This remarkable appliance has taken the culinary world by storm, revolutionizing the way we prepare and enjoy our favorite dishes. In this comprehensive guide, we will delve into the Tower Air Fryer, exploring its features, benefits, functions, usage tips, and maintenance techniques.

Tower Air Frying vs. Deep Frying:
Before we dive into the specifics of the Tower Air Fryer, let's first understand the fundamental difference between air frying and deep frying. Traditional deep frying involves submerging food in a large quantity of hot oil. While this method undeniably produces crispy and indulgent results, it comes with several downsides, such as excessive oil absorption, calorie-dense meals, and potential health risks associated with consuming too much fried food.

On the other hand, Tower Air Frying is a revolutionary cooking technique that uses hot air to circulate around the food, creating a crispy exterior with minimal oil. In fact, Tower Air Fryers typically require just a fraction of the oil used in traditional deep frying, making it a healthier alternative. The result? Crispy, golden-brown delights that retain the delicious flavors and textures we love, all while reducing the negative health impacts of excessive oil consumption.

Benefits of Tower Air Frying:
1. Healthier Eating:
One of the most significant advantages of using a Tower Air Fryer is the promotion of healthier eating habits. By requiring minimal oil to achieve that coveted crispy texture, this appliance allows you to enjoy your favorite fried foods with significantly reduced fat content. This translates to fewer calories and a lower risk of heart-related issues, making it an ideal choice for those who want to maintain a balanced diet without sacrificing taste.

2. Versatility:
Tower Air Fryers are incredibly versatile appliances that can do much more than just fry. They can also bake, roast, grill, and even reheat food efficiently. This versatility means you can use your Tower Air Fryer for a wide range of recipes, from crispy French fries to tender roasted vegetables and succulent grilled chicken.

3. Time Efficiency:
Tower Air Fryers are designed to save you time in the kitchen. They preheat quickly, and their rapid air circulation ensures even cooking and faster cooking times compared to traditional ovens. This means you can whip up a delicious meal in less time, perfect for busy individuals and families.

4. Easy Cleanup:
Say goodbye to the hassle of dealing with a pot of hot oil and the greasy aftermath of deep frying. Tower Air Fryers are easy to clean, with removable, dishwasher-safe parts. This not only simplifies the cleanup process but also encourages you to use your appliance more frequently.

5. Energy Efficiency:
Tower Air Fryers are energy-efficient appliances, requiring less power than conventional ovens and stovetops. This means you can cook your favorite dishes while reducing your energy consumption, contributing to a greener and more sustainable kitchen.

Functions of a Tower Air Fryer:
Tower Air Fryers come equipped with a variety of functions and features that make them versatile and user-friendly:

1. Temperature Control:

The Ultimate Tower Air Fryer Cookbook

You can adjust the cooking temperature to suit your recipe's requirements. This feature ensures precise cooking, allowing you to achieve the perfect results every time.

2. Timer:
The built-in timer lets you set the cooking duration, preventing overcooking or burning. Once the timer reaches zero, the Tower Air Fryer automatically turns off, ensuring your food is cooked to perfection.

3. Cooking Presets:
Many Tower Air Fryers come with pre-programmed cooking presets for popular dishes like French fries, chicken wings, and fish. These presets take the guesswork out of cooking and make it incredibly convenient to prepare your favorite meals.

4. Rapid Air Circulation:
The unique design of Tower Air Fryers ensures that hot air circulates rapidly around your food, cooking it evenly and efficiently. This technology eliminates the need for flipping or stirring during the cooking process.

Tips on How to Use a Tower Air Fryer:
To make the most of your Tower Air Fryer and achieve consistently delicious results, consider the following tips:

1. Preheat:
Preheating your Tower Air Fryer for a few minutes before adding your food helps ensure even cooking and a crispier texture.

2. Use the Right Amount of Oil:
While Tower Air Fryers require less oil than traditional frying methods, a light coating of oil can enhance the flavor and texture of your dishes. Use an oil spray or a brush to apply a thin layer to your food.

3. Avoid Overcrowding:
To allow proper air circulation, avoid overcrowding the fryer basket. Cook food in batches if necessary, ensuring each piece has enough space to cook evenly.

4. Shake or Flip:
For recipes that benefit from even browning, like French fries or chicken wings, consider shaking the basket or flipping the food halfway through the cooking time.

5. Check for Doneness:
Use a food thermometer or perform a visual check to ensure your food is cooked to the desired level of doneness. Different foods have different recommended internal temperatures, so be sure to consult a cooking guide or recipe for guidance.

Cleaning and Maintenance of a Tower Air Fryer:
Proper cleaning and maintenance are essential for keeping your Tower Air Fryer in optimal working condition. Here's how to care for your appliance:

1. Unplug and Cool Down:
Always unplug your Tower Air Fryer and allow it to cool down before starting the cleaning process. Safety should be a top priority.

2. Remove and Clean Removable Parts:
Most Tower Air Fryers have removable components like the fryer basket and pan. Remove these parts and wash them with warm, soapy water. They are usually dishwasher-safe for added convenience.

3. Wipe Down the Interior:
Use a damp cloth or sponge to wipe down the interior of the fryer. Be gentle and avoid abrasive materials to prevent damage.

4. Clean the Exterior:
Wipe the exterior of the Tower Air Fryer with a damp cloth to remove any grease or food residue. Ensure that the control panel remains dry to prevent electrical issues.

5. Regular Maintenance:
Check the user manual for any specific maintenance recommendations from the manufacturer. This may include inspecting the heating element or other internal components periodically.

In conclusion, the Tower Air Fryer is a game-changer in the world of healthy cooking, offering numerous benefits over traditional deep frying methods. With its versatility, time efficiency, and energy-saving features, it has become a must-have kitchen appliance for health-conscious individuals and food enthusiasts alike. By following the tips for usage and proper cleaning and maintenance, you can ensure that your Tower Air Fryer continues to deliver delicious, crispy results for years to come. Say goodbye to the guilt of indulging in your favorite fried dishes and embrace a healthier, more convenient way of cooking with the Tower Air Fryer..

Chapter 2: Measurement Conversions

BASIC KITCHEN CONVERSIONS & EQUIVALENTS

DRY MEASUREMENTS CONVERSION CHART
3 TEASPOONS = 1 TABLESPOON = 1/16 CUP
6 TEASPOONS = 2 TABLESPOONS = 1/8 CUP
12 TEASPOONS = 4 TABLESPOONS = 1/4 CUP
24 TEASPOONS = 8 TABLESPOONS = 1/2 CUP
36 TEASPOONS = 12 TABLESPOONS = 3/4 CUP
48 TEASPOONS = 16 TABLESPOONS = 1 CUP

METRIC TO US COOKING CONVERSIONS
OVEN TEMPERATURES
120 °C = 250 °F
160 °C = 320 °F
180° C = 360 °F
205 °C = 400 °F
220 °C = 425 °F

LIQUID MEASUREMENTS CONVERSION CHART
8 FLUID OUNCES = 1 CUP = 1/2 PINT = 1/4 QUART
16 FLUID OUNCES = 2 CUPS = 1 PINT = 1/2 QUART
32 FLUID OUNCES = 4 CUPS = 2 PINTS = 1 QUART = 1/4 GALLON
128 FLUID OUNCES = 16 CUPS = 8 PINTS = 4 QUARTS
= 1 GALLON

BAKING IN GRAMS
1 CUP FLOUR = 140 GRAMS
1 CUP SUGAR = 150 GRAMS
1 CUP POWDERED SUGAR = 160 GRAMS
1 CUP HEAVY CREAM = 235 GRAMS

VOLUME
1 MILLILITER = 1/5 TEASPOON
5 ML = 1 TEASPOON
15 ML = 1 TABLESPOON
240 ML = 1 CUP OR 8 FLUID OUNCES
1 LITER = 34 FL. OUNCES

WEIGHT
1 GRAM = .035 OUNCES
100 GRAMS = 3.5 OUNCES
500 GRAMS = 1.1 POUNDS
1 KILOGRAM = 35 OUNCES

US TO METRIC COOKING CONVERSIONS
1/5 TSP = 1 ML
1 TSP = 5 ML
1 TBSP = 15 ML
1 FL OUNCE = 30 ML
1 CUP = 237 ML
1 PINT (2 CUPS) = 473 ML
1 QUART (4 CUPS) = .95 LITER
1 GALLON (16 CUPS) = 3.8 LITERS
1 OZ = 28 GRAMS
1 POUND = 454 GRAMS

BUTTER
1 CUP BUTTER = 2 STICKS = 8 OUNCES = 230 GRAMS = 8 TABLESPOONS

WHAT DOES 1 CUP EQUAL
1 CUP = 8 FLUID OUNCES
1 CUP = 16 TABLESPOONS
1 CUP = 48 TEASPOONS
1 CUP = 1/2 PINT
1 CUP = 1/4 QUART
1 CUP = 1/16 GALLON
1 CUP = 240 ML

BAKING PAN CONVERSIONS
1 CUP ALL-PURPOSE FLOUR = 4.5 OZ
1 CUP ROLLED OATS = 3 OZ 1 LARGE EGG = 1.7 OZ
1 CUP BUTTER = 8 OZ 1 CUP MILK = 8 OZ
1 CUP HEAVY CREAM = 8.4 OZ
1 CUP GRANULATED SUGAR = 7.1 OZ
1 CUP PACKED BROWN SUGAR = 7.75 OZ
1 CUP VEGETABLE OIL = 7.7 OZ
1 CUP UNSIFTED POWDERED SUGAR = 4.4 OZ

BAKING PAN CONVERSIONS
9-INCH ROUND CAKE PAN = 12 CUPS
10-INCH TUBE PAN =16 CUPS
11-INCH BUNDT PAN = 12 CUPS
9-INCH SPRINGFORM PAN = 10 CUPS
9 X 5 INCH LOAF PAN = 8 CUPS
9-INCH SQUARE PAN = 8 CUPS

Chapter 3: Bread And Breakfast Recipes

Classic Cinnamon Rolls

Servings: 4
Cooking Time: 6 Minutes
Ingredients:
- 1½ cups all-purpose flour
- 1 tablespoon granulated sugar
- 2 teaspoons baking powder
- ½ teaspoon salt
- 4 tablespoons butter, divided
- ½ cup buttermilk
- 2 tablespoons brown sugar
- 1 teaspoon cinnamon
- 1 cup powdered sugar
- 2 tablespoons milk

Directions:
1. Preheat the air fryer to 360°F.
2. In a large bowl, stir together the flour, sugar, baking powder, and salt. Cut in 3 tablespoons of the butter with a pastry blender or two knives until coarse crumbs remain. Stir in the buttermilk until a dough forms.
3. Place the dough onto a floured surface and roll out into a square shape about ½ inch thick.
4. Melt the remaining 1 tablespoon of butter in the microwave for 20 seconds. Using a pastry brush or your fingers, spread the melted butter onto the dough.
5. In a small bowl, mix together the brown sugar and cinnamon. Sprinkle the mixture across the surface of the dough. Roll the dough up, forming a long log. Using a pastry cutter or sharp knife, cut 10 cinnamon rolls.
6. Carefully place the cinnamon rolls into the air fryer basket. Then bake at 360°F for 6 minutes or until golden brown.
7. Meanwhile, in a small bowl, whisk together the powdered sugar and milk.
8. Plate the cinnamon rolls and drizzle the glaze over the surface before serving.

Banana-pecan French Toast

Servings: 8
Cooking Time: 10 Minutes
Ingredients:
- 8 slices of whole-grain bread
- ¾ cup of any milk you like
- 1 sliced banana
- 1 cup of rolled oats
- 1 cup of pecan, chopped
- 2 tablespoons of ground flax seeds
- 1 teaspoon of cinnamon

Directions:
1. At 350 degrees F/ 175 degrees C, preheat your air fryer.
2. Mix nuts, cinnamon, oats, and flax seeds into a food processor and pulse until crumbly.
3. Pour milk into a deep and wide bowl.
4. Soak 1–2 pieces of bread for almost 15-30 seconds per side.
5. Transfer the soaked bread pieces to the oats mixture and cover with it from per side.
6. Set the prepared soak bread slices into the air fryer basket in 1 layer.
7. Cook them at 350 degrees F/ 175 degrees C for 3 minutes, flip, and continue cooking for 3 more minutes.
8. Repeat the same steps with the remaining bread slices.
9. Serve with maple syrup and banana slices.
10. Enjoy your Banana-Nut French Toast!

Chicken Saltimbocca Sandwiches

Servings: 3
Cooking Time: 11 Minutes
Ingredients:
- 3 5- to 6-ounce boneless skinless chicken breasts
- 6 Thin prosciutto slices
- 6 Provolone cheese slices
- 3 Long soft rolls, such as hero, hoagie, or Italian sub rolls (gluten-free, if a concern), split open lengthwise
- 3 tablespoons Pesto, purchased or homemade

Directions:
1. Preheat the air fryer to 400°F.
2. Wrap each chicken breast with 2 prosciutto slices, spiraling the prosciutto around the breast and overlapping the slices a bit to cover the breast. The prosciutto will stick to the chicken more readily than bacon does.
3. When the machine is at temperature, set the wrapped chicken breasts in the basket and air-fry undisturbed for 10 minutes, or until the prosciutto is frizzled and the chicken is cooked through.
4. Overlap 2 cheese slices on each breast. Air-fry undisturbed for 1 minute, or until melted. Take the basket out of the machine.
5. Smear the insides of the rolls with the pesto, then use kitchen tongs to put a wrapped and cheesy chicken breast in each roll.

Cajun Breakfast Potatoes

Servings: 4
Cooking Time: 20 Minutes
Ingredients:
- 1 pound roasting potatoes (like russet), scrubbed clean
- 1 tablespoon vegetable oil
- 2 teaspoons paprika
- ½ teaspoon garlic powder
- ¼ teaspoon onion powder
- ¼ teaspoon ground cumin
- 1 teaspoon thyme
- 1 teaspoon sea salt
- ½ teaspoon black pepper

Directions:
1. Cut the potatoes into 1-inch cubes.
2. In a large bowl, toss the cut potatoes with vegetable oil.

The Ultimate Tower Air Fryer Cookbook

3. Sprinkle paprika, garlic powder, onion powder, cumin, thyme, salt, and pepper onto the potatoes, and toss to coat well.
4. Preheat the air fryer to 400°F for 4 minutes.
5. Add the potatoes to the air fryer basket and bake for 10 minutes. Stir or toss the potatoes and continue baking for an additional 5 minutes. Stir or toss again and continue baking for an additional 5 minutes or until the desired crispness is achieved.

Parsley Egg Scramble With Cottage Cheese

Servings: 2
Cooking Time: 15 Minutes
Ingredients:
- 1 tbsp cottage cheese, crumbled
- 4 eggs
- Salt and pepper to taste
- 2 tsp heavy cream
- 1 tbsp chopped parsley

Directions:
1. Preheat air fryer to 400°F. Grease a baking pan with olive oil. Beat the eggs, salt, and pepper in a bowl. Pour it into the pan, place the pan in the frying basket, and Air Fry for 5 minutes. Using a silicone spatula, stir in heavy cream, cottage cheese, and half of parsley and Air Fry for another 2 minutes. Scatter with parsley to serve.

Shakshuka-style Pepper Cups

Servings: 4
Cooking Time: 35 Minutes
Ingredients:
- 2 tbsp ricotta cheese crumbles
- 1 tbsp olive oil
- ½ yellow onion, diced
- 2 cloves garlic, minced
- ¼ tsp turmeric
- 1 can diced tomatoes
- 1 tbsp tomato paste
- ½ tsp smoked paprika
- ½ tsp salt
- ½ tsp granular sugar
- ¼ tsp ground cumin
- ¼ tsp ground coriander
- ⅛ tsp cayenne pepper
- 4 bell peppers
- 4 eggs
- 2 tbsp chopped basil

Directions:
1. Warm the olive oil in a saucepan over medium heat. Stir-fry the onion for 10 minutes or until softened. Stir in the garlic and turmeric for another 1 minute. Add diced tomatoes, tomato paste, paprika, salt, sugar, cumin, coriander, and cayenne. Remove from heat and stir.
2. Preheat air fryer to 350°F. Slice the tops off the peppers, and carefully remove the core and seeds. Put the bell peppers in the frying basket. Divide the tomato mixture among bell peppers. Crack 1 egg into tomato mixture in each pepper. Bake for 8-10 minutes. Sprinkle with ricotta cheese and cook for 1 more minute. Let rest 5 minutes. Garnish with fresh basil and serve immediately.

Salmon And Brown Rice Frittata

Servings: 4
Cooking Time: 15 Minutes
Ingredients:
- Olive oil, for greasing the pan
- 1 egg
- 4 egg whites
- ½ teaspoon dried thyme
- ½ cup cooked brown rice
- ½ cup cooked, flaked salmon (about 3 ounces)
- ½ cup fresh baby spinach (see Tip)
- ¼ cup chopped red bell pepper
- 1 tablespoon grated Parmesan cheese

Directions:
1. Rub a 6-by-2-inch pan with a bit of olive oil and set aside.
2. In a small bowl, beat the egg, egg whites, and thyme until well mixed.
3. In the prepared pan, stir together the brown rice, salmon, spinach, and red bell pepper.
4. Pour the egg mixture over the rice mixture and sprinkle with the Parmesan cheese.
5. Bake for about 15 minutes, or until the frittata is puffed and golden brown. Serve.

Sweet Potato & Mushroom Hash

Servings: 6
Cooking Time: 35 Minutes
Ingredients:
- 2 peeled sweet potatoes, cubed
- 4 oz baby Bella mushrooms, diced
- ½ red bell pepper, diced
- ½ red onion, diced
- 2 tbsp olive oil
- 1 garlic clove, minced
- Salt and pepper to taste
- ½ tbsp chopped marjoram

Directions:
1. Preheat air fryer to 380°F. Place all ingredients in a large bowl and toss until the vegetables are well coated. Pour the vegetables into the frying basket. Bake for 8-10 minutes, then shake the vegetables. Cook for 8-10 more minutes. Serve and enjoy!

Cranberry Beignets

Servings: 16
Cooking Time: 10 Minutes
Ingredients:
- 1½ cups flour
- 2 teaspoons baking soda
- ¼ teaspoon salt
- 3 tablespoons brown sugar
- ⅓ cup chopped dried cranberries
- ½ cup buttermilk
- 1 egg

- 3 tablespoons melted unsalted butter

Directions:
1. In a medium bowl, combine the flour, baking soda, salt, and brown sugar, and mix well. Stir in dried cranberries.
2. In a small bowl, combine the buttermilk and egg, and beat until smooth. Stir into the dry ingredients just until moistened.
3. Pat the dough into an 8-by-8-inch square and cut into 16 pieces. Coat each piece lightly with melted butter.
4. Place in a single layer in the air fryer basket, making sure the pieces don't touch. You may have to cook in batches depending on the size of your air fryer basket. Air-fry for 5 to 8 minutes or until puffy and golden brown. Dust with powdered sugar before serving, if desired.
5. Did You Know? Using unsalted butter ensures food will not stick to the air fryer basket when cooking. Salt in butter can make foods stick, which is not what you want.

Apricot-cheese Mini Pies

Servings: 6
Cooking Time: 35 Minutes
Ingredients:
- 2 refrigerated piecrusts
- 1/3 cup apricot preserves
- 1 tsp cornstarch
- ½ cup vanilla yogurt
- 1 oz cream cheese
- 1 tsp sugar
- Rainbow sprinkles

Directions:
1. Preheat air fryer to 370°F. Lay out pie crusts on a flat surface. Cut each sheet of pie crust with a knife into three rectangles for a total of 6 rectangles. Mix apricot preserves and cornstarch in a small bowl. Cover the top half of one rectangle with 1 tbsp of the preserve mixture. Repeat for all rectangles. Fold the bottom of the crust over the preserve-covered top. Crimp and seal all edges with a fork.
2. Lightly coat each tart with cooking oil, then place into the air fryer without stacking. Bake for 10 minutes. Meanwhile, prepare the frosting by mixing yogurt, cream cheese, and sugar. When tarts are done, let cool completely in the air fryer. Frost the tarts and top with sprinkles. Serve.

Mashed Potato Taquitos With Hot Sauce

Servings: 4
Cooking Time: 30 Minutes
Ingredients:
- 1 potato, peeled and cubed
- 2 tbsp milk
- 2 garlic cloves, minced
- Salt and pepper to taste
- ½ tsp ground cumin
- 2 tbsp minced scallions
- 4 corn tortillas

- 1 cup red chili sauce
- 1 avocado, sliced
- 2 tbsp cilantro, chopped

Directions:
1. In a pot fitted with a steamer basket, cook the potato cubes for 15 minutes on the stovetop. Pour the potato cubes into a bowl and mash with a potato masher. Add the milk, garlic, salt, pepper, and cumin and stir. Add the scallions and cilantro and stir them into the mixture.
2. Preheat air fryer to 390°F. Run the tortillas under water for a second, then place them in the greased frying basket. Air Fry for 1 minute. Lay the tortillas on a flat surface. Place an equal amount of the potato filling in the center of each. Roll the tortilla sides over the filling and place seam-side down in the frying basket. Fry for 7 minutes or until the tortillas are golden and slightly crisp. Serve with chili sauce and avocado slices. Enjoy!

Awesome Everything Bagels

Servings: 2
Cooking Time: 10 Minutes
Ingredients:
- ½ cup self-rising flour
- ½ cup plain Greek yogurt
- 1 egg
- 1 tablespoon water
- 4 teaspoons everything bagel spice mix
- Cooking oil spray
- 1 tablespoon butter, melted

Directions:
1. In a suitable bowl, using a wooden spoon, stir together the flour and yogurt until a tacky dough forms.
2. Transfer the dough to a lightly-floured work surface and roll the dough into a ball.
3. Cut the prepared dough into 2 pieces and roll each piece into a log. Form each log into a bagel shape, pinching the ends together.
4. In a suitable bowl, whisk the egg and water. Brush the egg wash on the bagels.
5. Sprinkle 2 teaspoons of the spice mix over each bagel and gently press it into the dough.
6. Once your air fryer unit is preheated, spray the crisper plate with cooking spray.
7. Drizzle with the bagels with the butter and place them into the basket.
8. At 330 degrees F/ 165 degrees C, preheat your air fryer and cook for 10 minutes.
9. When the cooking is complete, the bagels should be lightly golden on the outside.
10. Serve warm.

Apple-cinnamon-walnut Muffins

Servings: 8
Cooking Time: 11 Minutes
Ingredients:
- 1 cup flour
- ⅓ cup sugar
- 1 teaspoon baking powder
- ¼ teaspoon baking soda

- ¼ teaspoon salt
- 1 teaspoon cinnamon
- ¼ teaspoon ginger
- ¼ teaspoon nutmeg
- 1 egg
- 2 tablespoons pancake syrup, plus 2 teaspoons
- 2 tablespoons melted butter, plus 2 teaspoons
- ¾ cup unsweetened applesauce
- ½ teaspoon vanilla extract
- ¼ cup chopped walnuts
- ¼ cup diced apple
- 8 foil muffin cups, liners removed and sprayed with cooking spray

Directions:
1. Preheat air fryer to 330°F.
2. In a large bowl, stir together flour, sugar, baking powder, baking soda, salt, cinnamon, ginger, and nutmeg.
3. In a small bowl, beat egg until frothy. Add syrup, butter, applesauce, and vanilla and mix well.
4. Pour egg mixture into dry ingredients and stir just until moistened.
5. Gently stir in nuts and diced apple.
6. Divide batter among the 8 muffin cups.
7. Place 4 muffin cups in air fryer basket and cook at 330°F for 11minutes.
8. Repeat with remaining 4 muffins or until toothpick inserted in center comes out clean.

Soufflé

Servings:4
Cooking Time: 22 Minutes
Ingredients:
- ⅓ cup butter, melted
- ¼ cup flour
- 1 cup milk
- 1 ounce (28 g) sugar
- 4 egg yolks
- 1 teaspoon vanilla extract
- 6 egg whites
- 1 teaspoon cream of tartar
- Cooking spray

Directions:
1. In a bowl, mix the butter and flour until a smooth consistency is achieved.
2. Pour the milk into a saucepan over medium-low heat. Add the sugar and allow to dissolve before raising the heat to boil the milk.
3. Pour in the flour and butter mixture and stir rigorously for 7 minutes to eliminate any lumps. Make sure the mixture thickens. Take off the heat and allow to cool for 15 minutes.
4. Preheat the air fryer to 320°F (160°C). Spritz 6 soufflé dishes with cooking spray.
5. Put the egg yolks and vanilla extract in a separate bowl and beat them together with a fork. Pour in the milk and combine well to incorporate everything.
6. In a smaller bowl mix the egg whites and cream of tartar with a fork. Fold into the egg yolks-milk mixture before adding in the flour mixture. Transfer equal amounts to the 6 soufflé dishes.
7. Put the dishes in the air fryer and bake for 15 minutes.
8. Serve warm.

Chorizo Sausage & Cheese Balls

Servings:4
Cooking Time: 25 Minutes
Ingredients:
- 1 egg white
- 1 lb chorizo ground sausage
- ¼ tsp smoked paprika
- 2 tbsp canned green chiles
- ¼ cup bread crumbs
- ¼ cup grated cheddar

Directions:
1. Preheat air fryer to 400°F. Mix all ingredients in a large bowl. Form into 16 balls. Put the sausage balls in the frying basket and Air Fry for 6 minutes. When done, shake the basket and cook for an additional 6 minutes. Transfer to a serving plate and serve.

Buttery Scallops

Servings: 2
Cooking Time: 8 Minutes
Ingredients:
- 1 lb jumbo scallops
- 1 tbsp fresh lemon juice
- 2 tbsp butter, melted

Directions:
1. Preheat the air fryer to 400°F.
2. In a small bowl, mix together lemon juice and butter.
3. Brush scallops with lemon juice and butter mixture and place into the air fryer basket.
4. Cook scallops for 4 minutes. Turn halfway through.
5. Again brush scallops with lemon butter mixture and cook for 4 minutes more. Turn halfway through.
6. Serve and enjoy.

Smoked Fried Tofu

Servings: 2
Cooking Time:22 Minutes
Ingredients:
- 1 tofu block; pressed and cubed
- 1 tbsp. smoked paprika
- 1/4 cup cornstarch
- Salt and black pepper to the taste
- Cooking spray

Directions:
1. Grease your air fryer's basket with cooking spray and heat the fryer at 370°F.
2. In a bowl; mix tofu with salt, pepper, smoked paprika and cornstarch and toss well.
3. Add tofu to you air fryer's basket and cook for 12 minutes shaking the fryer every 4 minutes. Divide into bowls and serve for breakfast.

Cheddar Tater Tot With Sausage

Servings: 4
Cooking Time: 20 Minutes
Ingredients:
- 4 eggs
- 1 cup milk
- 1 teaspoon onion powder
- Salt
- Black pepper
- Cooking oil
- 12 ounces ground chicken sausage
- 1-pound frozen tater tots
- ¾ cup shredded Cheddar cheese

Directions:
1. Beat the eggs with onion powder, milk, and black pepper and salt in a bowl.
2. Grease a suitable skillet with cooking oil and place it over medium-high heat.
3. Toss in the ground sausage and sauté for 4 minutes until brown.
4. Grease a suitable barrel pan with cooking oil.
5. Spread the tater tots in the prepared barrel pan. Air fry for 6 minutes almost.
6. Then add the egg and cooked sausage mixture, cook for 6 minutes more.
7. Sprinkle the cheese over the tater tot.
8. Cook for 2 to 3 minutes more.
9. Cool before serving.

Creamy Cinnamon Rolls

Servings: 8
Cooking Time: 9 Minutes
Ingredients:
- 1 pound (454 g) frozen bread dough, thawed
- ¼ cup butter, melted
- ¾ cup brown sugar
- 1½ tablespoons ground cinnamon
- Cream Cheese Glaze:
- 4 ounces (113 g) cream cheese, softened
- 2 tablespoons butter, softened
- 1¼ cups powdered sugar
- ½ teaspoon vanilla extract

Directions:
1. Let the bread dough come to room temperature on the counter. On a lightly floured surface, roll the dough into a 13-inch by 11-inch rectangle. Position the rectangle so the 13-inch side is facing you. Brush the melted butter all over the dough, leaving a 1-inch border uncovered along the edge farthest away from you.
2. Combine the brown sugar and cinnamon in a small bowl. Sprinkle the mixture evenly over the buttered dough, keeping the 1-inch border uncovered. Roll the dough into a log, starting with the edge closest to you. Roll the dough tightly, rolling evenly, and push out any air pockets. When you get to the uncovered edge of the dough, press the dough onto the roll to seal it together.
3. Cut the log into 8 pieces, slicing slowly with a sawing motion so you don't flatten the dough. Turn the slices on their sides and cover with a clean kitchen towel. Let the rolls sit in the warmest part of the kitchen for 1½ to 2 hours to rise.
4. To make the glaze, place the cream cheese and butter in a microwave-safe bowl. Soften the mixture in the microwave for 30 seconds at a time until it is easy to stir. Gradually add the powdered sugar and stir to combine. Add the vanilla extract and whisk until smooth. Set aside.
5. When the rolls have risen, preheat the air fryer to 350°F (177°C).
6. Transfer 4 of the rolls to the air fryer basket. Air fry for 5 minutes. Turn the rolls over and air fry for another 4 minutes. Repeat with the remaining 4 rolls.
7. Let the rolls cool for two minutes before glazing. Spread large dollops of cream cheese glaze on top of the warm cinnamon rolls, allowing some glaze to drip down the side of the rolls. Serve warm.

Bacon Puff Pastry Pinwheels

Servings: 8
Cooking Time: 10 Minutes
Ingredients:
- 1 sheet of puff pastry
- 2 tablespoons maple syrup
- ¼ cup brown sugar
- 8 slices bacon (not thick cut)
- coarsely cracked black pepper
- vegetable oil

Directions:
1. On a lightly floured surface, roll the puff pastry out into a square that measures roughly 10 inches wide by however long your bacon strips are. Cut the pastry into eight even strips.
2. Brush the strips of pastry with the maple syrup and sprinkle the brown sugar on top, leaving 1 inch of dough exposed at the far end of each strip. Place a slice of bacon on each strip of puff pastry, letting 1/8-inch of the length of bacon hang over the edge of the pastry. Season generously with coarsely ground black pepper.
3. With the exposed end of the pastry strips away from you, roll the bacon and pastry strips up into pinwheels. Dab a little water on the exposed end of the pastry and pinch it to the pinwheel to seal the pastry shut.
4. Preheat the air fryer to 360°F.
5. Brush or spray the air fryer basket with a little vegetable oil. Place the pinwheels into the basket and air-fry at 360°F for 8 minutes. Turn the pinwheels over and air-fry for another 2 minutes to brown the bottom. Serve warm.

Baked Eggs With Bacon-tomato Sauce

Servings: 1
Cooking Time: 12 Minutes
Ingredients:
- 1 teaspoon olive oil
- 2 tablespoons finely chopped onion
- 1 teaspoon chopped fresh oregano
- pinch crushed red pepper flakes

The Ultimate Tower Air Fryer Cookbook

- 1 (14-ounce) can crushed or diced tomatoes
- salt and freshly ground black pepper
- 2 slices of bacon, chopped
- 2 large eggs
- ¼ cup grated Cheddar cheese
- fresh parsley, chopped

Directions:
1. Start by making the tomato sauce. Preheat a medium saucepan over medium heat on the stovetop. Add the olive oil and sauté the onion, oregano and pepper flakes for 5 minutes. Add the tomatoes and bring to a simmer. Season with salt and freshly ground black pepper and simmer for 10 minutes.
2. Meanwhile, Preheat the air fryer to 400°F and pour a little water into the bottom of the air fryer drawer. (This will help prevent the grease that drips into the bottom drawer from burning and smoking.) Place the bacon in the air fryer basket and air-fry at 400°F for 5 minutes, shaking the basket every once in a while.
3. When the bacon is almost crispy, remove it to a paper-towel lined plate and rinse out the air fryer drawer, draining away the bacon grease.
4. Transfer the tomato sauce to a shallow 7-inch pie dish. Crack the eggs on top of the sauce and scatter the cooked bacon back on top. Season with salt and freshly ground black pepper and transfer the pie dish into the air fryer basket. You can use an aluminum foil sling to help with this by taking a long piece of aluminum foil, folding it in half lengthwise twice until it is roughly 26-inches by 3-inches. Place this under the pie dish and hold the ends of the foil to move the pie dish in and out of the air fryer basket. Tuck the ends of the foil beside the pie dish while it cooks in the air fryer.
5. Air-fry at 400°F for 5 minutes, or until the eggs are almost cooked to your liking. Sprinkle cheese on top and air-fry for an additional 2 minutes. When the cheese has melted, remove the pie dish from the air fryer, sprinkle with a little chopped parsley and let the eggs cool for a few minutes – just enough time to toast some buttered bread in your air fryer!

Viking Toast
Servings: 2
Cooking Time: 20 Minutes
Ingredients:
- 2 tbsp minced green chili pepper
- 1 avocado, pressed
- 1 clove garlic, minced
- ¼ tsp lemon juice
- Salt and pepper to taste
- 2 bread slices
- 2 plum tomatoes, sliced
- 4 oz smoked salmon
- ¼ diced peeled red onion

Directions:
1. Preheat air fryer at 350ºF. Combine the avocado, garlic, lemon juice, and salt in a bowl until you reach your desired consistency. Spread avocado mixture on the bread slices.
2. Top with tomato slices and sprinkle with black pepper. Place bread slices in the frying basket and Bake for 5 minutes. Transfer to a plate. Top each bread slice with salmon, green chili pepper, and red onion. Serve.

Sweet-hot Pepperoni Pizza
Servings: 2
Cooking Time: 18 Minutes
Ingredients:
- 1 (6- to 8-ounce) pizza dough ball*
- olive oil
- ½ cup pizza sauce
- ¾ cup grated mozzarella cheese
- ½ cup thick sliced pepperoni
- ⅓ cup sliced pickled hot banana peppers
- ¼ teaspoon dried oregano
- 2 teaspoons honey

Directions:
1. Preheat the air fryer to 390°F.
2. Cut out a piece of aluminum foil the same size as the bottom of the air fryer basket. Brush the foil circle with olive oil. Shape the dough into a circle and place it on top of the foil. Dock the dough by piercing it several times with a fork. Brush the dough lightly with olive oil and transfer it into the air fryer basket with the foil on the bottom.
3. Air-fry the plain pizza dough for 6 minutes. Turn the dough over, remove the aluminum foil and brush again with olive oil. Air-fry for an additional 4 minutes.
4. Spread the pizza sauce on top of the dough and sprinkle the mozzarella cheese over the sauce. Top with the pepperoni, pepper slices and dried oregano. Lower the temperature of the air fryer to 350°F and cook for 8 minutes, until the cheese has melted and lightly browned. Transfer the pizza to a cutting board and drizzle with the honey. Slice and serve.

Blueberry Pannenkoek (dutch Pancake)
Servings: 4
Cooking Time: 30 Minutes
Ingredients:
- 3 eggs, beaten
- ½ cup buckwheat flour
- ½ cup milk
- ½ tsp vanilla
- 1 ½ cups blueberries, crushed
- 2 tbsp powdered sugar

Directions:
1. Preheat air fryer to 330°F. Mix together eggs, buckwheat flour, milk, and vanilla in a bowl. Pour the batter into a greased baking pan and add it to the fryer. Bake until the pancake is puffed and golden, 12-16 minutes. Remove the pan and flip the pancake over onto a plate. Add blueberries and powdered sugar as a topping and serve.

Egg & Bacon Toasts

Servings: 4
Cooking Time: 25 Minutes
Ingredients:
- 4 French bread slices, cut diagonally
- 1 + tsp butter
- 4 eggs
- 2 tbsp milk
- ½ tsp dried thyme
- Salt and pepper to taste
- 4 oz cooked bacon, crumbled
- 2/3 cup grated Colby cheese

Directions:
1. Preheat the air fryer to 350°F. Spray each slice of bread with oil and Bake in the frying basket for 2-3 minutes until light brown; set aside. Beat together the eggs, milk, thyme, salt, and pepper in a bowl and add the melted butter. Transfer to a 6-inch cake pan and place the pan into the fryer. Bake for 7-8 minutes, stirring once or until the eggs are set. Transfer the egg mixture into a bowl.
2. Top the bread slices with egg mixture, bacon, and cheese. Return to the fryer and Bake for 4-8 minutes or until the cheese melts and browns in spots. Serve.

Banana-strawberry Cakecups

Servings: 6
Cooking Time: 25 Minutes
Ingredients:
- ½ cup mashed bananas
- ¼ cup maple syrup
- ½ cup Greek yogurt
- 1 tsp vanilla extract
- 1 egg
- 1 ½ cups flour
- 1 tbsp cornstarch
- ½ tsp baking soda
- ½ tsp baking powder
- ½ tsp salt
- ½ cup strawberries, sliced

Directions:
1. Preheat air fryer to 360°F. Place the mashed bananas, maple syrup, yogurt, vanilla, and egg in a large bowl and mix until smooth. Sift in 1 ½ cups of the flour, baking soda, baking powder, and salt, then stir to combine.
2. In a small bowl, toss the strawberries with the cornstarch. Fold the mixture into the muffin batter. Divide the mixture evenly between greased muffin cups and place into the air frying basket. Bake for 12-15 minutes until golden brown on top and a toothpick inserted into the middle of one of the muffins comes out clean. Leave to cool for 5 minutes. Serve and enjoy!

Cream Cheese Danish

Servings: 4
Cooking Time: 10 Minutes
Ingredients:
- 1 sheet frozen puff pastry dough, thawed
- 1 large egg, beaten
- 4 ounces full-fat cream cheese, softened
- ¼ cup confectioners' sugar
- 1 teaspoon vanilla extract
- ½ teaspoon lemon juice

Directions:
1. Preheat the air fryer to 320°F.
2. Unfold puff pastry and cut into four equal squares. For each pastry, fold all four corners partway to the center, leaving a 1" square in the center.
3. Brush egg evenly over folded puff pastry.
4. In a medium bowl, mix cream cheese, confectioners' sugar, vanilla, and lemon juice. Scoop 2 tablespoons of mixture into the center of each pastry square.
5. Place danishes directly in the air fryer basket and cook 10 minutes until puffy and golden brown. Cool 5 minutes before serving.

Cinnamon Rolls

Servings: 12
Cooking Time: 20 Minutes
Ingredients:
- 2½ cups shredded mozzarella cheese
- 2 ounces cream cheese, softened
- 1 cup blanched finely ground almond flour
- ½ teaspoon vanilla extract
- ½ cup confectioners' erythritol
- 1 tablespoon ground cinnamon

Directions:
1. In a large microwave-safe bowl, combine mozzarella cheese, cream cheese, and flour. Microwave the mixture on high 90 seconds until cheese is melted.
2. Add vanilla extract and erythritol, and mix 2 minutes until a dough forms.
3. Once the dough is cool enough to work with your hands, about 2 minutes, spread it out into a 12" × 4" rectangle on ungreased parchment paper. Evenly sprinkle dough with cinnamon.
4. Starting at the long side of the dough, roll lengthwise to form a log. Slice the log into twelve even pieces.
5. Divide rolls between two ungreased 6" round nonstick baking dishes. Place one dish into air fryer basket. Adjust the temperature to 375°F and set the timer for 10 minutes.
6. Cinnamon rolls will be done when golden around the edges and mostly firm. Repeat with second dish. Allow rolls to cool in dishes 10 minutes before serving.

Egg & Bacon Pockets

Servings: 4
Cooking Time: 50 Minutes
Ingredients:
- 2 tbsp olive oil
- 4 bacon slices, chopped
- ¼ red bell pepper, diced
- 1/3 cup scallions, chopped
- 4 eggs, beaten
- 1/3 cup grated Swiss cheese

- 1 cup flour
- 1 ½ tsp baking powder
- ½ tsp salt
- 1 cup Greek yogurt
- 1 egg white, beaten
- 2 tsp Italian seasoning
- 1 tbsp Tabasco sauce

Directions:
1. Warm the olive oil in a skillet over medium heat and add the bacon. Stir-fry for 3-4 minutes or until crispy. Add the bell pepper and scallions and sauté for 3-4 minutes. Pour in the beaten eggs and stir-fry to scramble them, 3 minutes. Stir in the Swiss cheese and set aside to cool.
2. Sift the flour, baking powder, and salt in a bowl. Add yogurt and mix together until combined. Transfer the dough to a floured workspace. Knead it for 3 minutes or until smooth. Form the dough into 4 equal balls. Roll out the balls into round discs. Divide the bacon-egg mixture between the rounds. Fold the dough over the filling and seal the edges with a fork. Brush the pockets with egg white and sprinkle with Italian seasoning.
3. Preheat air fryer to 350°F. Arrange the pockets on the greased frying basket and Bake for 9-11 minutes, flipping once until golden. Serve with Tabasco sauce.

Crispy Fish Sticks

Servings: 4
Cooking Time: 10 Minutes
Ingredients:
- 8 ounces cod fillet
- 1 egg, beaten
- ¼ cup coconut flour
- ¼ teaspoon ground coriander
- ¼ teaspoon ground paprika
- ¼ teaspoon ground cumin
- ¼ teaspoon Pink salt
- ⅓ cup coconut flakes
- 1 tablespoon mascarpone
- 1 teaspoon heavy cream
- Cooking spray

Directions:
1. Roughly chop the cod fillet. Then transfer into a blender.
2. Place in coconut flour, paprika, cumin, egg, salt, and ground coriander. Then mix the mixture together until smooth.
3. Then place the mixture into a bowl.
4. Place the fish mixture onto lined parchment paper and then shape into flat square.
5. Cut the square into sticks.
6. Whisk mascarpone and heavy cream together in a separate bowl.
7. Sprinkle the fish sticks with the mascarpone mixture and coat with coconut flakes.
8. At 400 degrees F/ 205 degrees C, heat your air fryer in advance.
9. Using cooking spray, spray the air fryer basket.
10. Place the fish sticks evenly inside the air fryer basket.
11. Cook the fish sticks in the preheated air fryer for 10 minutes.
12. Halfway through cooking, flip the fish sticks to the other side.
13. When cooked, remove from the air fryer and serve with your favorite dip.

Southwest Cornbread

Servings: 6
Cooking Time: 18 Minutes
Ingredients:
- cooking spray
- ½ cup yellow cornmeal
- ½ cup flour
- 2 teaspoons baking powder
- ½ teaspoon salt
- ½ cup frozen corn kernels, thawed and drained
- ¼ cup finely chopped onion
- 1 or 2 small jalapeño peppers, seeded and chopped
- 1 egg
- ½ cup milk
- 2 tablespoons melted butter
- 2 ounces sharp Cheddar cheese, grated

Directions:
1. Preheat air fryer to 360°F.
2. Spray air fryer baking pan with nonstick cooking spray.
3. In a medium bowl, stir together the cornmeal, flour, baking powder, and salt.
4. Stir in the corn, onion, and peppers.
5. In a small bowl, beat together the egg, milk, and butter. Stir into dry ingredients until well combined.
6. Spoon half the batter into prepared baking pan, spreading to edges. Top with grated cheese. Spoon remaining batter on top of cheese and gently spread to edges of pan so it completely covers the cheese.
7. Cook at 360°F for 18 minutes, until cornbread is done and top is crispy brown.

Strawberry Pastry

Servings: 8
Cooking Time: 15 Minutes Per Batch
Ingredients:
- 1 package refrigerated piecrust
- 1 cup strawberry jam
- 1 large egg, whisked
- ½ cup confectioners' sugar
- 2 tablespoons whole milk
- ½ teaspoon vanilla extract

Directions:
1. Preheat the air fryer to 320°F. Cut parchment paper to fit the air fryer basket.
2. On a lightly floured surface, lay piecrusts out flat. Cut each piecrust round into six 4" × 3" rectangles, reserving excess dough.

3. Form remaining dough into a ball, then roll out and cut four additional 4" × 3" rectangles, bringing the total to sixteen.
4. For each pastry, spread 2 tablespoons jam on a pastry rectangle, leaving a 1" border around the edges. Top with a second pastry rectangle and use a fork to gently press all four edges together. Repeat with remaining jam and pastry.
5. Brush tops of each pastry with egg and cut an X in the center of each to prevent excess steam from building up.
6. Place pastries on parchment in the air fryer basket, working in batches as necessary. Cook 12 minutes, then carefully flip and cook an additional 3 minutes until each side is golden brown. Let cool 10 minutes.
7. In a small bowl, whisk confectioners' sugar, milk, and vanilla. Brush each pastry with glaze, then place in the refrigerator 5 minutes to set before serving.

Green Onion Pancakes

Servings: 4
Cooking Time: 8 Minutes
Ingredients:
- 2 cup all-purpose flour
- ½ teaspoon salt
- ¾ cup hot water
- 1 tablespoon vegetable oil
- 1 tablespoon butter, melted
- 2 cups finely chopped green onions
- 1 tablespoon black sesame seeds, for garnish

Directions:
1. In a large bowl, whisk together the flour and salt. Make a well in the center and pour in the hot water. Quickly stir the flour mixture together until a dough forms. Knead the dough for 5 minutes; then cover with a warm, wet towel and set aside for 30 minutes to rest.
2. In a small bowl, mix together the vegetable oil and melted butter.
3. On a floured surface, place the dough and cut it into 8 pieces. Working with 1 piece of dough at a time, use a rolling pin to roll out the dough until it's ¼ inch thick; then brush the surface with the oil and butter mixture and sprinkle with green onions. Next, fold the dough in half and then in half again. Roll out the dough again until it's ¼ inch thick and brush with the oil and butter mixture and green onions. Fold the dough in half and then in half again and roll out one last time until it's ¼ inch thick. Repeat this technique with all 8 pieces.
4. Meanwhile, preheat the air fryer to 400°F.
5. Place 1 or 2 pancakes into the air fryer basket, and cook for 2 minutes or until crispy and golden brown. Repeat until all the pancakes are cooked. Top with black sesame seeds for garnish, if desired.

Mushroom And Asparagus Frittata

Servings: 4
Cooking Time: 10 Minutes
Ingredients:
- 6 eggs
- 3 mushrooms, sliced
- 10 asparagus, chopped
- ¼ cup half and half
- 2 teaspoons butter, melted
- 1 cup mozzarella cheese, shredded
- 1 teaspoon black pepper
- 1 teaspoon salt

Directions:
1. Toss mushrooms and asparagus with melted butter and add into the air fryer basket.
2. Cook mushrooms and asparagus at 350 degrees F/ 175 degrees C for 5 minutes. Shake basket twice.
3. Meanwhile, in a suitable bowl, whisk together eggs, half and half, black pepper, and salt.
4. Transfer cook mushrooms and asparagus into the air fryer basket.
5. Pour egg mixture over mushrooms and asparagus.
6. Place dish in the preheated air fryer and cook at almost 350 degrees F/ 175 degrees C for 5 minutes or until eggs are set.
7. Slice and serve.

Avocado Quesadillas

Servings: 4
Cooking Time: 11 Minutes
Ingredients:
- 4 eggs
- 2 tablespoons skim milk
- Salt and ground black pepper, to taste
- Cooking spray
- 4 flour tortillas
- 4 tablespoons salsa
- 2 ounces (57 g) Cheddar cheese, grated
- ½ small avocado, peeled and thinly sliced

Directions:
1. Preheat the air fryer to 270ºF (132ºC).
2. Beat together the eggs, milk, salt, and pepper.
3. Spray a baking pan lightly with cooking spray and add egg mixture.
4. Bake for 8 minutes, stirring every 1 to 2 minutes, until eggs are scrambled to the liking. Remove and set aside.
5. Spray one side of each tortilla with cooking spray. Flip over.
6. Divide eggs, salsa, cheese, and avocado among the tortillas, covering only half of each tortilla.
7. Fold each tortilla in half and press down lightly. Increase the temperature of the air fryer to 390ºF (199ºC).
8. Put 2 tortillas in air fryer basket and air fry for 3 minutes or until cheese melts and outside feels slightly crispy. Repeat with remaining two tortillas.
9. Cut each cooked tortilla into halves. Serve warm.

Chapter 4: Appetizers And Snacks Recipes

Root Vegetable Crisps

Servings: 4
Cooking Time: 8 Minutes
Ingredients:
- 1 small taro root, peeled and washed
- 1 small yucca root, peeled and washed
- 1 small purple sweet potato, washed
- 2 cups filtered water
- 2 teaspoons extra-virgin olive oil
- ½ teaspoon salt

Directions:
1. Using a mandolin, slice the taro root, yucca root, and purple sweet potato into ⅛-inch slices.
2. Add the water to a large bowl. Add the sliced vegetables and soak for at least 30 minutes.
3. Preheat the air fryer to 370°F.
4. Drain the water and pat the vegetables dry with a paper towel or kitchen cloth. Toss the vegetables with the olive oil and sprinkle with salt. Liberally spray the air fryer basket with olive oil mist.
5. Place the vegetables into the air fryer basket, making sure not to overlap the pieces.
6. Cook for 8 minutes, shaking the basket every 2 minutes, until the outer edges start to turn up and the vegetables start to brown. Remove from the basket and serve warm. Repeat with the remaining vegetable slices until all are cooked.

Garlic Mushroom Bites

Servings: 6
Cooking Time: 12 Minutes
Ingredients:
- Salt and black pepper to the taste
- 1 ¼ cups coconut flour
- 2 garlic clove, minced
- 1 tablespoons basil, minced
- ½ pound mushrooms, minced
- 1 egg, whisked

Directions:
1. In addition to the cooking spray, thoroughly mix up other ingredients and shape medium balls out of this mix.
2. Arrange the balls in the basket of your air fryer and grease them with cooking spray.
3. Air fry at 350 degrees F/ 175 degrees C for 6 minutes on each side.
4. Serve as an appetizer.

Tortilla Chips

Servings: 4
Cooking Time: 5 Minutes
Ingredients:
- 8 white corn tortillas
- ¼ cup olive oil
- 2 tablespoons lime juice
- ½ teaspoon salt

Directions:
1. Preheat the air fryer to 350°F.
2. Cut each tortilla into fourths and brush lightly with oil.
3. Place chips in a single layer in the air fryer basket, working in batches as necessary. Cook 5 minutes, shaking the basket halfway through cooking time.
4. Sprinkle with lime juice and salt. Serve warm.

Air Fried Pot Stickers

Servings: 30
Cooking Time: 18 To 20 Minutes
Ingredients:
- ½ cup finely chopped cabbage
- ¼ cup finely chopped red bell pepper
- 2 green onions, finely chopped
- 1 egg, beaten
- 2 tablespoons cocktail sauce
- 2 teaspoons low-sodium soy sauce
- 30 wonton wrappers
- 1 tablespoon water, for brushing the wrappers

Directions:
1. Preheat the air fryer to 360°F (182°C).
2. In a small bowl, combine the cabbage, pepper, green onions, egg, cocktail sauce, and soy sauce, and mix well.
3. Put about 1 teaspoon of the mixture in the center of each wonton wrapper. Fold the wrapper in half, covering the filling; dampen the edges with water, and seal. You can crimp the edges of the wrapper with your fingers so they look like the pot stickers you get in restaurants. Brush them with water.
4. Place the pot stickers in the air fryer basket and air fry in 2 batches for 9 to 10 minutes, or until the pot stickers are hot and the bottoms are lightly browned.
5. Serve hot.

Plantain Chips

Servings: 2
Cooking Time: 14 Minutes
Ingredients:
- 1 large green plantain
- 2½ cups filtered water, divided
- 2 teaspoons sea salt, divided
- Cooking spray

Directions:
1. Slice the plantain into 1-inch pieces. Place the plantains into a large bowl, cover with 2 cups water and 1 teaspoon salt. Soak the plantains for 30 minutes; then remove and pat dry.
2. Preheat the air fryer to 390°F.
3. Place the plantain pieces into the air fryer basket, leaving space between the plantain rounds. Cook the plantains for 5 minutes, and carefully remove them from the air fryer basket.
4. Add the remaining water to a small bowl.
5. Using a small drinking glass, dip the bottom of the glass into the water and mash the warm plantains until they're ¼-inch thick. Return the plantains to the air fryer basket, sprinkle with the remaining sea salt, and spray lightly with cooking spray.
6. Cook for another 6 to 8 minutes, or until lightly golden brown edges appear.

The Ultimate Tower Air Fryer Cookbook

Parmesan Cabbage Chips

Servings: 6
Cooking Time: 30 Minutes
Ingredients:
- 1 large cabbage head, tear cabbage leaves into pieces
- 2 tablespoons olive oil
- ¼ cup parmesan cheese, grated
- Black pepper
- Salt

Directions:
1. At 250 degrees F/ 120 degrees C, preheat your air fryer.
2. Add all the recipe ingredients into the suitable mixing bowl and toss well.
3. Grease its air fryer basket with cooking spray.
4. Divide cabbage in batches.
5. Add 1 cabbage chips batch in air fryer basket and cook for 25-30 minutes at 250 degrees F/ 120 degrees C or until chips are crispy and lightly golden brown.
6. Serve and enjoy.

Chinese-style Potstickers

Servings: 6
Cooking Time: 30 Minutes
Ingredients:
- 1 cup shredded Chinese cabbage
- ¼ cup chopped shiitake mushrooms
- ¼ cup grated carrots
- 2 tbsp minced chives
- 2 garlic cloves, minced
- 2 tsp grated fresh ginger
- 12 dumpling wrappers
- 2 tsp sesame oil

Directions:
1. Preheat air fryer to 370°F. Toss the Chinese cabbage, shiitake mushrooms, carrots, chives, garlic, and ginger in a baking pan and stir. Place the pan in the fryer and Bake for 3-6 minutes. Put a dumpling wrapper on a clean workspace, then top with a tablespoon of the veggie mix.
2. Fold the wrapper in half to form a half-circle and use water to seal the edges. Repeat with remaining wrappers and filling. Brush the potstickers with sesame oil and arrange them on the frying basket. Air Fry for 5 minutes until the bottoms should are golden brown. Take the pan out, add 1 tbsp of water, and put it back in the fryer to Air Fry for 4-6 minutes longer. Serve hot.

Home-style Taro Chips

Servings: 2
Cooking Time: 20 Minutes
Ingredients:
- 1 tbsp olive oil
- 1 cup thinly sliced taro
- Salt to taste
- ½ cup hummus

Directions:
1. Preheat air fryer to 325°F. Put the sliced taro in the greased frying basket, spread the pieces out, and drizzle with olive oil. Air Fry for 10-12 minutes, shaking the basket twice. Sprinkle with salt and serve with hummus.

Baked Ricotta

Servings:2
Cooking Time: 15 Minutes
Ingredients:
- 1 (15-ounce / 425-g) container whole milk Ricotta cheese
- 3 tablespoons grated Parmesan cheese, divided
- 2 tablespoons extra-virgin olive oil
- 1 teaspoon chopped fresh thyme leaves
- 1 teaspoon grated lemon zest
- 1 clove garlic, crushed with press
- ¼ teaspoon salt
- ¼ teaspoon pepper
- Toasted baguette slices or crackers, for serving

Directions:
1. Preheat the air fryer to 380ºF (193ºC).
2. To get the baking dish in and out of the air fryer, create a sling using a 24-inch length of foil, folded lengthwise into thirds.
3. Whisk together the Ricotta, 2 tablespoons of the Parmesan, oil, thyme, lemon zest, garlic, salt, and pepper. Pour into a baking dish. Cover the dish tightly with foil.
4. Place the sling under dish and lift by the ends into the air fryer, tucking the ends of the sling around the dish. Bake for 10 minutes. Remove the foil cover and sprinkle with the remaining 1 tablespoon of the Parmesan. Air fry for 5 more minutes, or until bubbly at edges and the top is browned.
5. Serve warm with toasted baguette slices or crackers.

Panko-breaded Onion Rings

Servings: 4
Cooking Time: 12 Minutes
Ingredients:
- 1 large sweet onion, cut into ½-inch slices and rings separated
- 2 cups ice water
- ½ cup all-purpose flour
- 1 teaspoon paprika
- 1 teaspoon salt
- ½ teaspoon black pepper
- ½ teaspoon garlic powder
- ¼ teaspoon onion powder
- 1 egg, whisked
- 2 tablespoons milk
- 1 cup breadcrumbs

Directions:
1. Preheat the air fryer to 400°F.
2. In a large bowl, soak the onion rings in the water for 5 minutes. Drain and pat dry with a towel.
3. In a medium bowl, place the flour, paprika, salt, pepper, garlic powder, and onion powder.
4. In a second bowl, whisk together the egg and milk.
5. In a third bowl, place the breadcrumbs.
6. To bread the onion rings, dip them first into the flour mixture, then into the egg mixture (shaking off the

excess), and then into the breadcrumbs. Place the coated onion rings onto a plate while you bread all the rings.
7. Place the onion rings into the air fryer basket in a single layer, sometimes nesting smaller rings into larger rings. Spray with cooking spray. Cook for 3 minutes, turn the rings over, and spray with more cooking spray. Cook for another 3 to 5 minutes. Cook the rings in batches; you may need to do 2 or 3 batches, depending on the size of your air fryer.

Crab-stuffed Mushrooms
Servings: 4
Cooking Time: 20 Minutes
Ingredients:
- ½ cup shredded mozzarella cheese
- 8 portobello mushrooms
- 1 tbsp olive oil
- ¼ tsp salt
- 3 oz lump crabmeat
- 3 tsp grated Parmesan cheese
- ¼ cup panko bread crumbs
- 1 tbsp ground walnuts
- 3 tsp mayonnaise
- 2 tbsp chopped chives
- 1 egg, beaten
- 1 garlic clove, minced
- ¼ tsp seafood seasoning
- 1 tbsp chopped cilantro

Directions:
1. Clean the mushrooms with a damp paper towel. Remove stems and chop them finely. Set aside. Take the mushroom caps and brush with oil before sprinkling with salt. Combine the remaining ingredients, excluding mozzarella, in a bowl. Spoon crab filling mixture into each mushroom cap. Top each cap with mozzarella and press down so that it may stick to the filling.
2. Preheat air fryer to 360°F. Place the stuffed mushrooms in the greased frying basket. Bake 8-10 minutes until the mushrooms are soft and the mozzarella is golden. Serve.

Stuffed Mushrooms With Bacon
Servings: 24
Cooking Time: 15 Minutes
Ingredients:
- 24 mushrooms, caps and stems diced
- 1 ½ tablespoon mozzarella cheese, shredded
- ½ cup sour cream
- 1 cup cheddar cheese, shredded
- 2 bacon slices, diced
- 1 small onion, diced
- ½ onion, diced
- ½ bell pepper, chopped

Directions:
1. Add bacon, carrot, diced mushrooms stems, onion, and bell pepper to pan and heat over medium heat.
2. Cook this vegetable mixture until softened, for about 5 minutes.
3. Add sour cream and cheddar cheese and cook until cheese is melted, about 2 minutes.

4. At 350 degrees F/ 175 degrees C, preheat your air fryer.
5. Divide the vegetable cheese mixture into the mushroom caps and place them in the air fryer basket.
6. Sprinkle mozzarella cheese on top.
7. Cook mushrooms for almost 8 minutes or until cheese is melted.
8. Serve and enjoy.

Bbq Cocktail Sausage
Servings: 6
Cooking Time: 15 Minutes
Ingredients:
- 1 pound beef cocktail wieners
- 10 ounces barbecue sauce, no sugar added

Directions:
1. At 380 degrees F/ 195 degrees C, preheat your air fryer.
2. Prick holes into your sausages using a fork and transfer them to the baking pan.
3. Cook for 13 minutes. Spoon the barbecue sauce into the pan and cook an additional 2 minutes.
4. Serve with toothpicks.

Bacon-wrapped Onion Rings
Servings: 8
Cooking Time: 10 Minutes
Ingredients:
- 1 large white onion, peeled and cut into 16 (¼"-thick) slices
- 8 slices sugar-free bacon

Directions:
1. Stack 2 slices onion and wrap with 1 slice bacon. Secure with a toothpick. Repeat with remaining onion slices and bacon.
2. Place onion rings into ungreased air fryer basket. Adjust the temperature to 350°F and set the timer for 10 minutes, turning rings halfway through cooking. Bacon will be crispy when done. Serve warm.

Roasted Nut Mixture
Servings: 6
Cooking Time: 20 Minutes
Ingredients:
- ½ cup walnuts
- ½ cup pecans
- ½ cup almonds
- 1 egg white
- 1 packet stevia
- ½-tablespoon ground cinnamon
- A pinch of cayenne pepper

Directions:
1. Mix up all of the ingredients in a bowl.
2. Arrange the nuts to the basket in the preheated air fryer (you can lay a piece of baking paper).
3. Cook the nuts for about 20 minutes at 320 degrees F/ 160 degrees C, stirring once halfway through.
4. Once done, transfer the hot nuts in a glass or steel bowl and serve.

Crunchy Spicy Chickpeas

Servings: 6
Cooking Time: 12 Minutes
Ingredients:
- 2½ cups Canned chickpeas, drained and rinsed
- 2½ tablespoons Vegetable or canola oil
- up to 1 tablespoon Cajun or jerk dried seasoning blend (see here for a Cajun blend, here for a jerk blend)
- up to ¾ teaspoon Table salt (optional)

Directions:
1. Preheat the air fryer to 400°F.
2. Toss the chickpeas, oil, seasoning blend, and salt (if using) in a large bowl until the chickpeas are evenly coated.
3. When the machine is at temperature, pour the chickpeas into the basket. Air-fry for 12 minutes, removing the basket at the 4- and 8-minute marks to toss and rearrange the chickpeas, until very aromatic and perhaps sizzling but not burned.
4. Pour the chickpeas into a large serving bowl. Cool for a couple of minutes, gently stirring once, before you dive in.

Crispy Old Bay Chicken Wings

Servings: 4
Cooking Time: 15 Minutes
Ingredients:
- Olive oil
- 2 tablespoons Old Bay seasoning
- 2 teaspoons baking powder
- 2 teaspoons salt
- 2 pounds chicken wings

Directions:
1. Spray a fryer basket lightly with olive oil.
2. In a large zip-top plastic bag, mix together the Old Bay seasoning, baking powder, and salt.
3. Pat the wings dry with paper towels.
4. Place the wings in the zip-top bag, seal, and toss with the seasoning mixture until evenly coated.
5. Place the seasoned wings in the fryer basket in a single layer. Lightly spray with olive oil. You may need to cook them in batches.
6. Air fry for 7 minutes. Turn the wings over, lightly spray them with olive oil, and air fry until the wings are crispy and lightly browned, 5 to 8 more minutes. Using a meat thermometer, check to make sure the internal temperature is 165°F or higher.

Cheesy Jalapeño Poppers

Servings: 4
Cooking Time: 10 Minutes
Ingredients:
- 8 jalapeño peppers
- ½ cup whipped cream cheese
- ¼ cup shredded Cheddar cheese

Directions:
1. Preheat the air fryer to 360°F (182°C).
2. Use a paring knife to carefully cut off the jalapeño tops, then scoop out the ribs and seeds. Set aside.
3. In a medium bowl, combine the whipped cream cheese and shredded Cheddar cheese. Place the mixture in a sealable plastic bag, and using a pair of scissors, cut off one corner from the bag. Gently squeeze some cream cheese mixture into each pepper until almost full.
4. Place a piece of parchment paper on the bottom of the air fryer basket and place the poppers on top, distributing evenly. Air fry for 10 minutes.
5. Allow the poppers to cool for 5 to 10 minutes before serving.

Cheesy Tortellini Bites

Servings: 8
Cooking Time: 10 Minutes
Ingredients:
- 1 large egg
- ½ teaspoon black pepper
- ½ teaspoon garlic powder
- 1 teaspoon Italian seasoning
- 12 ounces frozen cheese tortellini
- ½ cup panko breadcrumbs

Directions:
1. Preheat the air fryer to 380°F.
2. Spray the air fryer basket with an olive-oil-based spray.
3. In a medium bowl, whisk the egg with the pepper, garlic powder, and Italian seasoning.
4. Dip the tortellini in the egg batter and then coat with the breadcrumbs. Place each tortellini in the basket, trying not to overlap them. You may need to cook in batches to ensure the even crisp all around.
5. Bake for 5 minutes, shake the basket, and bake another 5 minutes.
6. Remove and let cool 5 minutes. Serve with marinara sauce, ranch, or your favorite dressing.

Honey-mustard Chicken Wings

Servings: 2
Cooking Time: 14 Minutes
Ingredients:
- 2 pounds chicken wings
- salt and freshly ground black pepper
- 2 tablespoons butter
- ¼ cup honey
- ¼ cup spicy brown mustard
- pinch ground cayenne pepper
- 2 teaspoons Worcestershire sauce

Directions:
1. Prepare the chicken wings by cutting off the wing tips and discarding (or freezing for chicken stock). Divide the drumettes from the wingettes by cutting through the joint. Place the chicken wing pieces in a large bowl.
2. Preheat the air fryer to 400°F.
3. Season the wings with salt and freshly ground black pepper and air-fry the wings in two batches for 10

minutes per batch, shaking the basket half way through the cooking process.
4. While the wings are air-frying, combine the remaining ingredients in a small saucepan over low heat.
5. When both batches are done, toss all the wings with the honey-mustard sauce and toss them all back into the basket for another 4 minutes to heat through and finish cooking. Give the basket a good shake part way through the cooking process to redistribute the wings. Remove the wings from the air fryer and serve.

Roasted Red Salsa

Servings: 4
Cooking Time: 10 Minutes
Ingredients:
- 10 medium Roma tomatoes, quartered
- 1 medium white onion, peeled and sliced
- 2 medium cloves garlic, peeled
- 2 tablespoons olive oil
- ¼ cup chopped fresh cilantro
- ½ teaspoon salt

Directions:
1. Preheat the air fryer to 340°F.
2. Place tomatoes, onion, and garlic into a 6" round baking dish. Drizzle with oil and toss to coat.
3. Place in the air fryer basket and cook 10 minutes, stirring twice during cooking, until vegetables start to turn dark brown and caramelize.
4. In a food processor, add roasted vegetables, cilantro, and salt. Pulse five times until vegetables are mostly broken down. Serve immediately.

String Bean Fries

Servings: 4
Cooking Time: 6 Minutes
Ingredients:
- ½ pound fresh string beans
- 2 eggs
- 4 teaspoons water
- ½ cup white flour
- ½ cup breadcrumbs
- ¼ teaspoon salt
- ¼ teaspoon ground black pepper
- ¼ teaspoon dry mustard (optional)
- oil for misting or cooking spray

Directions:
1. Preheat air fryer to 360°F.
2. Trim stem ends from string beans, wash, and pat dry.
3. In a shallow dish, beat eggs and water together until well blended.
4. Place flour in a second shallow dish.
5. In a third shallow dish, stir together the breadcrumbs, salt, pepper, and dry mustard if using.
6. Dip each string bean in egg mixture, flour, egg mixture again, then breadcrumbs.
7. When you finish coating all the string beans, open air fryer and place them in basket.
8. Cook for 3minutes.
9. Stop and mist string beans with oil or cooking spray.
10. Cook for 3 moreminutes or until string beans are crispy and nicely browned.

Veggie Salmon Nachos

Servings:6
Cooking Time: 9 To 12 Minutes
Ingredients:
- 2 ounces (57 g) baked no-salt corn tortilla chips
- 1 (5-ounce / 142-g) baked salmon fillet, flaked
- ½ cup canned low-sodium black beans, rinsed and drained
- 1 red bell pepper, chopped
- ½ cup grated carrot
- 1 jalapeño pepper, minced
- ⅓ cup shredded low-sodium low-fat Swiss cheese
- 1 tomato, chopped

Directions:
1. Preheat the air fryer to 360ºF (182ºC).
2. In a baking pan, layer the tortilla chips. Top with the salmon, black beans, red bell pepper, carrot, jalapeño, and Swiss cheese.
3. Bake in the air fryer for 9 to 12 minutes, or until the cheese is melted and starts to brown.
4. Top with the tomato and serve.

Bacon-wrapped Jalapeño Poppers

Servings:4
Cooking Time: 12 Minutes
Ingredients:
- 3 ounces full-fat cream cheese
- ½ cup shredded sharp Cheddar cheese
- ¼ teaspoon garlic powder
- 6 jalapeño peppers, trimmed and halved lengthwise, seeded and membranes removed
- 12 slices bacon

Directions:
1. Preheat the air fryer to 400°F.
2. In a large microwave-safe bowl, place cream cheese, Cheddar, and garlic powder. Microwave 20 seconds until softened and stir. Spoon cheese mixture into hollow jalapeño halves.
3. Wrap a bacon slice around each jalapeño half, completely covering pepper.
4. Place in the air fryer basket and cook 12 minutes, turning halfway through cooking time. Serve warm.

Veggie Chips

Servings: X
Cooking Time: X
Ingredients:
- sweet potato
- large parsnip
- large carrot
- turnip
- large beet
- vegetable or canola oil, in a spray bottle
- salt

The Ultimate Tower Air Fryer Cookbook

Directions:
1. You can do a medley of vegetable chips, or just select from the vegetables listed. Whatever you choose to do, scrub the vegetables well and then slice them paper-thin using a mandolin.
2. Preheat the air fryer to 400°F.
3. Air-fry the chips in batches, one type of vegetable at a time. Spray the chips lightly with oil and transfer them to the air fryer basket. The key is to NOT over-load the basket. You can overlap the chips a little, but don't pile them on top of each other. Doing so will make it much harder to get evenly browned and crispy chips. Air-fry at 400°F for the time indicated below, shaking the basket several times during the cooking process for even cooking.
4. Sweet Potato – 8 to 9 minutes
5. Parsnips – 5 minutes
6. Carrot – 7 minutes
7. Turnips – 8 minutes
8. Beets – 9 minutes
9. Season the chips with salt during the last couple of minutes of air-frying. Check the chips as they cook until they are done to your liking. Some will start to brown sooner than others.
10. You can enjoy the chips warm out of the air fryer or cool them to room temperature for crispier chips.

Bacon-wrapped Goat Cheese Poppers
Servings: 10
Cooking Time: 10 Minutes
Ingredients:
- 10 large jalapeño peppers
- 8 ounces goat cheese
- 10 slices bacon

Directions:
1. Preheat the air fryer to 380°F.
2. Slice the jalapeños in half. Carefully remove the veins and seeds of the jalapeños with a spoon.
3. Fill each jalapeño half with 2 teaspoons goat cheese.
4. Cut the bacon in half lengthwise to make long strips. Wrap the jalapeños with bacon, trying to cover the entire length of the jalapeño.
5. Place the bacon-wrapped jalapeños into the air fryer basket. Cook the stuffed jalapeños for 10 minutes or until bacon is crispy.

Crunchy Zucchini Fries With Parmesan
Servings: 4
Cooking Time: 10 Minutes
Ingredients:
- 2 medium zucchinis, cut into fry shape
- ½ teaspoon garlic powder
- 1 teaspoon Italian seasoning
- ½ cup parmesan cheese, grated
- ½ cup almond flour
- 1 egg, lightly beaten
- Black pepper
- Salt

Directions:
1. Add egg in a suitable bowl and whisk well.
2. In a shallow bowl, mix together almond flour, spices, parmesan cheese, black pepper, and salt.
3. Grease its air fryer basket with cooking spray.
4. Dip those zucchini fries in egg then coat with almond flour mixture and place in the air fryer basket.
5. Cook zucchini fries for almost 10 minutes at 400 degrees F/ 205 degrees C.
6. Serve and enjoy.

Tomato & Halloumi Bruschetta
Servings: 4
Cooking Time: 20 Minutes
Ingredients:
- 2 tbsp softened butter
- 8 French bread slices
- 1 cup grated halloumi cheese
- ½ cup basil pesto
- 12 chopped cherry tomatoes
- 2 green onions, thinly sliced

Directions:
1. Preheat air fryer to 350°F. Spread butter on one side of the bread. Place butter-side up in the frying basket. Bake until the bread is slightly brown, 3-5 minutes. Remove the bread and top it with halloumi cheese. Melt the cheese on the bread in the air fryer for another 1-3 minutes.
2. Meanwhile, mix pesto, cherry tomatoes, and green onions in a small bowl. When the cheese has melted, take the bread out of the fryer and arrange on a plate. Top with pesto mix and serve.

Jalapeño Cheese Balls
Servings:12
Cooking Time: 15 Minutes
Ingredients:
- 4 ounces cream cheese
- ⅓ cup shredded mozzarella cheese
- ⅓ cup shredded Cheddar cheese
- 2 jalapeños, finely chopped
- ½ cup bread crumbs
- 2 eggs
- ½ cup all-purpose flour
- Salt
- Pepper
- Cooking oil

Directions:
1. In a medium bowl, combine the cream cheese, mozzarella, Cheddar, and jalapeños. Mix well.
2. Form the cheese mixture into balls about an inch thick. Using a small ice cream scoop works well.
3. Arrange the cheese balls on a sheet pan and place in the freezer for 15 minutes. This will help the cheese balls maintain their shape while frying.
4. Spray the air fryer basket with cooking oil.
5. Place the bread crumbs in a small bowl. In another small bowl, beat the eggs. In a third small bowl, combine the flour with salt and pepper to taste, and mix well.

6. Remove the cheese balls from the freezer. Dip the cheese balls in the flour, then the eggs, and then the bread crumbs.
7. Place the cheese balls in the air fryer. (It is okay to stack them.) Spray with cooking oil. Cook for 8 minutes.
8. Open the air fryer and flip the cheese balls. I recommend flipping them instead of shaking so the balls maintain their form. Cook an additional 4 minutes.
9. Cool before serving.

Deviled Eggs With Ricotta
Servings: 4
Cooking Time: 17 Minutes
Ingredients:
- 2 eggs
- ½ teaspoon harissa
- ½ teaspoon chili flakes
- ¼ teaspoon chili powder
- 1 teaspoon ricotta cheese
- ½ teaspoon dried thyme

Directions:
1. At 250 degrees F/ 120 degrees C, preheat your air fryer.
2. Place 2 eggs in the air fryer basket and cook them for almost 17 minutes.
3. Then cool and peel the eggs. Cut the peeled eggs into halves and remove the egg yolks.
4. Stir the egg yolks with the help of the fork until they are smooth.
5. After this, add chili flakes, harissa, chili powder, ricotta cheese, and dried thyme.
6. Stir the mass until smooth. Fill the egg whites with hot egg yolk mixture.
7. Serve.

Garlic Edamame
Servings:4
Cooking Time: 10 Minutes
Ingredients:
- Olive oil
- 1 (16-ounce) bag frozen edamame in pods
- ½ teaspoon salt
- ½ teaspoon garlic salt
- ¼ teaspoon freshly ground black pepper
- ½ teaspoon red pepper flakes (optional)

Directions:
1. Spray a fryer basket lightly with olive oil.
2. In a medium bowl, add the frozen edamame and lightly spray with olive oil. Toss to coat.
3. In a small bowl, mix together the salt, garlic salt, black pepper, and red pepper flakes (if using). Add the mixture to the edamame and toss until evenly coated.
4. Place half the edamame in the fryer basket. Do not overfill the basket.
5. Air fry for 5 minutes. Shake the basket and cook until the edamame is starting to brown and get crispy, 3 to 5 more minutes.
6. Repeat with the remaining edamame and serve immediately.

Rumaki
Servings: 24
Cooking Time: 12 Minutes
Ingredients:
- 10 ounces raw chicken livers
- 1 can sliced water chestnuts, drained
- ¼ cup low-sodium teriyaki sauce
- 12 slices turkey bacon
- toothpicks

Directions:
1. Cut livers into 1½-inch pieces, trimming out tough veins as you slice.
2. Place livers, water chestnuts, and teriyaki sauce in small container with lid. If needed, add another tablespoon of teriyaki sauce to make sure livers are covered. Refrigerate for 1 hour.
3. When ready to cook, cut bacon slices in half crosswise.
4. Wrap 1 piece of liver and 1 slice of water chestnut in each bacon strip. Secure with toothpick.
5. When you have wrapped half of the livers, place them in the air fryer basket in a single layer.
6. Cook at 390°F for 12 minutes, until liver is done and bacon is crispy.
7. While first batch cooks, wrap the remaining livers. Repeat step 6 to cook your second batch.

Easy Crispy Prawns
Servings:4
Cooking Time:10 Minutes
Ingredients:
- 1 egg
- ½ pound nacho chips, crushed
- 18 prawns, peeled and deveined
- Salt and black pepper, to taste

Directions:
1. Preheat the Air fryer to 355°F and grease an Air fryer basket.
2. Crack egg in a shallow dish and beat well.
3. Place the crushed nacho chips in another shallow dish.
4. Coat prawns into egg and then roll into nacho chips.
5. Place the coated prawns into the Air fryer basket and cook for about 10 minutes.
6. Dish out and serve warm.

Parmesan Breaded Zucchini Chips
Servings: 5
Cooking Time: 20 Minutes
Ingredients:
- For the zucchini chips
- 2 medium zucchini
- 2 eggs
- ⅓ cup bread crumbs
- ⅓ cup grated Parmesan cheese
- Salt
- Pepper
- Cooking oil
- For the lemon aioli

- ½ cup mayonnaise
- ½ tablespoon olive oil
- Juice of ½ lemon
- 1 teaspoon minced garlic
- Salt
- Pepper

Directions:
1. Slice the zucchini into thin chips (about ⅛ inch thick) using a knife or mandoline.
2. In a small bowl, beat the eggs. In another small bowl, combine the bread crumbs, Parmesan cheese, and salt and pepper to taste.
3. Spray the air fryer basket with cooking oil.
4. Dip the zucchini slices one at a time in the eggs and then the bread crumb mixture. You can also sprinkle the bread crumbs onto the zucchini slices with a spoon.
5. Place the zucchini chips in the air fryer basket, but do not stack. Cook in batches. Spray the chips with cooking oil from a distance (otherwise, the breading may fly off). Cook for 10 minutes.
6. Remove the cooked zucchini chips from the air fryer, then repeat step 5 with the remaining zucchini.
7. While the zucchini is cooking, combine the mayonnaise, olive oil, lemon juice, and garlic in a small bowl, adding salt and pepper to taste. Mix well until fully combined.
8. Cool the zucchini and serve alongside the aioli.

Cheesy Green Dip

Servings: 6
Cooking Time: 30 Minutes
Ingredients:
- ½ cup canned artichoke hearts, chopped
- ½ cup cream cheese, softened
- 2 tbsp grated Romano cheese
- ¼ cup grated mozzarella
- ½ cup spinach, chopped
- ½ cup milk
- Salt and pepper to taste

Directions:
1. Preheat air fryer to 350°F. Whisk the milk, cream cheese, Romano cheese, spinach, artichoke hearts, salt, and pepper in a mixing bowl. Pour the mixture into a greased baking pan, and sprinkle the grated mozzarella cheese over the top. Bake in the air fryer for 20 minutes. Serve.

Potato Skin Bites

Servings: 25
Cooking Time: 20 Minutes
Ingredients:
- 4 slices bacon
- 4 large russet potatoes
- 1 tablespoon extra-virgin olive oil
- 1 teaspoon paprika
- Salt
- Pepper
- 1 cup shredded Cheddar cheese
- 2 teaspoons chopped chives
- 2 teaspoons chopped scallions, green parts (white parts optional)

Directions:
1. In a skillet over medium-high heat, cook the bacon for about 5 to 7 minutes, flipping to evenly crisp. Drain on paper towels, crumble, and set aside.
2. Cut the potatoes into ½-inch-thick rounds. Place the potato rounds in a large bowl with the olive oil and paprika, and season with salt and pepper to taste. Toss to fully coat.
3. Place the potatoes in the air fryer basket. It is okay stack them, but do not overcrowd the basket. You may need to cook the potatoes in two batches. Cook for 10 minutes.
4. Open the air fryer and shake the basket. Cook for an additional 5 to 8 minutes, until the potato skin bites are soft in the middle and crisp along the edges.
5. Transfer the potato skin bites to a serving dish. Top with the shredded cheese, crumbled bacon, chives, and scallions. Serve.

Corn With Coriander And Parmesan Cheese

Servings: 2
Cooking Time: 15 Minutes
Ingredients:
- 2 ears corn, husked and cleaned
- 1 tablespoon melted butter
- 1 tablespoon fresh coriander, finely chopped
- 2 tablespoons Parmesan cheese, finely chopped

Directions:
1. Butter the corn and then arrange the corn in the air fryer.
2. Cook for 14 minutes at 400 degrees F/ 205 degrees C.
3. When done, serve warm and top with the Parmesan cheese and fresh coriander.
4. Bon appétit!

Crispy Bacon Strips

Servings: 4
Cooking Time: 10 Minutes
Ingredients:
- 4 bacon strips, cut into small pieces
- ½ cup pork rinds, crushed
- ¼ cup hot sauce

Directions:
1. Add bacon pieces in a suitable bowl.
2. Add hot sauce and toss well.
3. Add crushed pork rinds and toss until bacon pieces are well coated.
4. Transfer bacon pieces in air fryer basket and cook at almost 350 degrees F/ 175 degrees C for almost 10 minutes.
5. Serve and enjoy.

Spicy Turkey Meatballs

Servings: 18
Cooking Time: 15 Minutes
Ingredients:
- 1 pound 85/15 ground turkey
- 1 large egg, whisked
- ¼ cup sriracha hot chili sauce
- ½ teaspoon salt
- ½ teaspoon paprika
- ¼ teaspoon ground black pepper

Directions:
1. Combine all ingredients in a large bowl. Roll mixture into eighteen meatballs, about 3 tablespoons each.
2. Place meatballs into ungreased air fryer basket. Adjust the temperature to 375°F and set the timer for 15 minutes, shaking the basket three times during cooking. Meatballs will be done when browned and internal temperature is at least 165°F. Serve warm.

Spicy Chickpeas With Paprika

Servings: 4
Cooking Time: 10 Minutes
Ingredients:
- 1 15-ounces can chickpeas, rinsed and drained
- 1 tablespoon olive oil
- ½ teaspoon ground cumin
- ½ teaspoon cayenne pepper
- ½ teaspoon smoked paprika
- Salt, to taste

Directions:
1. At 390 degrees F/ 200 degrees C, preheat your air fryer.
2. In a suitable bowl, add all the recipe ingredients and toss to coat well.
3. Add the chickpeas in an air fryer basket in 2 batches.
4. Air fry for about 8-10 minutes.
5. Serve.

Pesto Bruschetta

Servings: 4
Cooking Time: 4 To 8 Minutes
Ingredients:
- 8 slices French bread, ½ inch thick
- 2 tablespoons softened butter
- 1 cup shredded mozzarella cheese
- ½ cup basil pesto
- 1 cup chopped grape tomatoes
- 2 green onions, thinly sliced

Directions:
1. Spread the bread with the butter and place butter-side up in the air fryer basket. Bake for 3 to 5 minutes or until the bread is light golden brown.
2. Remove the bread from the basket and top each piece with some of the cheese. Return to the basket in batches and bake until the cheese melts, about 1 to 3 minutes.
3. Meanwhile, combine the pesto, tomatoes, and green onions in a small bowl.
4. When the cheese has melted, remove the bread from the air fryer and place on a serving plate. Top each slice with some of the pesto mixture and serve.

Buffalo French Fries

Servings: 6
Cooking Time: 35 Minutes
Ingredients:
- 3 large russet potatoes
- 2 tbsp buffalo sauce
- 2 tbsp extra-virgin olive oil
- Salt and pepper to taste

Directions:
1. Preheat air fryer to 380°F. Peel and cut potatoes lengthwise into French fries. Place them in a bowl, then coat with olive oil, salt and pepper. Air Fry them for 10 minutes. Shake the basket, then cook for five minutes. Serve drizzled with Buffalo sauce immediately.

Air Fried Pork With Fennel

Servings: 6
Cooking Time: 25 Minutes
Ingredients:
- 2 pounds pork belly, cut into strips
- 2 tablespoons olive oil
- 2 teaspoons fennel seeds
- A pinch of salt and black pepper
- A pinch of basil, dried

Directions:
1. Mix all the ingredients in a clean bowl.
2. Toss well and arrange the marinated pork strips to the basket of your air fryer.
3. Cook for 25 minutes at 425 degrees F/ 220 degrees C.
4. Before serving as a snack, divide into bowls.

Classic Chicken Wings

Servings: 8
Cooking Time: 20 Minutes
Ingredients:
- 16 chicken wings
- ¼ cup all-purpose flour
- ¼ teaspoon garlic powder
- ¼ teaspoon paprika
- ½ teaspoon salt
- ½ teaspoon black pepper
- ¼ cup butter
- ½ cup hot sauce
- ½ teaspoon Worcestershire sauce
- 2 ounces crumbled blue cheese, for garnish

Directions:
1. Preheat the air fryer to 380°F.
2. Pat the chicken wings dry with paper towels.
3. In a medium bowl, mix together the flour, garlic powder, paprika, salt, and pepper. Toss the chicken wings with the flour mixture, dusting off any excess.

The Ultimate Tower Air Fryer Cookbook

4. Place the chicken wings in the air fryer basket, making sure that the chicken wings aren't touching. Cook the chicken wings for 10 minutes, turn over, and cook another 5 minutes. Raise the temperature to 400°F and continue crisping the chicken wings for an additional 3 to 5 minutes.
5. Meanwhile, in a microwave-safe bowl, melt the butter and hot sauce for 1 to 2 minutes in the microwave. Remove from the microwave and stir in the Worcestershire sauce.
6. When the chicken wings have cooked, immediately transfer the chicken wings into the hot sauce mixture. Serve the coated chicken wings on a plate, and top with crumbled blue cheese.

Avocado Egg Rolls

Servings: 8
Cooking Time: 8 Minutes
Ingredients:
- 8 full-size egg roll wrappers
- 1 medium avocado, sliced into 8 pieces
- 1 cup cooked black beans, divided
- ½ cup mild salsa, divided
- ½ cup shredded Mexican cheese, divided
- ⅓ cup filtered water, divided
- ½ cup sour cream
- 1 teaspoon chipotle hot sauce

Directions:
1. Preheat the air fryer to 400°F.
2. Place the egg roll wrapper on a flat surface and place 1 strip of avocado down in the center.
3. Top the avocado with 2 tablespoons of black beans, 1 tablespoon of salsa, and 1 tablespoon of shredded cheese.
4. Place two of your fingers into the water, and then moisten the four outside edges of the egg roll wrapper with water (so the outer edges will secure shut).
5. Fold the bottom corner up, covering the filling. Then secure the sides over the top, remembering to lightly moisten them so they stick. Tightly roll the egg roll up and moisten the final flap of the wrapper and firmly press it into the egg roll to secure it shut.
6. Repeat Steps 2–5 until all 8 egg rolls are complete.
7. When ready to cook, spray the air fryer basket with olive oil spray and place the egg rolls into the basket. Depending on the size and type of air fryer you have, you may need to do this in two sets.
8. Cook for 4 minutes, flip, and then cook the remaining 4 minutes.
9. Repeat until all the egg rolls are cooked. Meanwhile, mix the sour cream with the hot sauce to serve as a dipping sauce.
10. Serve warm.

Grilled Cheese Sandwich Deluxe

Servings: 4
Cooking Time: 6 Minutes
Ingredients:
- 8 ounces Brie
- 8 slices oat nut bread
- 1 large ripe pear, cored and cut into ½-inch-thick slices
- 2 tablespoons butter, melted

Directions:
1. Spread a quarter of the Brie on each of four slices of bread.
2. Top Brie with thick slices of pear, then the remaining 4 slices of bread.
3. Lightly brush both sides of each sandwich with melted butter.
4. Cooking 2 at a time, place sandwiches in air fryer basket and cook at 360°F for 6 minutes or until cheese melts and outside looks golden brown.

Cauliflower Wings With Buffalo Sauce

Servings: 4
Cooking Time: 14 Minutes
Ingredients:
- 1 cauliflower head, cut into florets
- 1 tablespoon butter, melted
- ½ cup buffalo sauce
- Black pepper
- Salt

Directions:
1. Grease its air fryer basket with cooking spray.
2. In a suitable bowl, mix together buffalo sauce, butter, black pepper, and salt.
3. Add cauliflower florets into the air fryer basket and cook at almost 400 degrees F/ 205 degrees C for 7 minutes.
4. Transfer cauliflower florets into the buffalo sauce mixture and toss well.
5. Again, add cauliflower florets into the air fryer basket and cook for 7 minutes more at 400 degrees F/ 205 degrees C.
6. Serve and enjoy.

Antipasto-stuffed Cherry Tomatoes

Servings: 12
Cooking Time: 9 Minutes
Ingredients:
- 12 Large cherry tomatoes, preferably Campari tomatoes (about 1½ ounces each and the size of golf balls)
- ½ cup Seasoned Italian-style dried bread crumbs (gluten-free, if a concern)
- ¼ cup (about ¾ ounce) Finely grated Parmesan cheese
- ¼ cup Finely chopped pitted black olives
- ¼ cup Finely chopped marinated artichoke hearts
- 2 tablespoons Marinade from the artichokes
- 4 Sun-dried tomatoes (dry, not packed in oil), finely chopped
- Olive oil spray

Directions:
1. Preheat the air fryer to 400°F.

2. Cut the top off of each fresh tomato, exposing the seeds and pulp. (The tops can be saved for a snack, sprinkled with some kosher salt, to tide you over while the stuffed tomatoes cook.) Cut a very small slice off the bottom of each tomato (no cutting into the pulp) so it will stand up flat on your work surface. Use a melon baller to remove and discard the seeds and pulp from each tomato.
3. Mix the bread crumbs, cheese, olives, artichoke hearts, marinade, and sun-dried tomatoes in a bowl until well combined. Stuff this mixture into each prepared tomato, about 1½ tablespoons in each. Generously coat the tops of the tomatoes with olive oil spray.
4. Set the tomatoes stuffing side up in the basket. Air-fry undisturbed for 9 minutes, or until the stuffing has browned a bit and the tomatoes are blistered in places.
5. Remove the basket and cool the tomatoes in it for 5 minutes. Then use kitchen tongs to gently transfer the tomatoes to a serving platter.

Fried Cheese Ravioli With Marinara Sauce

Servings: 4
Cooking Time: 7 Minutes
Ingredients:
- 1 pound cheese ravioli, fresh or frozen
- 2 eggs, lightly beaten
- 1 cup plain breadcrumbs
- ½ teaspoon paprika
- ½ teaspoon dried oregano
- ½ teaspoon salt
- grated Parmesan cheese
- chopped fresh parsley
- 1 to 2 cups marinara sauce (jarred or homemade)

Directions:
1. Bring a stockpot of salted water to a boil. Boil the ravioli according to the package directions and then drain. Let the cooked ravioli cool to a temperature where you can comfortably handle them.
2. While the pasta is cooking, set up a dredging station with two shallow dishes. Place the eggs into one dish. Combine the breadcrumbs, paprika, dried oregano and salt in the other dish.
3. Preheat the air fryer to 380°F.
4. Working with one at a time, dip the cooked ravioli into the egg, coating all sides. Then press the ravioli into the breadcrumbs, making sure that all sides are covered. Transfer the ravioli to the air fryer basket, cooking in batches, one layer at a time. Air-fry at 380°F for 7 minutes.
5. While the ravioli is air-frying, bring the marinara sauce to a simmer on the stovetop. Transfer to a small bowl.
6. Sprinkle a little Parmesan cheese and chopped parsley on top of the fried ravioli and serve warm with the marinara sauce on the side for dipping.

Air Fry Bacon

Servings: 11
Cooking Time: 10 Minutes
Ingredients:
- 11 bacon slices

Directions:
1. Place half bacon slices in air fryer basket.
2. Cook at 400°F for 10 minutes.
3. Cook remaining half bacon slices using same steps.
4. Serve and enjoy.

Buffalo Cauliflower Snacks

Servings: 6
Cooking Time: 5 Minutes
Ingredients:
- 1 large head cauliflower, separated into small florets
- 1 tablespoon olive oil
- ½ teaspoon garlic powder
- ⅓ cup low-sodium hot wing sauce
- ⅔ cup nonfat Greek yogurt
- ½ teaspoons Tabasco sauce
- 1 celery stalk, chopped
- 1 tablespoon crumbled blue cheese

Directions:
1. In a large bowl, toss the cauliflower florets with the olive oil. Sprinkle with the garlic powder and toss again to coat. Put half of the cauliflower in the air fryer basket. Air-fry for 5 to 7 minutes, until the cauliflower is browned, shaking the basket once during cooking.
2. Transfer to a serving bowl and toss with half of the wing sauce. Repeat with the remaining cauliflower and wing sauce.
3. In a small bowl, stir together the yogurt, Tabasco sauce, celery, and blue cheese. Serve with the cauliflower for dipping.

Chives Meatballs

Servings: 6
Cooking Time: 20 Minutes
Ingredients:
- 1 pound beef meat, ground
- 1 teaspoon onion powder
- 1 teaspoon garlic powder
- A pinch of salt and black pepper
- 2 tablespoons chives, chopped
- Cooking spray

Directions:
1. In a bowl, mix all the ingredients except the cooking spray, stir well and shape medium meatballs out of this mix. Pace them in your lined air fryer's basket, grease with cooking spray and cook at 360°F for 20 minutes. Serve as an appetizer.

Savory Eggplant Fries

Servings: 4
Cooking Time: 20 Minutes
Ingredients:
- 1 eggplant, sliced

- 2 ½ tbsp shoyu
- 2 tsp garlic powder
- 2 tsp onion powder
- 4 tsp olive oil
- 2 tbsp fresh basil, chopped

Directions:
1. Preheat air fryer to 390°F. Place the eggplant slices in a bowl and sprinkle the shoyu, garlic, onion, and oil on top. Coat the eggplant evenly. Place the eggplant in a single layer in the greased frying basket and Air Fry for 5 minutes. Remove and put the eggplant in the bowl again. Toss the eggplant slices to coat evenly with the remaining liquid and put back in the fryer. Roast for another 3 minutes. Remove the basket and flip the pieces over to ensure even cooking. Roast for another 5 minutes or until the eggplant is golden. Top with basil and serve.

Greek Street Tacos

Servings: 8
Cooking Time: 3 Minutes
Ingredients:
- 8 small flour tortillas
- 8 tablespoons hummus
- 4 tablespoons crumbled feta cheese
- 4 tablespoons chopped kalamata or other olives (optional)
- olive oil for misting

Directions:
1. Place 1 tablespoon of hummus or tapenade in the center of each tortilla. Top with 1 teaspoon of feta crumbles and 1 teaspoon of chopped olives, if using.
2. Using your finger or a small spoon, moisten the edges of the tortilla all around with water.
3. Fold tortilla over to make a half-moon shape. Press center gently. Then press the edges firmly to seal in the filling.
4. Mist both sides with olive oil.
5. Place in air fryer basket very close but try not to overlap.
6. Cook at 390°F for 3 minutes, just until lightly browned and crispy.

Garlic Parmesan Kale Chips

Servings: 2
Cooking Time: 6 Minutes
Ingredients:
- 16 large kale leaves, washed and thick stems removed
- 1 tablespoon avocado oil
- ½ teaspoon garlic powder
- 1 teaspoon soy sauce or tamari
- ¼ cup grated Parmesan cheese

Directions:
1. Preheat the air fryer to 370°F.
2. Make a stack of kale leaves and cut them into 4 pieces.
3. Place the kale pieces into a large bowl. Drizzle the avocado oil onto the kale and rub to coat. Add the garlic powder, soy sauce or tamari, and cheese, tossing to coat.
4. Pour the chips into the air fryer basket and cook for 3 minutes, shake the basket, and cook another 3 minutes, checking for crispness every minute. When done cooking, pour the kale chips onto paper towels and cool at least 5 minutes before serving.

Chapter 5: Fish And Seafood Recipes

Very Easy Lime-garlic Shrimps

Servings: 1
Cooking Time: 6 Minutes
Ingredients:
- 1 clove of garlic, minced
- 1 cup raw shrimps
- 1 lime, juiced and zested
- Salt and pepper to taste

Directions:
1. In a mixing bowl, combine all Ingredients and give a good stir.
2. Preheat the air fryer to 390°F.
3. Skewer the shrimps onto the metal skewers that come with the double layer rack accessory.
4. Place on the rack and cook for 6 minutes.

French Grouper Nicoise

Servings: 4
Cooking Time: 20 Minutes
Ingredients:
- 4 grouper fillets
- Salt to taste
- ½ tsp ground cumin
- 3 garlic cloves, minced
- 1 tomato, sliced
- ¼ cup sliced Nicoise olives
- ¼ cup dill, chopped
- 1 lemon, juiced
- ¼ cup olive oil

Directions:
1. Preheat air fryer to 380°F. Sprinkle the grouper fillets with salt and cumin. Arrange them on the greased frying basket and top with garlic, tomato slices, olives, and fresh dill. Drizzle with lemon juice and olive oil. Bake for 10-12 minutes. Serve and enjoy!

Chili-lime Shrimp

Servings: 4
Cooking Time: 10 Minutes
Ingredients:
- 1 pound medium shrimp, peeled and deveined
- ½ cup lime juice
- 2 tablespoons olive oil
- 2 tablespoons sriracha
- 1 teaspoon salt
- ¼ teaspoon ground black pepper

Directions:
1. Preheat the air fryer to 375°F.
2. In an 6" round cake pan, combine all ingredients.
3. Place pan in the air fryer and cook 10 minutes, stirring halfway through cooking time, until the inside of shrimp are pearly white and opaque and internal temperature reaches at least 145°F. Serve warm.

Horseradish-crusted Salmon Fillets

Servings: 3
Cooking Time: 8 Minutes
Ingredients:
- ½ cup Fresh bread crumbs
- 4 tablespoons (¼ cup/½ stick) Butter, melted and cooled
- ¼ cup Jarred prepared white horseradish
- Vegetable oil spray
- 4 6-ounce skin-on salmon fillets

Directions:
1. Preheat the air fryer to 400°F.
2. Mix the bread crumbs, butter, and horseradish in a bowl until well combined.
3. Take the basket out of the machine. Generously spray the skin side of each fillet. Pick them up one by one with a nonstick-safe spatula and set them in the basket skin side down with as much air space between them as possible. Divide the bread-crumb mixture between the fillets, coating the top of each fillet with an even layer. Generously coat the bread-crumb mixture with vegetable oil spray.
4. Return the basket to the machine and air-fry undisturbed for 8 minutes, or until the topping has lightly browned and the fish is firm but not hard.
5. Use a nonstick-safe spatula to transfer the salmon fillets to serving plates. Cool for 5 minutes before serving. Because of the butter in the topping, it will stay very hot for quite a while. Take care, especially if you're serving these fillets to children.

Cilantro Sea Bass

Servings: 2
Cooking Time: 15 Minutes
Ingredients:
- Salt and pepper to taste
- 1 tsp olive oil
- 2 sea bass fillets
- ½ tsp berbere seasoning
- 2 tsp chopped cilantro
- 1 tsp dried thyme
- ½ tsp garlic powder
- 4 lemon quarters

Directions:
1. Preheat air fryer at 375°F. Rub sea bass fillets with olive oil, thyme, garlic powder, salt and black pepper. Season with berbere seasoning. Place fillets in the greased frying basket and Air Fry for 6-8 minutes. Let rest for 5 minutes on a serving plate. Scatter with cilantro and serve with lemon quarters on the side.

Peppery Tilapia Roulade

Servings: 4
Cooking Time: 25 Minutes
Ingredients:
- 4 jarred roasted red pepper slices
- 1 egg
- ½ cup breadcrumbs
- Salt and pepper to taste
- 4 tilapia fillets
- 2 tbsp butter, melted
- 4 lime wedges

- 1 tsp dill

Directions:
1. Preheat air fryer at 350°F. Beat the egg and 2 tbsp of water in a bowl. In another bowl, mix the breadcrumbs, salt, and pepper. Place a red pepper slice and sprinkle with dill on each fish fillet. Tightly roll tilapia fillets from one short end to the other. Secure with toothpicks. Roll each fillet in the egg mixture, then dredge them in the breadcrumbs. Place fish rolls in the greased frying basket and drizzle the tops with melted butter. Roast for 6 minutes. Let rest in a serving dish for 5 minutes before removing the toothpicks. Serve with lime wedges. Enjoy!

Coriander Cod And Green Beans

Servings: 4
Cooking Time: 15 Minutes
Ingredients:
- 12 oz cod fillet
- ½ cup green beans, trimmed and halved
- 1 tablespoon avocado oil
- 1 teaspoon salt
- 1 teaspoon ground coriander

Directions:
1. Cut the cod fillet on 4 servings and sprinkle every serving with salt and ground coriander. After this, place the fish on 4 foil squares. Top them with green beans and avocado oil and wrap them into parcels. Preheat the air fryer to 400°F. Place the cod parcels in the air fryer and cook them for 15 minutes.

Stevia Cod

Servings: 4
Cooking Time: 14 Minutes
Ingredients:
- 1/3 cup stevia
- 2 tablespoons coconut aminos
- 4 cod fillets, boneless
- A pinch of salt and black pepper

Directions:
1. In a pan that fits the air fryer, combine all the ingredients and toss gently. Introduce the pan in the fryer and cook at 350°F for 14 minutes, flipping the fish halfway. Divide everything between plates and serve.

Bang Bang Shrimp

Servings: 4 Servings
Cooking Time: 30 Minutes
Ingredients:
- 1 pound of peeled jumbo shrimp
- 1 cup of mayonnaise
- 1 cup of bread crumbs
- ¾ cup of corn starch
- ½ cup of buttermilk
- ¼ cup of sweet chili sauce
- ½ teaspoon of sriracha
- Chopped fresh parsley, for garnishing

Directions:
1. Preheat your air fryer to 400°F. Spray some oil inside the air fryer basket.
2. Add mayonnaise, sweet chili sauce, and sriracha in a small bowl. Mix it well until combined.
3. Take 6–8 shrimp at a time, generously coat in cornstarch. Then dip in buttermilk and finally roll them in bread crumbs until fully covered. Transfer the coated shrimp in the air fryer in a single layer; avoid them touching.
4. Cook at 400°F for 5 minutes, spray tops with some oil, flip them, and cook for extra 5 minutes. Remove and set aside. Repeat the last 2 steps with the remaining part of the shrimp.
5. Put all cooked shrimp in a medium mixing bowl, pour in the mayonnaise-chili sauce, and toss* until the shrimp are fully covered.
6. Top with fresh parsley, serve warm,** and enjoy your Bang Bang Shrimp!

Snapper Fillets With Thai Sauce

Servings: 2
Cooking Time: 30 Minutes + Marinating Time
Ingredients:
- 1/2 cup full-fat coconut milk
- 2 tablespoons lemon juice
- 1 teaspoon fresh ginger, grated
- 2 snapper fillets
- 1 tablespoon olive oil
- Salt and white pepper, to taste

Directions:
1. Place the milk, lemon juice, and ginger in a glass bowl; add fish and let it marinate for 1 hour.
2. Removed the fish from the milk mixture and place in the Air Fryer basket. Drizzle olive oil all over the fish fillets.
3. Cook in the preheated Air Fryer at 390°F for 15 minutes.
4. Meanwhile, heat the milk mixture over medium-high heat; bring to a rapid boil, stirring continuously. Reduce to simmer and add the salt, and pepper; continue to cook 12 minutes more.
5. Spoon the sauce over the warm snapper fillets and serve immediately. Bon appétit!

Halibut Soy Treat With Rice

Servings: 4
Cooking Time: 12 Minutes
Ingredients:
- 16-ounce Halibut steak
- To make the marinade:
- ⅔ cup soy sauce
- ½ cup cooking vine
- ¼ cup sugar
- 2 tablespoon lime juice
- ¼ cup orange juice
- ¼ teaspoon red pepper flakes, crushed
- ¼ teaspoon ginger ground
- 1 clove garlic (smashed)

Directions:
1. Add the marinade ingredients in a medium-size saucepan.
2. Heat the pan over medium heat for a few minutes. Cool down completely.
3. To marinate, in a zip-lock bag, combine the steak and marinade. Seal and refrigerate for 30-40 minutes.
4. Coat the air-frying basket gently with cooking oil or spray.
5. Place the steak in the basket of your air fryer and cook for 12 minutes at 355 degrees F/ 180 degrees C.
6. When done, serve warm with cooked rice!

Chinese Firecracker Shrimp
Servings: 4
Cooking Time: 20 Minutes
Ingredients:
- 1 lb peeled shrimp, deveined
- 2 green onions, chopped
- 2 tbsp sesame seeds
- Salt and pepper to taste
- 1 egg
- ½ cup all-purpose flour
- ¾ cup panko bread crumbs
- 1/3 cup sour cream
- 2 tbsp Sriracha sauce
- ¼ cup sweet chili sauce

Directions:
1. Preheat air fryer to 400°F. Set out three small bowls. In the first, add flour. In the second, beat the egg. In the third, add the crumbs. Season the shrimp with salt and pepper. Dip the shrimp in the flour, then dredge in the egg, and finally in the bread crumbs. Place the shrimp in the greased frying basket and Air Fry for 8 minutes, flipping once until crispy. Combine sour cream, Sriracha, and sweet chili sauce in a bowl. Top the shrimp with sesame seeds and green onions and serve with the chili sauce.

Cornmeal Shrimp Po'boy
Servings: 4
Cooking Time: 10 Minutes
Ingredients:
- For the shrimp
- 1 pound shrimp, peeled and deveined (see Prep tip, here)
- 1 egg
- ½ cup flour
- ¾ cup cornmeal
- Salt
- Pepper
- Cooking oil
- For the remoulade
- ½ cup mayonnaise
- 1 teaspoon mustard (I use Dijon)
- 1 teaspoon Worcestershire
- 1 teaspoon minced garlic
- Juice of ½ lemon
- 1 teaspoon Sriracha
- ½ teaspoon Creole seasoning (I use Tony Chachere's brand)
- For the po'boys
- 4 rolls
- 2 cups shredded lettuce
- 8 slices tomato

Directions:
1. Dry the shrimp with paper towels.
2. In a small bowl, beat the egg. In another small bowl, place the flour. Place the cornmeal in a third small bowl, and season with salt and pepper to taste.
3. Spray the air fryer basket with cooking oil.
4. Dip the shrimp in the flour, then the egg, and then the cornmeal.
5. Place the shrimp in the air fryer. Cook for 4 minutes. Open the basket and flip the shrimp. Cook for an additional 4 minutes, or until crisp.
6. Split the rolls and spread them with the remoulade.
7. Let the shrimp cool slightly before assembling the po'boys.
8. Fill each roll with a quarter of the shrimp, ½ cup of shredded lettuce, and 2 slices of tomato. Serve.

Cajun Lobster Tails
Servings: 4
Cooking Time: 10 Minutes
Ingredients:
- 4 lobster tails
- 2 tablespoons salted butter, melted
- 2 teaspoons lemon juice
- 1 tablespoon Cajun seasoning

Directions:
1. Preheat the air fryer to 400°F.
2. Carefully cut open lobster tails with kitchen scissors and pull back the shell a little to expose the meat. Drizzle butter and lemon juice over each tail, then sprinkle with Cajun seasoning.
3. Place tails in the air fryer basket and cook 10 minutes until lobster shells are bright red and internal temperature reaches at least 145°F. Serve warm.

Oyster Shrimp With Fried Rice
Servings: 4
Cooking Time: 40 Minutes
Ingredients:
- 1 lb peeled shrimp, deveined
- 1 shallot, chopped
- 2 garlic cloves, minced
- 1 tbsp olive oil
- 1 tbsp butter
- 2 eggs, beaten
- 2 cups cooked rice
- 1 cup baby peas
- 2 tbsp fish sauce
- 1 tbsp oyster sauce

Directions:

1. Preheat the air fryer to 370°F. Combine the shrimp, shallot, garlic, and olive oil in a cake pan. Put the cake pan in the air fryer and Bake the shrimp for 5-7 minutes, stirring once until shrimp are no pinker. Remove into a bowl, and set aside. Put the butter in the hot cake pan to melt. Add the eggs and return to the fryer. Bake for 4-6 minutes, stirring once until the eggs are set. Remove the eggs from the pan and set aside.
2. Add the rice, peas, oyster sauce, and fish sauce to the pan and return it to the fryer. Bake for 12-15 minutes, stirring once halfway through. Pour in the shrimp and eggs and stir. Cook for 2-3 more minutes until everything is hot.

Almond-crusted Fish

Servings: 4
Cooking Time: 10 Minutes
Ingredients:
- 4 4-ounce fish fillets
- ¾ cup breadcrumbs
- ¼ cup sliced almonds, crushed
- 2 tablespoons lemon juice
- ⅛ teaspoon cayenne
- salt and pepper
- ¾ cup flour
- 1 egg, beaten with 1 tablespoon water
- oil for misting or cooking spray

Directions:
1. Split fish fillets lengthwise down the center to create 8 pieces.
2. Mix breadcrumbs and almonds together and set aside.
3. Mix the lemon juice and cayenne together. Brush on all sides of fish.
4. Season fish to taste with salt and pepper.
5. Place the flour on a sheet of wax paper.
6. Roll fillets in flour, dip in egg wash, and roll in the crumb mixture.
7. Mist both sides of fish with oil or cooking spray.
8. Spray air fryer basket and lay fillets inside.
9. Cook at 390°F for 5minutes, turn fish over, and cook for an additional 5minutes or until fish is done and flakes easily.

Salmon On Bed Of Fennel And Carrot

Servings: 2
Cooking Time:13 To 14 Minutes
Ingredients:
- 1 fennel bulb, thinly sliced
- 1 large carrot, peeled and sliced
- 1 small onion, thinly sliced
- ¼ cup low-fat sour cream
- ¼ teaspoon coarsely ground pepper
- 2 (5 ounce) salmon fillets

Directions:
1. Combine the fennel, carrot, and onion in a bowl and toss.
2. Put the vegetable mixture into a 6-inch metal pan. Roast in the air fryer for 4 minutes or until the vegetables are crisp tender.
3. Remove the pan from the air fryer. Stir in the sour cream and sprinkle the vegetables with the pepper.
4. Top with the salmon fillets.
5. Return the pan to the air fryer. Roast for another 9 to 10 minutes or until the salmon just barely flakes when tested with a fork.

Zesty Garlic Scallops

Servings:4
Cooking Time: 15 Minutes
Ingredients:
- 2 teaspoons olive oil, plus more for spraying
- 1 packet dry zesty Italian dressing mix
- 1 teaspoon minced garlic
- 16 ounces small scallops, thawed, patted dry

Directions:
1. Spray a fryer basket lightly with olive oil.
2. In a large zip-top plastic bag, combine the olive oil, Italian dressing mix, and garlic.
3. Add the scallops, seal the zip-top bag, and coat the scallops in the seasoning mixture.
4. Place the scallops in the fryer basket and lightly spray with olive oil.
5. Air fry for 5 minutes, shake the basket, and cook until the scallops reach an internal temperature of 120°F, for 5 to 10 more minutes.

Pasta Shrimp

Servings: 4
Cooking Time: 5 Minutes
Ingredients:
- ½ teaspoon hot paprika
- 2 garlic cloves, peeled and minced
- 1 teaspoon onion powder
- ½ teaspoon salt
- 1 teaspoon lemon-pepper seasoning
- 18 shrimps, shelled and deveined
- 2 tablespoons extra-virgin olive oil
- ¼ teaspoon cumin powder
- 2 tablespoons squeezed lemon juice
- ½ cup parsley, coarsely chopped

Directions:
1. Thoroughly mix the ingredients in a medium-size bowl, then cover it with a foil and refrigerate for 30-45 minutes.
2. Place the shrimps in the basket that has been coated with cooking oil or spray.
3. Arrange the basket to the air fryer and cook at 400 degrees F/ 205 degrees C for 5 minutes or until turn pink.
4. Serve warm with cooked pasta or just shrimps!

Kid´s Flounder Fingers

Servings: 4
Cooking Time: 45 Minutes
Ingredients:
- 1 lb catfish flounder fillets, cut into 1-inch chunks

- ½ cup seasoned fish fry breading mix

Directions:
1. Preheat air fryer to 400°F. In a resealable bag, add flounder and breading mix. Seal bag and shake until the fish is coated. Place the nuggets in the greased frying basket and Air Fry for 18-20 minutes, shaking the basket once until crisp. Serve warm and enjoy!

Honey Pecan Shrimp

Servings: 4
Cooking Time: 10 Minutes
Ingredients:
- ¼ cup cornstarch
- ¾ teaspoon sea salt, divided
- ¼ teaspoon pepper
- 2 egg whites
- ⅔ cup finely chopped pecans
- 1 pound raw, peeled, and deveined shrimp
- ¼ cup honey
- 2 tablespoons mayonnaise

Directions:
1. In a small bowl, whisk together the cornstarch, ½ teaspoon of the salt, and the pepper.
2. In a second bowl, whisk together the egg whites until soft and foamy. (They don't need to be whipped to peaks or even soft peaks, just frothy.)
3. In a third bowl, mix together the pecans and the remaining ¼ teaspoon of sea salt.
4. Pat the shrimp dry with paper towels. Working in small batches, dip the shrimp into the cornstarch, then into the egg whites, and then into the pecans until all the shrimp are coated with pecans.
5. Preheat the air fryer to 330°F.
6. Place the coated shrimp inside the air fryer basket and spray with cooking spray. Cook for 5 minutes, toss the shrimp, and cook another 5 minutes.
7. Meanwhile, place the honey in a microwave-safe bowl and microwave for 30 seconds. Whisk in the mayonnaise until smooth and creamy. Pour the honey sauce into a serving bowl. Add the cooked shrimp to the serving bowl while hot and toss to coat. Serve immediately.

King Prawns Al Ajillo

Servings: 4
Cooking Time: 15 Minutes
Ingredients:
- 1 ¼ lb peeled king prawns, deveined
- ½ cup grated Parmesan
- 1 tbsp olive oil
- 1 tbsp lemon juice
- ½ tsp garlic powder
- 2 garlic cloves, minced

Directions:
1. Preheat the air fryer to 350°F. In a large bowl, add the prawns and sprinkle with olive oil, lemon juice, and garlic powder. Toss in the minced garlic and Parmesan, then toss to coat. Put the prawns in the frying basket and Air Fry for 10-15 minutes or until the prawns cook through. Shake the basket once while cooking. Serve immediately.

Shrimp Al Pesto

Servings: 4
Cooking Time: 10 Minutes
Ingredients:
- 1 lb peeled shrimp, deveined
- ¼ cup pesto sauce
- 1 lime, sliced
- 2 cups cooked farro

Directions:
1. Preheat air fryer to 360°F. Coat the shrimp with the pesto sauce in a bowl. Put the shrimp in a single layer in the frying basket. Put the lime slices over the shrimp and Roast for 5 minutes. Remove lime and discard. Serve the shrimp over a bed of farro pilaf. Enjoy!

Garlic Salmon Patties

Servings: 2
Cooking Time: 7 Minutes
Ingredients:
- 8 ounces salmon fillet, minced
- 1 lemon, sliced
- ½ teaspoon garlic powder
- 1 egg, lightly beaten
- ⅛ teaspoon salt

Directions:
1. Add all the recipe ingredients except lemon slices into the bowl and mix until well combined.
2. Grease its air fryer basket with cooking spray.
3. Place lemon slice into the air fryer basket.
4. Make the equal shape of patties from salmon mixture and place on top of lemon slices into the air fryer basket.
5. Cook at almost 390 degrees F/ 200 degrees C for 7 minutes.
6. Serve and enjoy.

Bean Burritos With Cheddar Cheese

Servings: 4
Cooking Time: 15 Minutes
Ingredients:
- 4 tortillas
- 1 can beans
- 1 cup cheddar cheese, grated
- ¼-teaspoon paprika
- ¼-teaspoon chili powder
- ¼-teaspoon garlic powder
- Salt and pepper to taste

Directions:
1. Heat the Air Fryer to 350 degrees F/ 175 degrees C ahead of time.
2. Mix up the paprika, chili powder, garlic powder, salt and pepper in a suitable bowl.
3. Before adding the spice mixture and cheddar cheese, fill each tortilla with an equal portion of beans.

4. Roll the tortilla wraps into burritos.
5. Use the parchment paper to cover the base of a baking dish.
6. Arrange the burritos to the baking dish and place the dish in the air fryer.
7. Cook the burritos for about 5 minutes at 350 degrees F/ 175 degrees C.
8. When cooked, serve hot.

Snow Crab Legs

Servings:6
Cooking Time: 15 Minutes Per Batch
Ingredients:
- 8 pounds fresh shell-on snow crab legs
- 2 tablespoons olive oil
- 2 teaspoons Old Bay Seasoning
- 4 tablespoons salted butter, melted
- 2 teaspoons lemon juice

Directions:
1. Preheat the air fryer to 400°F.
2. Drizzle crab legs with oil and sprinkle with Old Bay. Place in the air fryer basket, working in batches as necessary. Cook 15 minutes, turning halfway through cooking time, until crab turns a bright red-orange.
3. In a small bowl, whisk together butter and lemon juice. Serve as a dipping sauce with warm crab legs.

Yummy Salmon Burgers With Salsa Rosa

Servings: 4
Cooking Time: 35 Minutes + Chilling Time
Ingredients:
- ¼ cup minced red onion
- ¼ cup slivered onions
- ½ cup mayonnaise
- 2 tsp ketchup
- 1 tsp brandy
- 2 tsp orange juice
- 1 lb salmon fillets
- 5 tbsp panko bread crumbs
- 1 garlic clove, minced
- 1 large egg, lightly beaten
- 1 tbsp Dijon mustard
- 1 tsp fresh lemon juice
- 1 tbsp chopped parsley
- Salt to taste
- 4 buns
- 8 Boston lettuce leaves

Directions:
1. Mix the mayonnaise, ketchup, brandy, and orange juice in a bowl until blended. Set aside the resulting salsa rosa until ready to serve. Cut a 4-oz section of salmon and place in a food processor. Pulse until it turns into a paste. Chop the remaining salmon into cubes and transfer to a bowl along with the salmon paste. Add the panko, minced onion, garlic, egg, mustard, lemon juice, parsley, and salt. Toss to combine. Divide into 5 patties about ¾-inch thick. Refrigerate for 30 minutes.
2. Preheat air fryer to 400°F. Place the patties in the greased frying basket. Air Fry for 12-14 minutes, flipping once until golden. Serve each patty on a bun, 2 lettuce leaves, 2 tbsp of salsa rosa, and slivered onions. Enjoy!

Air Fried Calamari

Servings:3
Cooking Time: 30 Minutes
Ingredients:
- ½ cup cornmeal or cornstarch
- 2 large eggs, beaten
- 2 mashed garlic cloves
- 1 cup breadcrumbs
- lemon juice

Directions:
1. Coat calamari with the cornmeal. The first mixture is prepared by mixing the eggs and garlic. Dip the calamari in the eggs' mixture. Then dip them in the breadcrumbs. Put the rings in the fridge for 2 hours.
2. Then, line them in the air fryer and add oil generously. Fry for 10 to 13 minutes at 390°F, shaking once halfway through. Serve with garlic mayonnaise and top with lemon juice.

Mojo Sea Bass

Servings:2
Cooking Time: 15 Minutes
Ingredients:
- 1 tbsp butter, melted
- ¼ tsp chili powder
- 2 cloves garlic, minced
- 1 tbsp lemon juice
- ¼ tsp salt
- 2 sea bass fillets
- 2 tsp chopped cilantro

Directions:
1. Preheat air fryer to 370°F. Whisk the butter, chili powder, garlic, lemon juice, and salt in a bowl. Rub mixture over the tops of each fillet. Place the fillets in the frying basket and Air Fry for 7 minutes. Let rest for 5 minutes. Divide between 2 plates and garnish with cilantro to serve.

Garlic-lemon Scallops

Servings:4
Cooking Time: 12 Minutes
Ingredients:
- ¼ teaspoon salt
- ¼ teaspoon ground black pepper
- 8 sea scallops, rinsed and patted dry
- 4 tablespoons salted butter, melted
- 4 teaspoons finely minced garlic
- Zest and juice of ½ small lemon

Directions:
1. Preheat the air fryer to 375°F.
2. Sprinkle salt and pepper evenly over scallops. Spritz scallops lightly with cooking spray. Place in the air fryer

basket in a single layer and cook 12 minutes, turning halfway through cooking time, until scallops are opaque and firm and internal temperature reaches at least 130°F.
3. While scallops are cooking, in a small bowl, mix butter, garlic, lemon zest, and juice. Set aside.
4. When scallops are done, drizzle with garlic–lemon butter. Serve warm.

Speedy Shrimp Paella
Servings: 4
Cooking Time: 20 Minutes
Ingredients:
- 2 cups cooked rice
- 1 red bell pepper, chopped
- ¼ cup vegetable broth
- ½ tsp turmeric
- ½ tsp dried thyme
- 1 cup cooked small shrimp
- ½ cup baby peas
- 1 tomato, diced

Directions:
1. Preheat air fryer to 340°F. Gently combine rice, red bell pepper, broth, turmeric, and thyme in a baking pan. Bake in the air fryer until the rice is hot, about 9 minutes. Remove the pan from the air fryer and gently stir in shrimp, peas, and tomato. Return to the air fryer and cook until bubbling and all ingredients are hot, 5-8 minutes. Serve and enjoy!

Coconut Shrimp
Servings: 4
Cooking Time: 12 Minutes
Ingredients:
- 1 pound large shrimp (about 16 to 20), peeled and de-veined
- ½ cup flour
- salt and freshly ground black pepper
- 2 egg whites
- ½ cup fine breadcrumbs
- ½ cup shredded unsweetened coconut
- zest of one lime
- ½ teaspoon salt
- ⅛ to ¼ teaspoon ground cayenne pepper
- vegetable or canola oil
- sweet chili sauce or duck sauce (for serving)

Directions:
1. Set up a dredging station. Place the flour in a shallow dish and season well with salt and freshly ground black pepper. Whisk the egg whites in a second shallow dish. In a third shallow dish, combine the breadcrumbs, coconut, lime zest, salt and cayenne pepper.
2. Preheat the air fryer to 400°F.
3. Dredge each shrimp first in the flour, then dip it in the egg mixture, and finally press it into the breadcrumb-coconut mixture to coat all sides. Place the breaded shrimp on a plate or baking sheet and spray both sides with vegetable oil.
4. Air-fry the shrimp in two batches, being sure not to over-crowd the basket. Air-fry for 5 minutes, turning the shrimp over for the last minute or two. Repeat with the second batch of shrimp.
5. Lower the temperature of the air fryer to 340°F. Return the first batch of shrimp to the air fryer basket with the second batch and air-fry for an additional 2 minutes, just to re-heat everything.
6. Serve with sweet chili sauce, duck sauce or just eat them plain!

Delicious Grouper Filets
Servings: 3
Cooking Time: 10 Minutes
Ingredients:
- 1 pound grouper filets
- ¼ teaspoon shallot powder
- ¼ teaspoon porcini powder
- 1 teaspoon fresh garlic, minced
- ½ teaspoon cayenne pepper
- ½ teaspoon hot paprika
- ¼ teaspoon oregano
- ½ teaspoon marjoram
- ½ teaspoon sage
- 1 tablespoon butter, melted
- Sea salt and black pepper, to taste

Directions:
1. Use the kitchen towels to pat dry the grouper filets.
2. Mix up the remaining ingredients until well incorporated, then rub the grouper filets on all sides with the mixture.
3. Cook the grouper filets in the preheated Air Fryer at 400 degrees F/ 205 degrees C for 10 minutes, flipping halfway through.
4. Serve over hot rice if desired. Bon appétit!

Crab Cakes On A Budget
Servings: 4
Cooking Time: 12 Minutes
Ingredients:
- 8 ounces imitation crabmeat
- 4 ounces leftover cooked fish (such as cod, pollock, or haddock)
- 2 tablespoons minced green onion
- 2 tablespoons minced celery
- ¾ cup crushed saltine cracker crumbs
- 2 tablespoons light mayonnaise
- 1 teaspoon prepared yellow mustard
- 1 tablespoon Worcestershire sauce, plus 2 teaspoons
- 2 teaspoons dried parsley flakes
- ½ teaspoon dried dill weed, crushed
- ½ teaspoon garlic powder
- ½ teaspoon Old Bay Seasoning
- ½ cup panko breadcrumbs
- oil for misting or cooking spray

Directions:
1. Use knives or a food processor to finely shred crabmeat and fish.

2. In a large bowl, combine all ingredients except panko and oil. Stir well.
3. Shape into 8 small, fat patties.
4. Carefully roll patties in panko crumbs to coat. Spray both sides with oil or cooking spray.
5. Place patties in air fryer basket and cook at 390°F for 12 minutes or until golden brown and crispy.

Simple Salmon

Servings: 2
Cooking Time: 10 Minutes
Ingredients:
- 2 salmon fillets
- Salt and black pepper, as required
- 1 tablespoon olive oil

Directions:
1. Preheat the Air fryer to 390°F and grease an Air fryer basket.
2. Season each salmon fillet with salt and black pepper and drizzle with olive oil.
3. Arrange salmon fillets into the Air fryer basket and cook for about 10 minutes.
4. Remove from the Air fryer and dish out the salmon fillets onto the serving plates.

Trimmed Mackerel With Spring Onions

Servings: 5
Cooking Time: 20 Minutes
Ingredients:
- 1 pound mackerel, trimmed
- 1 tablespoon ground paprika
- 1 green bell pepper
- ½ cup spring onions, chopped
- 1 tablespoon avocado oil
- 1 teaspoon apple cider vinegar
- ½-teaspoon salt

Directions:
1. Sprinkle the clean mackerel with ground paprika.
2. Chop the green bell pepper.
3. Fill the mackerel with bell pepper and spring onion.
4. After this, sprinkle the fish with avocado oil, salt and apple cider vinegar.
5. At 375 degrees F/ 190 degrees C, heat your air fryer in advance.
6. Place the mackerel in the basket and arrange the basket to the air fryer.
7. Cook the mackerel for 20 minutes at 375 degrees F/ 190 degrees C.
8. When cooked, serve and enjoy.

Korean-style Fried Calamari

Servings: 4
Cooking Time: 25 Minutes
Ingredients:
- 2 tbsp tomato paste
- 1 tbsp gochujang
- 1 tbsp lime juice
- 1 tsp lime zest
- 1 tsp smoked paprika
- ½ tsp salt
- 1 cup bread crumbs
- 1/3 lb calamari rings

Directions:
1. Preheat air fryer to 400°F. Whisk tomato paste, gochujang, lime juice and zest, paprika, and salt in a bowl. In another bowl, add in the bread crumbs. Dredge calamari rings in the tomato mixture, shake off excess, then roll through the crumbs. Place calamari rings in the greased frying basket and Air Fry for 4-5 minutes, flipping once. Serve.

Almond Topped Trout

Servings: 4
Cooking Time: 20 Minutes
Ingredients:
- 4 trout fillets
- 2 tbsp olive oil
- Salt and pepper to taste
- 2 garlic cloves, sliced
- 1 lemon, sliced
- 1 tbsp flaked almonds

Directions:
1. Preheat air fryer to 380°F. Lightly brush each fillet with olive oil on both sides and season with salt and pepper. Put the fillets in a single layer in the frying basket. Put the sliced garlic over the tops of the trout fillets, then top with lemon slices and cook for 12-15 minutes. Serve topped with flaked almonds and enjoy!

Flavor Moroccan Harissa Shrimp

Servings: 3
Cooking Time: 10 Minutes
Ingredients:
- 1-pound breaded shrimp, frozen
- 1 teaspoon extra-virgin olive oil
- Sea salt, to taste
- Ground black pepper, to taste
- 1 teaspoon coriander seeds
- 1 teaspoon caraway seeds
- 1 teaspoon crushed red pepper
- 1 teaspoon fresh garlic, minced

Directions:
1. Arrange the breaded shrimp tossed with olive oil to the cooking basket and then arrange the basket to the air fryer.
2. Cook the shrimp at 400 degrees F/ 205 degrees C for 5 minutes.
3. After 5 minutes, shake the basket and cook an additional 4 minutes.
4. During cooking, mix the remaining ingredients until well combined.
5. Taste and adjust seasonings.
6. Toss the warm shrimp with the harissa sauce and serve immediately. Enjoy!

Zesty Mahi Mahi

Servings: 3
Cooking Time: 8 Minutes
Ingredients:
- 1½ pounds Mahi Mahi fillets
- 1 lemon, cut into slices
- 1 tablespoon fresh dill, chopped
- ½ teaspoon red chili powder
- Salt and ground black pepper, as required

Directions:
1. Preheat the Air fryer to 375°F and grease an Air fryer basket.
2. Season the Mahi Mahi fillets evenly with chili powder, salt, and black pepper.
3. Arrange the Mahi Mahi fillets into the Air fryer basket and top with the lemon slices.
4. Cook for about 8 minutes and dish out
5. Place the lemon slices over the salmon the salmon fillets in the serving plates.
6. Garnish with fresh dill and serve warm.

Fried Catfish Fillets

Servings: 2
Cooking Time: 40 Minutes
Ingredients:
- 3 tbsp breadcrumbs
- 1 tsp cayenne pepper
- 1 tsp dry fish seasoning, of choice
- 2 sprigs parsley, chopped
- Salt to taste, optional
- Cooking spray

Directions:
1. Preheat air fryer to 400°F. Pour all the dry ingredients, except the parsley, in a zipper bag. Pat dry and add the fish pieces. Close the bag and shake to coat the fish well. Do this with one fish piece at a time.
2. Lightly spray the fish with olive oil. Arrange them in the fryer basket, one at a time depending on the size of the fish. Close the air fryer and cook for 10 minutes. Flip the fish and cook further for 10 minutes. For extra crispiness, cook for 3 more minutes. Garnish with parsley and serve.

Autenthic Greek Fish Pitas

Servings: 4
Cooking Time: 25 Minutes
Ingredients:
- 1 lb pollock, cut into 1-inch pieces
- ¼ cup olive oil
- 1 tsp salt
- ½ tsp dried oregano
- ½ tsp dried thyme
- ½ tsp garlic powder
- ¼ tsp chili powder
- 4 pitas
- 1 cup grated lettuce
- 4 Kalamata olives, chopped
- 2 tomatoes, diced
- 1 cup Greek yogurt

Directions:
1. Preheat air fryer to 380°F. Coat the pollock with olive oil, salt, oregano, thyme, garlic powder, and chili powder in a bowl. Put the pollock into the frying basket and Air Fry for 15 minutes. Serve inside pitas with lettuce, tomato, olives and Greek yogurt. Enjoy!

Crispy Fish Tacos

Servings: 5 Servings
Cooking Time: 40 Minutes
Ingredients:
- 1 pound of the firm and white fish
- 3 eggs
- 2 cups of sour cream
- ¾ cup of AP flour
- 1 package of corn tortillas
- 1 cup of panko bread crumbs
- 1–2 limes
- 1 teaspoon of cumin
- 1 teaspoon of onion powder
- 1 teaspoon of garlic powder
- 1 teaspoon of salt
- 1 teaspoon of black pepper
- 1 teaspoon of red chili flakes (optional)
- 1 teaspoon of lemon pepper (optional)
- Lettuce leaves, salsa, avocado, tomatoes, radishes, cabbage, and/or hot sauce, for serving

Directions:
1. Thaw the fish fillets and dry them with a paper towel. Cut into 2–3 pieces depending on the size of the fillets. Season both sides with pepper and salt.
2. Add AP flour in one bowl. Whisk 3 eggs in a separate bowl. Mix the panko bread crumbs, lemon pepper, cumin, red chili flakes, onion powder, garlic powder, ½ teaspoon of salt and pepper in a third bowl.
3. Dip the fish piece into the flour, then into the whisked eggs, and finally into the bread crumb mixture, lightly pressing it. Put the coated fillet on a big plate. Repeat this step with the remaining part of the fish.
4. Preheat your air fryer to 370ºF. Spray some oil inside the air fryer basket.
5. Transfer the coated fillets into the preheated basket; avoid them touching. Cook at 370ºF for 6 minutes. Gently flip it and cook for another 6 minutes. Remove and set aside. Repeat this step until all pieces of fish are cooked.
6. To cook the lime crema: Add the sour cream in a small bowl. Add in zest and juice from 2 limes. Season with a pinch of salt and whisk it with a fork.
7. To serve: Warm tortillas in a microwave or on the pan. Put the crispy fish in the middle. Top with the prepared lime crema and add vegetables or hot sauce you like.*
8. Serve warm and enjoy your Crispy Fish Tacos!

Catfish Fillets With Tortilla Chips

Servings: 4
Cooking Time: 30 Minutes
Ingredients:
- 2 catfish fillets [catfish]
- 1 medium egg, beaten
- 1 cup bread crumbs
- 1 cup tortilla chips
- 1 lemon, juiced and peeled
- 1 teaspoon parsley
- Salt and pepper to taste

Directions:
1. Slice the catfish fillets neatly and then drizzle lightly with the lemon juice.
2. Mix up the bread crumbs with the lemon rind, parsley, tortillas, salt and pepper in a bowl, then pour into your food processor and pulse.
3. Distributes the fillets evenly on the base of the cooking tray.
4. Cover the fish fillets well with the prepared mixture.
5. Arrange the tray to your air fryer and cook the fillets at 350 degrees F/ 175 degrees C for 15 minutes.
6. When done, serve with chips and a refreshing drink.

Fish-in-chips

Servings:4
Cooking Time: 11 Minutes
Ingredients:
- 1 cup All-purpose flour or potato starch
- 2 Large egg(s), well beaten
- 1½ cups Crushed plain potato chips, preferably thick-cut or ruffled (gluten-free, if a concern)
- 4 4-ounce skinless cod fillets

Directions:
1. Preheat the air fryer to 400°F.
2. Set up and fill three shallow soup plates or small pie plates on your counter: one for the flour, one for the beaten egg(s), and one for the crushed potato chips.
3. Dip a piece of cod in the flour, turning it to coat on all sides, even the ends and sides. Gently shake off any excess flour, then dip it in the beaten egg(s). Gently turn to coat it on all sides, then let any excess egg slip back into the rest. Set the fillet in the crushed potato chips and turn several times and onto all sides, pressing gently to coat the fish. Dip it back in the egg(s), coating all sides but taking care that the coating doesn't slip off; then dip it back in the potato chips for a thick, even coating. Set it aside and coat more fillets in the same way.
4. When the machine is at temperature, set the fillets in the basket with as much air space between them as possible. Air-fry undisturbed for 11 minutes, until golden brown and firm but not hard.
5. Use kitchen tongs to transfer the fillets to a wire rack. Cool for just a minute or two before serving.

Pecan-crusted Tilapia

Servings: 4
Cooking Time: 8 Minutes
Ingredients:
- 1 pound skinless, boneless tilapia filets
- ¼ cup butter, melted
- 1 teaspoon minced fresh or dried rosemary
- 1 cup finely chopped pecans
- 1 teaspoon sea salt
- ¼ teaspoon paprika
- 2 tablespoons chopped parsley
- 1 lemon, cut into wedges

Directions:
1. Pat the tilapia filets dry with paper towels.
2. Pour the melted butter over the filets and flip the filets to coat them completely.
3. In a medium bowl, mix together the rosemary, pecans, salt, and paprika.
4. Preheat the air fryer to 350°F.
5. Place the tilapia filets into the air fryer basket and top with the pecan coating. Cook for 6 to 8 minutes. The fish should be firm to the touch and flake easily when fully cooked.
6. Remove the fish from the air fryer. Top the fish with chopped parsley and serve with lemon wedges.

Lemon Jumbo Scallops

Servings: 4
Cooking Time: 11 Minutes
Ingredients:
- 8 jumbo scallops
- 1 teaspoon sesame oil
- Sea salt and red pepper flakes, to season
- 1 tablespoon coconut oil
- 1 Thai chili, deveined and minced
- 1 teaspoon garlic, minced
- 1 tablespoon oyster sauce
- 1 tablespoon soy sauce
- ¼ cup coconut milk
- 2 tablespoons fresh lime juice

Directions:
1. Mix up the 1 teaspoon of sesame oil, salt, red pepper and the jumbo scallops that have been patted dry in advance.
2. Cook the jumbo scallops in your Air Fryer at 400 degrees F/ 205 degrees C for 4 minutes.
3. After that, turn them over and cook an additional 3 minutes.
4. While cooking the scallops, in a frying pan, heat the coconut oil over medium-high heat.
5. Once hot, add the Thai chili, garlic and cook for 1 minute or so until just tender and fragrant.
6. Add in the soy sauce, coconut milk, and oyster sauce and continue to simmer, partially covered, for 5 minutes longer.
7. Lastly, add fresh lime juice and stir to combine well.
8. Add the warm scallops to the sauce and serve immediately.

The Ultimate Tower Air Fryer Cookbook

Cajun Fish Cakes

Servings: 4
Cooking Time: 30 Minutes
Ingredients:
- 2 catfish fillets
- 1 cup all-purpose flour
- 1 ounce butter
- 1 teaspoon baking powder
- 1 teaspoon baking soda
- ½ cup buttermilk
- 1 teaspoon Cajun seasoning
- 1 cup Swiss cheese, shredded

Directions:
1. Boil a pot of water, the put in the fish fillets and boil for 5 minutes or until it is opaque.
2. When done, flake the fish into small pieces.
3. In a bowl, mix up the other ingredients, then add the fish and mix them well.
4. Form 12 fish patties from the mixture.
5. Place the patties to the cooking pan and arrange the pan to your air fryer.
6. Cook at 380 degrees F/ 195 degrees C for 15 minutes.
7. Working in batches is suggested.
8. Enjoy!

Snapper Scampi

Servings:4
Cooking Time: 8 To 10 Minutes
Ingredients:
- 4 (6-ounce) skinless snapper or arctic char fillets
- 1 tablespoon olive oil
- 3 tablespoons lemon juice, divided
- ½ teaspoon dried basil
- Pinch salt
- Freshly ground black pepper
- 2 tablespoons butter
- 2 cloves garlic, minced

Directions:
1. Rub the fish fillets with olive oil and 1 tablespoon of the lemon juice. Sprinkle with the basil, salt, and pepper, and place in the air fryer basket.
2. Grill the fish for 7 to 8 minutes or until the fish just flakes when tested with a fork. Remove the fish from the basket and put on a serving plate. Cover to keep warm.
3. In a 6-by-6-by-2-inch pan, combine the butter, remaining 2 tablespoons lemon juice, and garlic. Cook in the air fryer for 1 to 2 minutes or until the garlic is sizzling. Pour this mixture over the fish and serve.
4. Did You Know? You can buy bottled lemon and lime juice at the supermarket, but for recipes such as this one, where the flavor is so important, squeeze the juice from a lemon yourself just before you make the recipe.

Baltimore Crab Cakes

Servings: 4
Cooking Time: 35 Minutes
Ingredients:
- ½ lb lump crabmeat, shells discarded
- 2 tbsp mayonnaise
- ½ tsp yellow mustard
- ½ tsp lemon juice
- ½ tbsp minced shallot
- ¼ cup bread crumbs
- 1 egg
- Salt and pepper to taste
- 4 poached eggs
- ½ cup bechamel sauce
- 2 tsp chopped chives
- 1 lemon, cut into wedges

Directions:
1. Preheat air fryer at 400°F. Combine all ingredients, except eggs, sauce, and chives, in a bowl. Form mixture into 4 patties. Place crab cakes in the greased frying basket and Air Fry for 10 minutes, flipping once. Transfer them to a serving dish. Top each crab cake with 1 poached egg, drizzle with Bechamel sauce and scatter with chives and lemon wedges. Serve and enjoy!

Five Spice Red Snapper With Green Onions And Orange Salsa

Servings: 2
Cooking Time: 8 Minutes
Ingredients:
- 2 oranges, peeled, segmented and chopped
- 1 tablespoon minced shallot
- 1 to 3 teaspoons minced red Jalapeño or Serrano pepper
- 1 tablespoon chopped fresh cilantro
- lime juice, to taste
- salt, to taste
- 2 (5- to 6-ounce) red snapper fillets
- ½ teaspoon Chinese five spice powder
- salt and freshly ground black pepper
- vegetable or olive oil, in a spray bottle
- 4 green onions, cut into 2-inch lengths

Directions:
1. Start by making the salsa. Cut the peel off the oranges, slicing around the oranges to expose the flesh. Segment the oranges by cutting in between the membranes of the orange. Chop the segments roughly and combine in a bowl with the shallot, Jalapeño or Serrano pepper, cilantro, lime juice and salt. Set the salsa aside.
2. Preheat the air fryer to 400°F.
3. Season the fish fillets with the five-spice powder, salt and freshly ground black pepper. Spray both sides of the fish fillets with oil. Toss the green onions with a little oil.
4. Transfer the fish to the air fryer basket and scatter the green onions around the fish. Air-fry at 400°F for 8 minutes.
5. Remove the fish from the air fryer, along with the fried green onions. Serve with white rice and a spoonful of the salsa on top.

Basil Crab Cakes With Fresh Salad

Servings: 2
Cooking Time: 25 Minutes
Ingredients:
- 8 oz lump crabmeat
- 2 tbsp mayonnaise
- ½ tsp Dijon mustard
- ½ tsp lemon juice
- ½ tsp lemon zest
- 2 tsp minced yellow onion
- ¼ tsp prepared horseradish
- ¼ cup flour
- 1 egg white, beaten
- 1 tbsp basil, minced
- 1 tbsp olive oil
- 2 tsp white wine vinegar
- Salt and pepper to taste
- 4 oz arugula
- ½ cup blackberries
- ¼ cup pine nuts
- 2 lemon wedges

Directions:
1. Preheat air fryer to 400°F. Combine the crabmeat, mayonnaise, mustard, lemon juice and zest, onion, horseradish, flour, egg white, and basil in a bowl. Form mixture into 4 patties. Place the patties in the lightly greased frying basket and Air Fry for 10 minutes, flipping once. Combine olive oil, vinegar, salt, and pepper in a bowl. Toss in the arugula and share into 2 medium bowls. Add 2 crab cakes to each bowl and scatter with blackberries, pine nuts, and lemon wedges. Serve warm.

Country Shrimp "boil"

Servings: 4
Cooking Time: 20 Minutes
Ingredients:
- 2 tablespoons olive oil, plus more for spraying
- 1 pound large shrimp, deveined, tail on
- 1 pound smoked turkey sausage, cut into thick slices
- 2 corn cobs, quartered
- 1 zucchini, cut into bite-sized pieces
- 1 red bell pepper, cut into chunks
- 1 tablespoon Old Bay seasoning

Directions:
1. Spray the fryer basket lightly with olive oil.
2. In a large bowl, mix together the shrimp, turkey sausage, corn, zucchini, bell pepper, and Old Bay seasoning, and toss to coat with the spices. Add the 2 tablespoons of olive oil and toss again until evenly coated.
3. Spread the mixture in the fryer basket in a single layer. You will need to cook in batches.
4. Air fry until cooked through, 15 to 20 minutes, shaking the basket every 5 minutes for even cooking.

Maple Balsamic Glazed Salmon

Servings: 4
Cooking Time: 10 Minutes
Ingredients:
- 4 fillets of salmon
- salt and freshly ground black pepper
- vegetable oil
- ¼ cup pure maple syrup
- 3 tablespoons balsamic vinegar
- 1 teaspoon Dijon mustard

Directions:
1. Preheat the air fryer to 400°F.
2. Season the salmon well with salt and freshly ground black pepper. Spray or brush the bottom of the air fryer basket with vegetable oil and place the salmon fillets inside. Air-fry the salmon for 5 minutes.
3. While the salmon is air-frying, combine the maple syrup, balsamic vinegar and Dijon mustard in a small saucepan over medium heat and stir to blend well. Let the mixture simmer while the fish is cooking. It should start to thicken slightly, but keep your eye on it so it doesn't burn.
4. Brush the glaze on the salmon fillets and air-fry for an additional 5 minutes. The salmon should feel firm to the touch when finished and the glaze should be nicely browned on top. Brush a little more glaze on top before removing and serving with rice and vegetables, or a nice green salad.

Southwestern Prawns With Asparagus

Servings: 3
Cooking Time: 5 Minutes
Ingredients:
- 1-pound prawns, deveined
- ½ pound asparagus spears, cut into 1-inch chinks
- 1 teaspoon butter, melted
- ¼ teaspoon oregano
- ½ teaspoon mixed peppercorns, crushed
- Salt, to taste
- 1 ripe avocado
- 1 lemon, sliced
- ½ cup chunky-style salsa

Directions:
1. Toss your prawns and asparagus with melted butter, oregano, salt and mixed peppercorns.
2. Cook the prawns and asparagus at 400 degrees F/ 205 degrees C for 5 minutes, shaking the air fryer basket halfway through the cooking time.
3. Divide the prawns and asparagus between serving plates and garnish with avocado and lemon slices. Serve with the salsa on the side. Bon appétit!

Chapter 6: Poultry Recipes

Cheddar Chicken Stuffed Mushrooms
Servings: 4
Cooking Time: 9 Minutes
Ingredients:
- 9 medium-sized button mushrooms, cleaned and steams removed
- ½ pound chicken white meat, ground
- 2 ounces goat cheese, room temperature
- 2 ounces cheddar cheese, grated
- 1 teaspoon soy sauce
- 2 tablespoons scallions, finely chopped
- 1 teaspoon fresh garlic, finely chopped
- Sea salt and red pepper, to season

Directions:
1. Dry the mushrooms and set aside.
2. Combine chicken, goat cheese, soy sauce, scallions, fresh garlic, sea salt, and red pepper in a mixing bowl. Stir them together until well combined.
3. Then stuff the mushrooms with the mixture.
4. Cook in your air fryer at 370 degrees F/ 185 degrees C for 5 minutes.
5. Sprinkle cheddar cheese on the top and continue cooking for 3 to 4 minutes or until the cheese melts.
6. Enjoy!

Marjoram Butter Chicken
Servings: 2
Cooking Time: 30 Minutes
Ingredients:
- 2 skinless, boneless small chicken breasts
- 2 tablespoons butter
- 1 teaspoon sea salt
- ½ teaspoon red pepper flakes, crushed
- 2 teaspoon marjoram
- ¼ teaspoon lemon pepper

Directions:
1. Before cooking, heat your air fryer to 390 degrees F/ 200 degrees C.
2. Combine chicken breasts, butter, sea salt, red pepper flakes, marjoram, and lemon pepper together in a bowl and toss together to coat well.
3. Let it marinate for 30 to 60 minutes.
4. Cook in your air fryer for 20 minutes, and flip the chicken halfway through cooking. Check the doneness with an instant-read thermometer.
5. When cooked, serve with jasmine rice.

Chicken Breast Burgers
Servings: 4
Cooking Time: 35 Minutes
Ingredients:
- 2 chicken breasts
- 1 cup dill pickle juice
- 1 cup buttermilk
- 1 egg
- ½ cup flour
- Salt and pepper to taste
- 4 buns
- 2 pickles, sliced

Directions:
1. Cut the chicken into cutlets by cutting them in half horizontally on a cutting board. Transfer them to a large bowl along with pickle juice and ½ cup of buttermilk. Toss to coat, then marinate for 30 minutes in the fridge.
2. Preheat air fryer to 370°F. In a shallow bowl, beat the egg and the rest of the buttermilk to combine. In another shallow bowl, mix flour, salt, and pepper. Dip the marinated cutlet in the egg mixture, then dredge in flour. Place the cutlets in the greased frying basket and Air Fry for 12 minutes, flipping once halfway through. Remove the cutlets and pickles on buns and serve.

Buffalo Egg Rolls
Servings: 8
Cooking Time: 9 Minutes Per Batch
Ingredients:
- 1 teaspoon water
- 1 tablespoon cornstarch
- 1 egg
- 2½ cups cooked chicken, diced or shredded (see opposite page)
- ⅓ cup chopped green onion
- ⅓ cup diced celery
- ⅓ cup buffalo wing sauce
- 8 egg roll wraps
- oil for misting or cooking spray
- Blue Cheese Dip
- 3 ounces cream cheese, softened
- ⅓ cup blue cheese, crumbled
- 1 teaspoon Worcestershire sauce
- ¼ teaspoon garlic powder
- ¼ cup buttermilk (or sour cream)

Directions:
1. Mix water and cornstarch in a small bowl until dissolved. Add egg, beat well, and set aside.
2. In a medium size bowl, mix together chicken, green onion, celery, and buffalo wing sauce.
3. Divide chicken mixture evenly among 8 egg roll wraps, spooning ½ inch from one edge.
4. Moisten all edges of each wrap with beaten egg wash.
5. Fold the short ends over filling, then roll up tightly and press to seal edges.
6. Brush outside of wraps with egg wash, then spritz with oil or cooking spray.
7. Place 4 egg rolls in air fryer basket.
8. Cook at 390°F for 9minutes or until outside is brown and crispy.
9. While the rolls are cooking, prepare the Blue Cheese Dip. With a fork, mash together cream cheese and blue cheese.
10. Stir in remaining ingredients.
11. Dip should be just thick enough to slightly cling to egg rolls. If too thick, stir in buttermilk or milk 1

The Ultimate Tower Air Fryer Cookbook

tablespoon at a time until you reach the desired consistency.
12. Cook remaining 4 egg rolls as in steps 7 and 8.
13. Serve while hot with Blue Cheese Dip, more buffalo wing sauce, or both.

Rosemary Partridge

Servings: 4
Cooking Time: 14 Minutes
Ingredients:
- 10 oz partridges
- 1 teaspoon dried rosemary
- 1 tablespoon butter, melted
- 1 teaspoon salt

Directions:
1. Cut the partridges into the halves and sprinkle with dried rosemary and salt. Then brush them with melted butter. Preheat the air fryer to 385°F. Put the partridge halves in the air fryer and cook them for 8 minutes. Then flip the poultry on another side and cook for 6 minutes more.

Spinach And Feta Stuffed Chicken Breasts

Servings: 4
Cooking Time: 27 Minutes
Ingredients:
- 1 package frozen spinach, thawed and drained well
- 1 cup feta cheese, crumbled
- ½ teaspoon freshly ground black pepper
- 4 boneless chicken breasts
- salt and freshly ground black pepper
- 1 tablespoon olive oil

Directions:
1. Prepare the filling. Squeeze out as much liquid as possible from the thawed spinach. Rough chop the spinach and transfer it to a mixing bowl with the feta cheese and the freshly ground black pepper.
2. Prepare the chicken breast. Place the chicken breast on a cutting board and press down on the chicken breast with one hand to keep it stabilized. Make an incision about 1-inch long in the fattest side of the breast. Move the knife up and down inside the chicken breast, without poking through either the top or the bottom, or the other side of the breast. The inside pocket should be about 3-inches long, but the opening should only be about 1-inch wide. If this is too difficult, you can make the incision longer, but you will have to be more careful when cooking the chicken breast since this will expose more of the stuffing.
3. Once you have prepared the chicken breasts, use your fingers to stuff the filling into each pocket, spreading the mixture down as far as you can.
4. Preheat the air fryer to 380°F.
5. Lightly brush or spray the air fryer basket and the chicken breasts with olive oil. Transfer two of the stuffed chicken breasts to the air fryer. Air-fry for 12 minutes, turning the chicken breasts over halfway through the cooking time. Remove the chicken to a resting plate and air-fry the second two breasts for 12 minutes. Return the first batch of chicken to the air fryer with the second batch and air-fry for 3 more minutes. When the chicken is cooked, an instant read thermometer should register 165°F in the thickest part of the chicken, as well as in the stuffing.
6. Remove the chicken breasts and let them rest on a cutting board for 2 to 3 minutes. Slice the chicken on the bias and serve with the slices fanned out.

Chicken Pesto Pizzas

Servings:4
Cooking Time: 12 Minutes
Ingredients:
- 1 pound ground chicken thighs
- ¼ teaspoon salt
- ⅛ teaspoon ground black pepper
- ¼ cup basil pesto
- 1 cup shredded mozzarella cheese
- 4 grape tomatoes, sliced

Directions:
1. Cut four squares of parchment paper to fit into your air fryer basket.
2. Place ground chicken in a large bowl and mix with salt and pepper. Divide mixture into four equal sections.
3. Wet your hands with water to prevent sticking, then press each section into a 6" circle onto a piece of ungreased parchment. Place each chicken crust into air fryer basket, working in batches if needed.
4. Adjust the temperature to 350°F and set the timer for 10 minutes, turning crusts halfway through cooking.
5. When the timer beeps, spread 1 tablespoon pesto across the top of each crust, then sprinkle with ¼ cup mozzarella and top with 1 sliced tomato. Continue cooking at 350°F for 2 minutes. Cheese will be melted and brown when done. Serve warm.

Maewoon Chicken Legs

Servings: 4
Cooking Time: 30 Minutes + Chilling Time
Ingredients:
- 4 scallions, sliced, whites and greens separated
- ¼ cup tamari
- 2 tbsp sesame oil
- 1 tsp sesame seeds
- ¼ cup honey
- 2 tbsp gochujang
- 2 tbsp ketchup
- 4 cloves garlic, minced
- ½ tsp ground ginger
- Salt and pepper to taste
- 1 tbsp parsley
- 1 ½ lb chicken legs

Directions:
1. Whisk all ingredients, except chicken and scallion greens, in a bowl. Reserve ¼ cup of marinade. Toss

chicken legs in the remaining marinade and chill for 30 minutes.
2. Preheat air fryer at 400ºF. Place chicken legs in the greased frying basket and Air Fry for 10 minutes. Turn chicken. Cook for 8 more minutes. Let sit in a serving dish for 5 minutes. Coat the cooked chicken with the reserved marinade and scatter with scallion greens, sesame seeds and parsley to serve.

Turkey And Cranberry Quesadillas
Servings:4
Cooking Time: 4 To 8 Minutes
Ingredients:
- 6 low-sodium whole-wheat tortillas
- ⅓ cup shredded low-sodium low-fat Swiss cheese
- ¾ cup shredded cooked low-sodium turkey breast
- 2 tablespoons cranberry sauce
- 2 tablespoons dried cranberries
- ½ teaspoon dried basil
- Olive oil spray, for spraying the tortillas

Directions:
1. Preheat the air fryer to 400ºF (204ºC).
2. Put 3 tortillas on a work surface.
3. Evenly divide the Swiss cheese, turkey, cranberry sauce, and dried cranberries among the tortillas. Sprinkle with the basil and top with the remaining tortillas.
4. Spray the outsides of the tortillas with olive oil spray.
5. One at a time, air fry the quesadillas in the air fryer for 4 to 8 minutes, or until crisp and the cheese is melted. Cut into quarters and serve.

Simple Grilled Chicken
Servings: 4
Cooking Time: 35 Minutes
Ingredients:
- 2 pounds' chicken wings
- Black pepper and salt, to taste
- Cooking spray

Directions:
1. Flavor the chicken wings with black pepper and salt.
2. Grease its air fryer basket with cooking spray.
3. Add chicken wings and cook at 400 degrees F/ 205 degrees C for 35 minutes.
4. Flip 3 times during cooking for even cooking.
5. Serve.

Herb-buttermilk Chicken Breast
Servings:2
Cooking Time: 40 Minutes
Ingredients:
- 1 large bone-in, skin-on chicken breast
- 1 cup buttermilk
- 1½ teaspoons dried parsley
- 1½ teaspoons dried chives
- ¾ teaspoon kosher salt
- ½ teaspoon dried dill
- ½ teaspoon onion powder
- ¼ teaspoon garlic powder
- ¼ teaspoon dried tarragon
- Cooking spray

Directions:
1. Place the chicken breast in a bowl and pour over the buttermilk, turning the chicken in it to make sure it's completely covered. Let the chicken stand at room temperature for at least 20 minutes or in the refrigerator for up to 4 hours.
2. Meanwhile, in a bowl, stir together the parsley, chives, salt, dill, onion powder, garlic powder, and tarragon.
3. Preheat the air fryer to 300ºF (149ºC).
4. Remove the chicken from the buttermilk, letting the excess drip off, then place the chicken skin-side up directly in the air fryer. Sprinkle the seasoning mix all over the top of the chicken breast, then let stand until the herb mix soaks into the buttermilk, at least 5 minutes.
5. Spray the top of the chicken with cooking spray. Bake for 10 minutes, then increase the temperature to 350ºF (177ºC) and bake until an instant-read thermometer inserted into the thickest part of the breast reads 160ºF (71ºC) and the chicken is deep golden brown, 30 to 35 minutes.
6. Transfer the chicken breast to a cutting board, let rest for 10 minutes, then cut the meat off the bone and cut into thick slices for serving.

Popcorn Chicken Tenders With Vegetables
Servings: 4
Cooking Time: 30 Minutes
Ingredients:
- 2 tbsp cooked popcorn, ground
- Salt and pepper to taste
- 1 lb chicken tenders
- ½ cup bread crumbs
- ½ tsp dried thyme
- 1 tbsp olive oil
- 2 carrots, sliced
- 12 baby potatoes

Directions:
1. Preheat air fryer to 380°F. Season the chicken tenders with salt and pepper. In a shallow bowl, mix the crumbs, popcorn, thyme, and olive oil until combined. Coat the chicken with mixture. Press firmly, so the crumbs adhere. Arrange the carrots and baby potatoes in the greased frying basket and top them with the chicken tenders. Bake for 9-10 minutes. Shake the basket and continue cooking for another 9-10 minutes, until the vegetables are tender. Serve and enjoy!

Chicken Tenderloins With Parmesan Cheese
Servings: 6
Cooking Time: 12 Minutes
Ingredients:
- 1 lime
- 2 pounds' chicken tenderloins cut up

- 1 cup cornflakes, crushed
- ½ cup Parmesan cheese, grated
- 1 tablespoon olive oil
- Salt and black pepper, to taste
- 1 teaspoon cayenne pepper
- ⅓ teaspoon ground cumin
- 1 teaspoon chili powder
- 1 egg

Directions:
1. Squeeze and rub the lime juice all over the chicken.
2. Spritz the cooking basket with a nonstick cooking spray.
3. In a suitable mixing bowl, thoroughly combine the cornflakes, Parmesan, olive oil, salt, black pepper, cayenne pepper, cumin, and chili powder.
4. In a suitable shallow bowl, whisk the egg until well beaten.
5. Dip the chicken tenders in the egg, then in cornflakes mixture.
6. Transfer the coated chicken to the prepared cooking basket.
7. Cook in the preheated Air Fryer at about 380 degrees F/ 195 degrees C for 12 minutes almost.
8. Flip them halfway through the cooking time.
9. Serve immediately.

Healthy Chicken With Veggies

Servings: 4 Servings
Cooking Time: 20 Minutes
Ingredients:
- 1 pound of chopped chicken breast
- 1 chopped zucchini
- 1 cup of broccoli florets
- 1 cup of chopped bell peppers
- ½ chopped onion
- 2 minced garlic cloves
- 2 tablespoons of olive oil
- 1 tablespoon of Italian seasonings
- ½ teaspoon of garlic powder
- ½ teaspoon of chili powder (optional)
- Pinch of salt and black pepper, to taste

Directions:
1. Preheat your air fryer to 400ºF.
2. Put the chopped vegetables with chicken breast into a large mixing bowl. Add seasonings with oil and mix it well.
3. Transfer all the ingredients into the air fry basket and cook at 400ºF for 10 minutes. Toss halfway through cooking. If it's not ready, cook for 3–5 minutes more.
4. Serve warm and enjoy your Healthy Chicken with Veggies!

Chipotle Drumsticks

Servings:4
Cooking Time: 25 Minutes
Ingredients:
- 1 tablespoon tomato paste
- ½ teaspoon chipotle powder
- ¼ teaspoon apple cider vinegar
- ¼ teaspoon garlic powder
- 8 chicken drumsticks
- ½ teaspoon salt
- ⅛ teaspoon ground black pepper

Directions:
1. In a small bowl, combine tomato paste, chipotle powder, vinegar, and garlic powder.
2. Sprinkle drumsticks with salt and pepper, then place into a large bowl and pour in tomato paste mixture. Toss or stir to evenly coat all drumsticks in mixture.
3. Place drumsticks into ungreased air fryer basket. Adjust the temperature to 400°F and set the timer for 25 minutes, turning drumsticks halfway through cooking. Drumsticks will be dark red with an internal temperature of at least 165°F when done. Serve warm.

Chicken Burgers With Ham And Cheese

Servings:4
Cooking Time: 13 To 16 Minutes
Ingredients:
- ⅓ cup soft bread crumbs
- 3 tablespoons milk
- 1 egg, beaten
- ½ teaspoon dried thyme
- Pinch salt
- Freshly ground black pepper, to taste
- 1¼ pounds (567 g) ground chicken
- ¼ cup finely chopped ham
- ⅓ cup grated Havarti cheese
- Olive oil for misting

Directions:
1. Preheat the air fryer to 350ºF (177ºC).
2. In a medium bowl, combine the bread crumbs, milk, egg, thyme, salt, and pepper. Add the chicken and mix gently but thoroughly with clean hands.
3. Form the chicken into eight thin patties and place on waxed paper.
4. Top four of the patties with the ham and cheese. Top with remaining four patties and gently press the edges together to seal, so the ham and cheese mixture is in the middle of the burger.
5. Place the burgers in the basket and mist with olive oil. Bake for 13 to 16 minutes or until the chicken is thoroughly cooked to 165ºF (74ºC) as measured with a meat thermometer. Serve immediately.

Easy Turkey Meatballs

Servings: 4
Cooking Time: 20 Minutes
Ingredients:
- 1 lb ground turkey
- ½ celery stalk, chopped
- 1 egg
- ¼ tsp red pepper flakes
- ¼ cup bread crumbs
- Salt and pepper to taste

The Ultimate Tower Air Fryer Cookbook

- ½ tsp garlic powder
- ½ tsp onion powder
- ½ tsp cayenne pepper

Directions:
1. Preheat air fryer to 360°F. Add all of the ingredients to a bowl and mix well. Shape the mixture into 12 balls and arrange them on the greased frying basket. Air Fry for 10-12 minutes or until the meatballs are cooked through and browned. Serve and enjoy!

Sweet Marinated Chicken Wings

Servings: 6-8
Cooking Time: 12 Minutes
Ingredients:
- 16 chicken wings
- To make the marinade:
- 2 tablespoons honey
- 2 tablespoons light soya sauce
- ½ teaspoon sea salt
- ¼ teaspoon black pepper
- ¼ teaspoon white pepper, ground
- 2 tablespoons lemon juice

Directions:
1. To marinate, combine the marinade ingredients with the chicken wings in the zip-log bag. Then seal and refrigerate for 4 to 6 minutes.
2. On a flat kitchen surface, plug your air fryer and turn it on.
3. Before cooking, heat the air fryer to 355 degrees F/ 180 degrees C for 4 to 5 minutes.
4. Gently coat the air fryer basket with cooking oil or spray.
5. Place the chicken wings inside the air fryer basket. Cook in your air fryer for 5 to 6 minutes.
6. When cooked, remove the air fryer basket from the air fryer and serve warm with lemon wedges as you like.

Chicken Cordon Bleu

Servings: 2
Cooking Time: 16 Minutes
Ingredients:
- 2 boneless, skinless chicken breasts
- ¼ teaspoon salt
- 2 teaspoons Dijon mustard
- 2 ounces deli ham
- 2 ounces Swiss, fontina, or Gruyère cheese
- ⅓ cup all-purpose flour
- 1 egg
- ½ cup breadcrumbs

Directions:
1. Pat the chicken breasts with a paper towel. Season the chicken with the salt. Pound the chicken breasts to 1½ inches thick. Create a pouch by slicing the side of each chicken breast. Spread 1 teaspoon Dijon mustard inside the pouch of each chicken breast. Wrap a 1-ounce slice of ham around a 1-ounce slice of cheese and place into the pouch. Repeat with the remaining ham and cheese.
2. In a medium bowl, place the flour.
3. In a second bowl, whisk the egg.
4. In a third bowl, place the breadcrumbs.
5. Dredge the chicken in the flour and shake off the excess. Next, dip the chicken into the egg and then in the breadcrumbs. Set the chicken on a plate and repeat with the remaining chicken piece.
6. Preheat the air fryer to 360°F.
7. Place the chicken in the air fryer basket and spray liberally with cooking spray. Cook for 8 minutes, turn the chicken breasts over, and liberally spray with cooking spray again; cook another 6 minutes. Once golden brown, check for an internal temperature of 165°F.

Simple & Delicious Chicken Wings

Servings: 8
Cooking Time: 20 Minutes
Ingredients:
- 1 ½ pounds chicken wings
- 2 tablespoons olive oil
- Black pepper
- Salt

Directions:
1. Toss chicken wings with oil and place in the air fryer basket.
2. Cook chicken wings at 370 degrees F/ 185 degrees C for almost 15 minutes.
3. Shake basket and cook at 400 degrees F/ 205 degrees C for 5 minutes more.
4. Season cooked chicken wings with black pepper and salt.
5. Serve and enjoy.

Jerk Chicken Kebabs

Servings: 4
Cooking Time: 14 Minutes
Ingredients:
- 8 ounces boneless, skinless chicken thighs, cut into 1" cubes
- 2 tablespoons jerk seasoning
- 2 tablespoons coconut oil
- ½ medium red bell pepper, seeded and cut into 1" pieces
- ¼ medium red onion, peeled and cut into 1" pieces
- ½ teaspoon salt

Directions:
1. Place chicken in a medium bowl and sprinkle with jerk seasoning and coconut oil. Toss to coat on all sides.
2. Using eight 6" skewers, build skewers by alternating chicken, pepper, and onion pieces, about three repetitions per skewer.
3. Sprinkle salt over skewers and place into ungreased air fryer basket. Adjust the temperature to 370°F and set the timer for 14 minutes, turning skewers halfway through cooking. Chicken will be golden and have an internal temperature of at least 165°F when done. Serve warm.

Garlic-roasted Chicken With Creamer Potatoes

Servings: 4
Cooking Time: 25 Minutes
Ingredients:
- 1 (2½- to 3-pound) broiler-fryer whole chicken
- 2 tablespoons olive oil
- ½ teaspoon garlic salt
- 8 cloves garlic, peeled
- 1 slice lemon
- ½ teaspoon dried thyme
- ½ teaspoon dried marjoram
- 12 to 16 creamer potatoes, scrubbed

Directions:
1. Do not wash the chicken before cooking. Remove it from its packaging and pat the chicken dry.
2. Combine the olive oil and salt in a small bowl. Rub half of this mixture on the inside of the chicken, under the skin, and on the chicken skin. Place the garlic cloves and lemon slice inside the chicken. Sprinkle the chicken with the thyme and marjoram.
3. Put the chicken in the air fryer basket. Surround with the potatoes and drizzle the potatoes with the remaining olive oil mixture.
4. Roast for 25 minutes, then test the temperature of the chicken. It should be 160°F. Test at the thickest part of the breast, making sure the probe doesn't touch bone. If the chicken isn't done yet, return it to the air fryer and roast it for 4 to 5 minutes, or until the temperature is 160°F.
5. When the chicken is done, transfer it and the potatoes to a serving platter and cover with foil. Let the chicken rest for 5 minutes before serving.

Lemon Herb Whole Cornish Hen

Servings: 2
Cooking Time: 50 Minutes
Ingredients:
- 1 Cornish hen
- ¼ cup olive oil
- 2 tbsp lemon juice
- 2 tbsp sage, chopped
- 2 tbsp thyme, chopped
- 4 garlic cloves, chopped
- Salt and pepper to taste
- 1 celery stalk, chopped
- ½ small onion
- ½ lemon, juiced and zested
- 2 tbsp chopped parsley

Directions:
1. Preheat air fryer to 380°F. Whisk the olive oil, lemon juice, sage, thyme, garlic, salt, and pepper in a bowl. Rub the mixture on the tops and sides of the hen. Pour any excess inside the cavity of the bird. Stuff the celery, onion, and lemon juice and zest into the cavity of the hen. Put in the frying basket and Roast for 40-45 minutes. Cut the hen in half and serve garnished with parsley.

Gluten-free Nutty Chicken Fingers

Servings: 4
Cooking Time: 10 Minutes
Ingredients:
- ½ cup gluten-free flour
- ½ teaspoon garlic powder
- ¼ teaspoon onion powder
- ¼ teaspoon black pepper
- ¼ teaspoon salt
- 1 cup walnuts, pulsed into coarse flour
- ½ cup gluten-free breadcrumbs
- 2 large eggs
- 1 pound boneless, skinless chicken tenders

Directions:
1. Preheat the air fryer to 400°F.
2. In a medium bowl, mix the flour, garlic, onion, pepper, and salt. Set aside.
3. In a separate bowl, mix the walnut flour and breadcrumbs.
4. In a third bowl, whisk the eggs.
5. Liberally spray the air fryer basket with olive oil spray.
6. Pat the chicken tenders dry with a paper towel. Dredge the tenders one at a time in the flour, then dip them in the egg, and toss them in the breadcrumb coating. Repeat until all tenders are coated.
7. Set each tender in the air fryer, leaving room on each side of the tender to allow for flipping.
8. When the basket is full, cook 5 minutes, flip, and cook another 5 minutes. Check the internal temperature after cooking completes; it should read 165°F. If it does not, cook another 2 to 4 minutes.
9. Remove the tenders and let cool 5 minutes before serving. Repeat until all the tenders are cooked.

Ham And Cheese Stuffed Chicken Burgers

Servings: 4
Cooking Time: 13 To 16 Minutes
Ingredients:
- ⅓ cup soft bread crumbs
- 3 tablespoons milk
- 1 egg, beaten
- ½ teaspoon dried thyme
- Pinch salt
- Freshly ground black pepper
- 1¼ pounds ground chicken
- ¼ cup finely chopped ham
- ⅓ cup grated Havarti cheese
- Olive oil for misting

Directions:
1. In a medium bowl, combine the bread crumbs, milk, egg, thyme, salt, and pepper. Add the chicken and mix gently but thoroughly with clean hands.

2. Form the chicken into eight thin patties and place on waxed paper.
3. Top four of the patties with the ham and cheese. Top with remaining four patties and gently press the edges together to seal, so the ham and cheese mixture is in the middle of the burger.
4. Place the burgers in the basket and mist with olive oil. Grill for 13 to 16 minutes or until the chicken is thoroughly cooked to 165°F as measured with a meat thermometer.

Israeli Chicken Schnitzel

Servings:4
Cooking Time: 10 Minutes
Ingredients:
- 2 large boneless, skinless chicken breasts, each weighing about 1 pound (454 g)
- 1 cup all-purpose flour
- 2 teaspoons garlic powder
- 2 teaspoons kosher salt
- 1 teaspoon black pepper
- 1 teaspoon paprika
- 2 eggs beaten with 2 tablespoons water
- 2 cups panko bread crumbs
- Vegetable oil spray
- Lemon juice, for serving

Directions:
1. Preheat the air fryer to 375°F (191°C).
2. Place 1 chicken breast between 2 pieces of plastic wrap. Use a mallet or a rolling pin to pound the chicken until it is ¼ inch thick. Set aside. Repeat with the second breast. Whisk together the flour, garlic powder, salt, pepper, and paprika on a large plate. Place the panko in a separate shallow bowl or pie plate.
3. Dredge 1 chicken breast in the flour, shaking off any excess, then dip it in the egg mixture. Dredge the chicken breast in the panko, making sure to coat it completely. Shake off any excess panko. Place the battered chicken breast on a plate. Repeat with the second chicken breast.
4. Spray the air fryer basket with oil spray. Place 1 of the battered chicken breasts in the basket and spray the top with oil spray. Air fry until the top is browned, about 5 minutes. Flip the chicken and spray the second side with oil spray. Air fry until the second side is browned and crispy and the internal temperature reaches 165°F (74°C). Remove the first chicken breast from the air fryer and repeat with the second chicken breast.
5. Serve hot with lemon juice.

Nacho Chicken Fries

Servings: 4
Cooking Time: 7 Minutes
Ingredients:
- 1 pound chicken tenders
- salt
- ¼ cup flour
- 2 eggs
- ¾ cup panko breadcrumbs
- ¾ cup crushed organic nacho cheese tortilla chips
- oil for misting or cooking spray
- Seasoning Mix
- 1 tablespoon chili powder
- 1 teaspoon ground cumin
- ½ teaspoon garlic powder
- ½ teaspoon onion powder

Directions:
1. Stir together all seasonings in a small cup and set aside.
2. Cut chicken tenders in half crosswise, then cut into strips no wider than about ½ inch.
3. Preheat air fryer to 390°F.
4. Salt chicken to taste. Place strips in large bowl and sprinkle with 1 tablespoon of the seasoning mix. Stir well to distribute seasonings.
5. Add flour to chicken and stir well to coat all sides.
6. Beat eggs together in a shallow dish.
7. In a second shallow dish, combine the panko, crushed chips, and the remaining 2 teaspoons of seasoning mix.
8. Dip chicken strips in eggs, then roll in crumbs. Mist with oil or cooking spray.
9. Chicken strips will cook best if done in two batches. They can be crowded and overlapping a little but not stacked in double or triple layers.
10. Cook for 4minutes. Shake basket, mist with oil, and cook 3 moreminutes, until chicken juices run clear and outside is crispy.
11. Repeat step 10 to cook remaining chicken fries.

Flavorful Chicken With Bacon

Servings: 4
Cooking Time: 25 Minutes
Ingredients:
- 4 medium-sized skin-on chicken drumsticks
- 1 ½ teaspoons herbs de Provence
- 1 tablespoon rice vinegar
- 2 tablespoons olive oil
- Salt and pepper as needed
- 2 garlic cloves, crushed
- 12 ounces crushed canned tomatoes
- 1 leek, thinly sliced
- 2 slices smoked bacon, chopped

Directions:
1. Mix thoroughly the herbs de Provence, salt, chicken, and pepper in a medium sized bowl.
2. Then add rice vinegar and olive oil inside and mix to toss well.
3. On a flat kitchen surface, plug your air fryer and turn it on.
4. Before cooking, heat your air fryer to 360 degrees F/ 180 degrees C for about 4 to 5 minutes.
5. Gently coat an air fryer basket with cooking oil or spray.
6. Then add the chicken mixture inside.
7. Insert the basket inside your air fryer and cook for 10 minutes.

8. When cooked, remove the basket from the air fryer and then add the remaining ingredients inside. Stir well.
9. Cook in the air fryer for 15 more minutes.
10. Serve the chicken warm with lemon wedges or steamed rice.

Betty's Baked Chicken

Servings: 1
Cooking Time: 70 Minutes
Ingredients:
- ½ cup butter
- 1 tsp. pepper
- 3 tbsp. garlic, minced
- 1 whole chicken

Directions:
1. Pre-heat your fryer at 350°F.
2. Allow the butter to soften at room temperature, then mix well in a small bowl with the pepper and garlic.
3. Massage the butter into the chicken. Any remaining butter can go inside the chicken.
4. Cook the chicken in the fryer for half an hour. Flip, then cook on the other side for another thirty minutes.
5. Test the temperature of the chicken by sticking a meat thermometer into the fat of the thigh to make sure it has reached 165°F. Take care when removing the chicken from the fryer. Let sit for ten minutes before you carve it and serve.

Herbs Chicken Drumsticks With Tamari Sauce

Servings: 6
Cooking Time: 35 Minutes
Ingredients:
- 6 chicken drumsticks
- Sauce:
- 6 oz. hot sauce
- 3 tablespoons olive oil
- 3 tablespoons tamari sauce
- 1 teaspoon dried thyme
- ½ teaspoon dried oregano

Directions:
1. Spritz a nonstick cooking spray over the sides and bottom of the cooking basket.
2. Cook the chicken drumsticks at 380 degrees F/ 195 degrees C for 35 minutes, flipping them over halfway through.
3. Meanwhile, heat the hot sauce, olive oil, tamari sauce, thyme, and oregano in a pan over medium-low heat; reserve.
4. Drizzle the sauce over the prepared chicken drumsticks; toss to coat well and serve.

Fiesta Chicken Plate

Servings: 4
Cooking Time: 15 Minutes
Ingredients:
- 1 pound boneless, skinless chicken breasts (2 large breasts)
- 2 tablespoons lime juice
- 1 teaspoon cumin
- ½ teaspoon salt
- ½ cup grated Pepper Jack cheese
- 1 16-ounce can refried beans
- ½ cup salsa
- 2 cups shredded lettuce
- 1 medium tomato, chopped
- 2 avocados, peeled and sliced
- 1 small onion, sliced into thin rings
- sour cream
- tortilla chips (optional)

Directions:
1. Split each chicken breast in half lengthwise.
2. Mix lime juice, cumin, and salt together and brush on all surfaces of chicken breasts.
3. Place in air fryer basket and cook at 390°F for 15 minutes, until well done.
4. Divide the cheese evenly over chicken breasts and cook for an additional minute to melt cheese.
5. While chicken is cooking, heat refried beans on stovetop or in microwave.
6. When ready to serve, divide beans among 4 plates. Place chicken breasts on top of beans and spoon salsa over. Arrange the lettuce, tomatoes, and avocados artfully on each plate and scatter with the onion rings.
7. Pass sour cream at the table and serve with tortilla chips if desired.

Seasoned Chicken Thighs With Italian Herbs

Servings: 4
Cooking Time: 20 Minutes
Ingredients:
- 4 skin-on bone-in chicken thighs
- 2 tablespoons unsalted butter, melted
- 3 teaspoons Italian herbs
- ½ teaspoon garlic powder
- ¼ teaspoon onion powder

Directions:
1. Using a brush, coat the chicken thighs with the melted butter.
2. Combine the herbs with the garlic powder and onion powder, then massage into the chicken thighs.
3. Place the thighs your air fryer's basket.
4. Cook at almost exactly 380 degrees F/ 195 degrees C for 20 minutes, turning the chicken halfway through to cook on the other side.
5. Once the inner temperature has reached 165 degrees F/ 75 degrees C, remove from the fryer and serve.

Ginger Turmeric Chicken Thighs

Servings:4
Cooking Time: 25 Minutes
Ingredients:
- 4 boneless, skin-on chicken thighs
- 2 tablespoons coconut oil, melted
- ½ teaspoon ground turmeric

- ½ teaspoon salt
- ½ teaspoon garlic powder
- ½ teaspoon ground ginger
- ¼ teaspoon ground black pepper

Directions:
1. Place chicken thighs in a large bowl and drizzle with coconut oil. Sprinkle with remaining ingredients and toss to coat both sides of thighs.
2. Place thighs skin side up into ungreased air fryer basket. Adjust the temperature to 400°F and set the timer for 25 minutes. After 10 minutes, turn thighs. When 5 minutes remain, flip thighs once more. Chicken will be done when skin is golden brown and the internal temperature is at least 165°F. Serve warm.

Mediterranean Fried Chicken

Servings: 2
Cooking Time: 21 Minutes
Ingredients:
- 2 (6-ounce) boneless skinless chicken breast halves
- 3 tablespoons olive oil
- 6 pitted Greek or ripe olives, sliced
- 2 tablespoons. capers, drained
- ½-pint grape tomatoes
- ¼ teaspoon salt
- ¼ teaspoon. pepper

Directions:
1. Before cooking, heat your air fryer to 390 degrees F/ 200 degrees C.
2. Using the cooking spray, gently grease a baking pan that fits in your air fryer.
3. To season, add salt and pepper, as well as the chicken inside the baking pan and toss well.
4. Brown in the preheated air fryer for 6 minutes, flipping to the other side halfway through cooking.
5. Add olives, oil, capers, and tomatoes in the baking pan and stir to combine.
6. Cook in your air fryer at 330 degrees F/ 165 degrees C for 15 minutes.
7. When cooked, remove from the air fryer and serve.

French Mustard Chicken Thighs

Servings: 4
Cooking Time: 15 Minutes
Ingredients:
- 1-pound bone-in or boneless, skinless chicken thighs
- Black pepper and salt to taste
- 2 garlic cloves, minced
- ½ cup honey
- ¼ cup French mustard
- 2 tablespoons butter
- 2 tablespoon dill, chopped
- Herbs de Provence seasoning, as needed

Directions:
1. At 390 degrees F/ 200 degrees C, preheat your Air fryer.
2. Grease its air fryer basket with cooking spray.
3. In a suitable bowl, mix the Herbs de Provence seasoning, salt, and black pepper. Rub the chicken with this mixture.
4. Transfer to the cooking basket.
5. Cook for almost 15 minutes, flipping once halfway through.
6. Meanwhile, melt the butter in a suitable saucepan over medium heat.
7. Add honey, French mustard, and garlic; cook until reduced to a thick consistency, about 3 minutes.
8. Serve the chicken drizzled with the honey-mustard sauce.

Grilled Chicken Legs With Coconut Cream

Servings: 4
Cooking Time: 25 Minutes
Ingredients:
- 4 big chicken legs
- 5 teaspoons turmeric powder
- 2 tablespoons ginger grated
- Black pepper and salt to taste
- 4 tablespoons coconut cream

Directions:
1. In a suitable bowl, mix salt, black pepper, ginger, turmeric, and cream, whisk well.
2. Add chicken pieces, coat and marinate for 2 hours.
3. Transfer chicken to the preheated air fryer and cook at almost 370 degrees F/ 185 degrees C for 25 minutes.
4. Serve.

Crispy Cordon Bleu

Servings: 4
Cooking Time: 25 Minutes
Ingredients:
- 4 deli ham slices, halved lengthwise
- 2 tbsp grated Parmesan
- 4 chicken breast halves
- Salt and pepper to taste
- 8 Swiss cheese slices
- 1 egg
- 2 egg whites
- ¾ cup bread crumbs
- 1 tsp garlic powder
- 1 tsp onion powder
- 1 tsp mustard powder

Directions:
1. Preheat air fryer to 400°F. Season the chicken cutlets with salt and pepper. On one cutlet, put a half slice of ham and cheese on the top. Roll the chicken tightly, then set aside. Beat the eggs and egg whites in a shallow bowl. Put the crumbs, Parmesan, garlic, onion, and mustard powder, in a second bowl. Dip the cutlet in the egg bowl and then in the crumb mix. Press so that they stick to the chicken. Put the rolls of chicken seam side down in the greased frying basket and Air Fry for 12-14 minutes, flipping once until golden and cooked through. Serve.

Tandoori Chicken

Servings: 4
Cooking Time: 18 To 23 Minutes
Ingredients:
- ⅔ cup plain low-fat yogurt
- 2 tablespoons freshly squeezed lemon juice
- 2 teaspoons curry powder (see Tip)
- ½ teaspoon ground cinnamon
- 2 garlic cloves, minced
- 2 teaspoons olive oil
- 4 (5-ounce) low-sodium boneless skinless chicken breasts

Directions:
1. In a medium bowl, whisk the yogurt, lemon juice, curry powder, cinnamon, garlic, and olive oil.
2. With a sharp knife, cut thin slashes into the chicken. Add it to the yogurt mixture and turn to coat. Let stand for 10 minutes at room temperature. You can also prepare this ahead of time and marinate the chicken in the refrigerator for up to 24 hours.
3. Remove the chicken from the marinade and shake off any excess liquid. Discard any remaining marinade.
4. Roast the chicken for 10 minutes. With tongs, carefully turn each piece. Roast for 8 to 13 minutes more, or until the chicken reaches an internal temperature of 165°F on a meat thermometer. Serve immediately.

Chicago-style Turkey Meatballs

Servings: 6
Cooking Time: 15 Minutes
Ingredients:
- 1 lb ground turkey
- 1 tbsp orange juice
- Salt and pepper to taste
- ½ tsp smoked paprika
- ½ tsp chili powder
- 1 tsp cumin powder
- ¼ red bell pepper, diced
- 1 diced jalapeño pepper
- 2 garlic cloves, minced

Directions:
1. Preheat air fryer to 400°F. Combine all of the ingredients in a large bowl. Shape into meatballs. Transfer the meatballs into the greased frying basket. Air Fry for 4 minutes, then flip the meatballs. Air Fry for another 3 minutes until cooked through. Serve immediately.

Windsor's Chicken Salad

Servings: 4
Cooking Time: 30 Minutes
Ingredients:
- ½ cup halved seedless red grapes
- 2 chicken breasts, cubed
- Salt and pepper to taste
- ¾ cup mayonnaise
- 1 tbsp lemon juice
- 2 tbsp chopped parsley
- ½ cup chopped celery
- 1 shallot, diced

Directions:
1. Preheat air fryer to 350°F. Sprinkle chicken with salt and pepper. Place the chicken cubes in the frying basket and Air Fry for 9 minutes, flipping once. In a salad bowl, combine the cooked chicken, mayonnaise, lemon juice, parsley, grapes, celery, and shallot and let chill covered in the fridge for 1 hour up to overnight.

Glazed Chicken Thighs

Servings: 4
Cooking Time: 25 Minutes
Ingredients:
- 1 lb boneless, skinless chicken thighs
- ¼ cup balsamic vinegar
- 3 tbsp honey
- 2 tbsp brown sugar
- 1 tsp whole-grain mustard
- ¼ cup soy sauce
- 3 garlic cloves, minced
- Salt and pepper to taste
- ½ tsp smoked paprika
- 2 tbsp chopped shallots

Directions:
1. Preheat air fryer to 375°F. Whisk vinegar, honey, sugar, soy sauce, mustard, garlic, salt, pepper, and paprika in a small bowl. Arrange the chicken in the frying basket and brush the top of each with some of the vinegar mixture. Air Fry for 7 minutes, then flip the chicken. Brush the tops with the rest of the vinegar mixture and Air Fry for another 5 to 8 minutes. Allow resting for 5 minutes before slicing. Serve warm sprinkled with shallots.

Parmesan Chicken Fingers

Servings: 2
Cooking Time: 19 Minutes
Ingredients:
- ½ cup flour
- 1 teaspoon salt
- freshly ground black pepper
- 2 eggs, beaten
- ¾ cup seasoned panko breadcrumbs
- ¾ cup grated Parmesan cheese
- 8 chicken tenders (about 1 pound)
- OR
- 2 to 3 boneless, skinless chicken breasts, cut into strips
- vegetable oil
- marinara sauce

Directions:
1. Set up a dredging station. Combine the flour, salt and pepper in a shallow dish. Place the beaten eggs in second shallow dish, and combine the panko breadcrumbs and Parmesan cheese in a third shallow dish.

2. Dredge the chicken tenders in the flour mixture. Then dip them into the egg, and finally place the chicken in the breadcrumb mixture. Press the coating onto both sides of the chicken tenders. Place the coated chicken tenders on a baking sheet until they are all coated. Spray both sides of the chicken fingers with vegetable oil.
3. Preheat the air fryer to 360°F.
4. Air-fry the chicken fingers in two batches. Transfer half the chicken fingers to the air fryer basket and air-fry for 9 minutes, turning the chicken over halfway through the cooking time. When the second batch of chicken fingers has finished cooking, return the first batch to the air fryer with the second batch and air-fry for one minute to heat everything through.
5. Serve immediately with marinara sauce, honey-mustard, ketchup or your favorite dipping sauce.

Cajun Chicken Drumsticks
Servings: 5
Cooking Time: 40 Minutes
Ingredients:
- 10 chicken drumsticks
- 1½ tablespoons Louisiana Cajun Seasoning
- Salt
- Pepper
- Cooking oil

Directions:
1. Season the drumsticks with the Cajun seasoning and salt and pepper to taste.
2. Spray the air fryer basket with cooking oil.
3. Place 5 drumsticks in the air fryer. Do not stack. Spray the drumsticks with cooking oil. Cook for 10 minutes.
4. Open the air fryer and flip the chicken. Cook for an additional 8 minutes.
5. Remove the cooked chicken from the air fryer, then repeat steps 3 and 4 for the remaining 5 drumsticks.
6. Cool before serving.

Homemade Chicken Sliders
Servings: 3
Cooking Time: 30 Minutes
Ingredients:
- ½ cup all-purpose flour
- 1 teaspoon garlic salt
- ½ teaspoon black pepper
- 1 teaspoon celery seeds
- ½ teaspoon mustard seeds
- ½ teaspoon dried basil
- 1 egg
- 2 chicken breasts, cut in thirds
- 6 small-sized dinner rolls

Directions:
1. In mixing bowl, thoroughly combine the flour and seasonings.
2. In a separate shallow bowl, beat the egg until frothy.
3. Dredge the cleaned chicken through the flour mixture, then into egg; afterwards, roll them over the flour mixture again.
4. Spritz the chicken pieces with a cooking spray on all sides. Transfer them to the cooking basket.
5. Cook in the preheated Air Fryer at 380 degrees F/ 195 degrees C for 15 minutes; flip them and continue cooking for 10 to 12 minutes.
6. Test for doneness and adjust the seasonings.
7. Serve immediately on dinner rolls.

Flavorful Spiced Chicken Pieces
Servings: 10
Cooking Time: 20 Minutes
Ingredients:
- 5 pounds' chicken, about 10 pieces
- 1 tablespoon coconut oil
- 2 ½ teaspoon white black pepper
- 1 teaspoon ground ginger
- 1 ½ teaspoon garlic salt
- 1 tablespoon paprika
- 1 teaspoon dried mustard
- 1 teaspoon black pepper
- 1 teaspoon celery salt
- ⅓ teaspoon oregano
- ½ teaspoon basil
- ½ teaspoon thyme
- 2 cups pork rinds, crushed
- 1 tablespoon vinegar
- 1 cup unsweetened almond milk
- ½ teaspoon salt

Directions:
1. Add chicken in a suitable mixing bowl.
2. Add milk and vinegar over chicken and place in the refrigerator for 2 hours.
3. In a shallow dish, mix together pork rinds, white black pepper, ginger, garlic salt, paprika, mustard, black pepper, celery salt, oregano, basil, thyme, and salt.
4. Coat air fryer basket with coconut oil.
5. Coat each chicken piece with pork rind mixture and place on a plate.
6. Place ½ coated chicken in the air fryer basket.
7. Cook chicken at 360 degrees F/ 180 degrees C for almost 10 minutes then turn chicken and continue cooking for almost 10 minutes more or until internal temperature reaches at 165 F.
8. Cook remaining chicken using the same method.
9. Serve and enjoy.

Paprika Chicken Drumettes
Servings: 2
Cooking Time: 30 Minutes
Ingredients:
- 1 lb chicken drumettes
- 1 cup buttermilk
- 3/4 cup bread crumbs
- ½ tsp smoked paprika
- 1 tsp chicken seasoning

The Ultimate Tower Air Fryer Cookbook

- ½ tsp garlic powder
- Salt and pepper to taste
- 3 tsp of lemon juice

Directions:
1. Mix drumettes and buttermilk in a bowl and let sit covered in the fridge overnight. Preheat air fryer at 350ºF. In a shallow bowl, combine the remaining ingredients. Shake excess buttermilk off drumettes and dip them in the breadcrumb mixture. Place breaded drumettes in the greased frying basket and Air Fry for 12 minutes. Increase air fryer temperature to 400ºF, toss chicken, and cook for 8 minutes. Let rest for 5 minutes before serving.

Mumbai Chicken Nuggets

Servings: 4
Cooking Time: 30 Minutes
Ingredients:
- 1 lb boneless, skinless chicken breasts
- 4 tsp curry powder
- Salt and pepper to taste
- 1 egg, beaten
- 2 tbsp sesame oil
- 1 cup panko bread crumbs
- ½ cup coconut yogurt
- 1/3 cup mango chutney
- ¼ cup mayonnaise

Directions:
1. Preheat the air fryer to 400°F. Cube the chicken into 1-inch pieces and sprinkle with 3 tsp of curry powder, salt, and pepper; toss to coat. Beat together the egg and sesame oil in a shallow bowl and scatter the panko onto a separate plate. Dip the chicken in the egg, then in the panko, and press to coat. Lay the coated nuggets on a wire rack as you work. Set the nuggets in the greased frying basket and Air Fry for 7-10 minutes, rearranging once halfway through cooking. While the nuggets are cooking, combine the yogurt, chutney, mayonnaise, and the remaining teaspoon of curry powder in a small bowl. Serve the nuggets with the dipping sauce.

The Ultimate Chicken Bulgogi

Servings: 4
Cooking Time: 30 Minutes
Ingredients:
- 1 ½ lb boneless, skinless chicken thighs, cubed
- 1 cucumber, thinly sliced
- ¼ cup apple cider vinegar
- 4 garlic cloves, minced
- ¼ tsp ground ginger
- ⅛ tsp red pepper flakes
- 2 tsp honey
- ⅛ tsp salt
- 2 tbsp tamari
- 2 tsp sesame oil
- 2 tsp granular honey
- 2 tbsp lemon juice
- ½ tsp lemon zest
- 3 scallions, chopped
- 2 cups cooked white rice
- 2 tsp roasted sesame seeds

Directions:
1. In a bowl, toss the cucumber, vinegar, half of the garlic, half of the ginger, pepper flakes, honey, and salt and store in the fridge covered. Combine the tamari, sesame oil, granular honey, lemon juice, remaining garlic, remaining ginger, and chicken in a large bowl. Toss to coat and marinate in the fridge for 10 minutes.
2. Preheat air fryer to 350ºF. Place chicken in the frying basket, do not discard excess marinade. Air Fry for 11 minutes, shaking once and pouring excess marinade over. Place the chicken bulgogi over the cooked rice and scatter with scallion greens, pickled cucumbers, and sesame seeds. Serve and enjoy!

Turkey Stuffed Bell Peppers

Servings: 4
Cooking Time: 15 Minutes
Ingredients:
- ½ pound (227 g) lean ground turkey
- 4 medium bell peppers
- 1 (15-ounce / 425-g) can black beans, drained and rinsed
- 1 cup shredded reduced-fat Cheddar cheese
- 1 cup cooked long-grain brown rice
- 1 cup mild salsa
- 1¼ teaspoons chili powder
- 1 teaspoon salt
- ½ teaspoon ground cumin
- ½ teaspoon freshly ground black pepper
- Olive oil spray
- Chopped fresh cilantro, for garnish

Directions:
1. Preheat the air fryer to 360ºF (182ºC).
2. In a large skillet over medium-high heat, cook the turkey, breaking it up with a spoon, until browned, about 5 minutes. Drain off any excess fat.
3. Cut about ½ inch off the tops of the peppers and then cut in half lengthwise. Remove and discard the seeds and set the peppers aside.
4. In a large bowl, combine the browned turkey, black beans, Cheddar cheese, rice, salsa, chili powder, salt, cumin, and black pepper. Spoon the mixture into the bell peppers.
5. Lightly spray the air fryer basket with olive oil spray.
6. Place the stuffed peppers in the air fryer basket. Air fry until heated through, 10 to 15 minutes. Garnish with cilantro and serve.

Daadi Chicken Salad

Servings: 2
Cooking Time: 30 Minutes
Ingredients:
- ½ cup chopped golden raisins
- 1 Granny Smith apple, grated
- 2 chicken breasts
- Salt and pepper to taste

- ¾ cup mayonnaise
- 1 tbsp lime juice
- 1 tsp curry powder
- ½ sliced avocado
- 1 scallion, minced
- 2 tbsp chopped pecans
- 1 tsp poppy seeds

Directions:
1. Preheat air fryer at 350ºF. Sprinkle chicken breasts with salt and pepper, place them in the greased frying basket, and Air Fry for 8-10 minutes, tossing once. Let rest for 5 minutes before cutting. In a salad bowl, combine chopped chicken, mayonnaise, lime juice, curry powder, raisins, apple, avocado, scallion, and pecans. Let sit covered in the fridge until ready to eat. Before serve sprinkled with the poppy seeds.

Family Chicken Fingers

Servings: 4
Cooking Time: 30 Minutes
Ingredients:
- 1 lb chicken breast fingers
- 1 tbsp chicken seasoning
- ½ tsp mustard powder
- Salt and pepper to taste
- 2 eggs
- 1 cup bread crumbs

Directions:
1. Preheat air fryer to 400°F. Add the chicken fingers to a large bowl along with chicken seasoning, mustard, salt, and pepper; mix well. Set up two small bowls. In one bowl, beat the eggs. In the second bowl, add the bread crumbs. Dip the chicken in the egg, then dredge in breadcrumbs. Place the nuggets in the air fryer. Lightly spray with cooking oil, then Air Fry for 8 minutes, shaking the basket once until crispy and cooked through. Serve warm.

Jerk Turkey Meatballs

Servings: 7
Cooking Time: 8 Minutes
Ingredients:
- 1 pound lean ground turkey
- ¼ cup chopped onion
- 1 teaspoon minced garlic
- ½ teaspoon dried thyme
- ¼ teaspoon ground cinnamon
- 1 teaspoon cayenne pepper
- ½ teaspoon paprika
- ½ teaspoon salt
- ⅛ teaspoon black pepper
- ¼ teaspoon red pepper flakes
- 2 teaspoons brown sugar
- 1 large egg, whisked
- ⅓ cup panko breadcrumbs
- 2⅓ cups cooked brown Jasmine rice
- 2 green onions, chopped
- ¾ cup sweet onion dressing

Directions:
1. Preheat the air fryer to 350°F.
2. In a medium bowl, mix the ground turkey with the onion, garlic, thyme, cinnamon, cayenne pepper, paprika, salt, pepper, red pepper flakes, and brown sugar. Add the whisked egg and stir in the breadcrumbs until the turkey starts to hold together.
3. Using a 1-ounce scoop, portion the turkey into meatballs. You should get about 28 meatballs.
4. Spray the air fryer basket with olive oil spray.
5. Place the meatballs into the air fryer basket and cook for 5 minutes, shake the basket, and cook another 2 to 4 minutes (or until the internal temperature of the meatballs reaches 165°F).
6. Remove the meatballs from the basket and repeat for the remaining meatballs.
7. Serve warm over a bed of rice with chopped green onions and spicy Caribbean jerk dressing.

Rosemary Chicken With Sweet Potatoes

Servings: 2
Cooking Time: 35 Minutes
Ingredients:
- 2 chicken legs, bone-in
- 2 garlic cloves, minced
- 1 teaspoon sesame oil
- Sea salt, to taste
- Ground black pepper, to taste
- 2 sprigs rosemary, leaves picked and crushed
- ½ pound sweet potatoes

Directions:
1. Before cooking, heat your air fryer to 380 degrees F/ 195 degrees C.
2. Rub the chicken legs with the garlic cloves.
3. Drizzle the sesame oil over the chicken legs and sweet potatoes. Then sprinkle rosemary and salt over them. Transfer the sweet potatoes and chicken legs inside the air fryer basket.
4. Then set the cooking temperature to 380 degrees F/ 195 degrees C and the timer for 30 minutes. Cook in your air fryer until the sweet potatoes are completely cooked and the internal temperature of the chicken legs is 165 degrees F/ 75 degrees C.
5. When cooked, remove from the air fryer and serve. Enjoy!

Buffalo Chicken Meatballs

Servings:5
Cooking Time: 12 Minutes
Ingredients:
- 1 pound ground chicken breast
- 1 packet dry ranch seasoning
- ⅓ cup plain bread crumbs
- 3 tablespoons mayonnaise
- 5 tablespoons buffalo sauce, divided

Directions:

1. Preheat the air fryer to 370°F.
2. In a large bowl, mix chicken, ranch seasoning, bread crumbs, and mayonnaise. Pour in 2 tablespoons buffalo sauce and stir to combine.
3. Roll meat mixture into balls, about 2 tablespoons for each, to make twenty meatballs.
4. Place meatballs in the air fryer basket and cook 12 minutes, shaking the basket twice during cooking, until brown and internal temperature reaches at least 165°F.
5. Toss meatballs in remaining buffalo sauce and serve.

Chicken Burgers With Blue Cheese Sauce

Servings: 4
Cooking Time: 40 Minutes
Ingredients:
- ¼ cup crumbled blue cheese
- ¼ cup sour cream
- 2 tbsp mayonnaise
- 1 tbsp red hot sauce
- Salt to taste
- 3 tbsp buffalo wing sauce
- 1 lb ground chicken
- 2 tbsp grated carrot
- 2 tbsp diced celery
- 1 egg white

Directions:
1. Whisk the blue cheese, sour cream, mayonnaise, red hot sauce, salt, and 1 tbsp of buffalo sauce in a bowl. Let sit covered in the fridge until ready to use.
2. Preheat air fryer at 350ºF. In another bowl, combine the remaining ingredients. Form mixture into 4 patties, making a slight indentation in the middle of each. Place patties in the greased frying basket and Air Fry for 13 minutes until you reach your desired doneness, flipping once. Serve with the blue cheese sauce.

Chapter 7: Beef, pork & Lamb Recipes

Mozzarella-stuffed Meatloaf

Servings: 6
Cooking Time: 30 Minutes
Ingredients:
- 1 pound 80/20 ground beef
- ½ medium green bell pepper, seeded and chopped
- ¼ medium yellow onion, peeled and chopped
- ½ teaspoon salt
- ¼ teaspoon ground black pepper
- 2 ounces mozzarella cheese, sliced into ¼"-thick slices
- ¼ cup low-carb ketchup

Directions:
1. In a large bowl, combine ground beef, bell pepper, onion, salt, and black pepper. Cut a piece of parchment to fit air fryer basket. Place half beef mixture on ungreased parchment and form a 9" × 4" loaf, about ½" thick.
2. Center mozzarella slices on beef loaf, leaving at least ¼" around each edge.
3. Press remaining beef into a second 9" × 4" loaf and place on top of mozzarella, pressing edges of loaves together to seal.
4. Place parchment with meatloaf into air fryer basket. Adjust the temperature to 350°F and set the timer for 30 minutes, carefully turning loaf and brushing top with ketchup halfway through cooking. Loaf will be browned and have an internal temperature of at least 180°F when done. Slice and serve warm.

Rice And Meatball Stuffed Bell Peppers

Servings: 4
Cooking Time: 11 To 17 Minutes
Ingredients:
- 4 bell peppers
- 1 tablespoon olive oil
- 1 small onion, chopped
- 2 cloves garlic, minced
- 1 cup frozen cooked rice, thawed
- 16 to 20 small frozen precooked meatballs, thawed
- ½ cup tomato sauce
- 2 tablespoons Dijon mustard

Directions:
1. To prepare the peppers, cut off about ½ inch of the tops. Carefully remove the membranes and seeds from inside the peppers. Set aside.
2. In a 6-by-6-by-2-inch pan, combine the olive oil, onion, and garlic. Bake in the air fryer for 2 to 4 minutes or until crisp and tender. Remove the vegetable mixture from the pan and set aside in a medium bowl.
3. Add the rice, meatballs, tomato sauce, and mustard to the vegetable mixture and stir to combine.
4. Stuff the peppers with the meat-vegetable mixture.
5. Place the peppers in the air fryer basket and bake for 9 to 13 minutes or until the filling is hot and the peppers are tender.

Pork And Pinto Bean Gorditas

Servings: 4
Cooking Time: 21 Minutes
Ingredients:
- 1 pound (454 g) lean ground pork
- 2 tablespoons chili powder
- 2 tablespoons ground cumin
- 1 teaspoon dried oregano
- 2 teaspoons paprika
- 1 teaspoon garlic powder
- ½ cup water
- 1 (15-ounce / 425-g) can pinto beans, drained and rinsed
- ½ cup taco sauce
- Salt and freshly ground black pepper, to taste
- 2 cups grated Cheddar cheese
- 5 (12-inch) flour tortillas
- 4 (8-inch) crispy corn tortilla shells
- 4 cups shredded lettuce
- 1 tomato, diced
- ⅓ cup sliced black olives
- Sour cream, for serving
- Tomato salsa, for serving
- Cooking spray

Directions:
1. Preheat the air fryer to 400°F (204°C). Spritz the air fryer basket with cooking spray.
2. Put the ground pork in the air fryer basket and air fry at 400°F (204°C) for 10 minutes, stirring a few times to gently break up the meat. Combine the chili powder, cumin, oregano, paprika, garlic powder and water in a small bowl. Stir the spice mixture into the browned pork. Stir in the beans and taco sauce and air fry for an additional minute. Transfer the pork mixture to a bowl. Season with salt and freshly ground black pepper.
3. Sprinkle ½ cup of the grated cheese in the center of the flour tortillas, leaving a 2-inch border around the edge free of cheese and filling. Divide the pork mixture among the four tortillas, placing it on top of the cheese. Put a crunchy corn tortilla on top of the pork and top with shredded lettuce, diced tomatoes, and black olives. Cut the remaining flour tortilla into 4 quarters. These quarters of tortilla will serve as the bottom of the gordita. Put one quarter tortilla on top of each gordita and fold the edges of the bottom flour tortilla up over the sides, enclosing the filling. While holding the seams down, brush the bottom of the gordita with olive oil and place the seam side down on the countertop while you finish the remaining three gorditas.
4. Preheat the air fryer to 380°F (193°C).
5. Air fry one gordita at a time. Transfer the gordita carefully to the air fryer basket, seam side down. Brush or spray the top tortilla with oil and air fry for 5 minutes. Carefully turn the gordita over and air fry for an additional 4 to 5 minutes until both sides are browned. When finished air frying all four gorditas, layer them back into the air fryer for an additional minute to make sure they are all warm before serving with sour cream and salsa.

Mustard Pork Tenderloin With Ground Walnuts

Servings: 4
Cooking Time: 16 Minutes
Ingredients:
- 3 tablespoons grainy mustard
- 2 teaspoons olive oil
- ¼ teaspoon dry mustard powder
- 1 1-pound pork tenderloin, excess fat trimmed
- 2 slices whole-wheat bread, crumbled
- ¼ cup ground walnuts
- 2 tablespoons cornstarch

Directions:
1. In a suitable bowl, stir together the mustard, olive oil, and mustard powder.
2. Spread this mixture over the pork.
3. On a plate, mix the bread crumbs, walnuts, and cornstarch. Dip the mustard-coated pork into the crumb mixture to coat.
4. Air-fry the pork for 12 to 16 minutes, or until it measures at least 145 degrees F/ 60 degrees C.
5. Slice to serve.

Roasted Pork Tenderloin

Servings: 6
Cooking Time: 1 Hour
Ingredients:
- 1 (3-pound) pork tenderloin
- 2 tablespoons extra-virgin olive oil
- 2 garlic cloves, minced
- 1 teaspoon dried basil
- 1 teaspoon dried oregano
- 1 teaspoon dried thyme
- Salt
- Pepper

Directions:
1. Drizzle the pork tenderloin with the olive oil.
2. Rub the garlic, basil, oregano, thyme, and salt and pepper to taste all over the tenderloin.
3. Place the tenderloin in the air fryer. Cook for 45 minutes.
4. Use a meat thermometer to test for doneness. (See Cooking tip.)
5. Open the air fryer and flip the pork tenderloin. Cook for an additional 15 minutes.
6. Remove the cooked pork from the air fryer and allow it to rest for 10 minutes before cutting.

Pork & Beef Egg Rolls

Servings: 8
Cooking Time: 8 Minutes
Ingredients:
- ¼ pound very lean ground beef
- ¼ pound lean ground pork
- 1 tablespoon soy sauce
- 1 teaspoon olive oil
- ½ cup grated carrots
- 2 green onions, chopped
- 2 cups grated Napa cabbage
- ¼ cup chopped water chestnuts
- ¼ teaspoon salt
- ¼ teaspoon garlic powder
- ¼ teaspoon black pepper
- 1 egg
- 1 tablespoon water
- 8 egg roll wraps
- oil for misting or cooking spray

Directions:
1. In a large skillet, brown beef and pork with soy sauce. Remove cooked meat from skillet, drain, and set aside.
2. Pour off any excess grease from skillet. Add olive oil, carrots, and onions. Sauté until barely tender, about 1 minute.
3. Stir in cabbage, cover, and cook for 1 minute or just until cabbage slightly wilts. Remove from heat.
4. In a large bowl, combine the cooked meats and vegetables, water chestnuts, salt, garlic powder, and pepper. Stir well. If needed, add more salt to taste.
5. Beat together egg and water in a small bowl.
6. Fill egg roll wrappers, using about ¼ cup of filling for each wrap. Roll up and brush all over with egg wash to seal. Spray very lightly with olive oil or cooking spray.
7. Place 4 egg rolls in air fryer basket and cook at 390°F for 4minutes. Turn over and cook 4 more minutes, until golden brown and crispy.
8. Repeat to cook remaining egg rolls.

Flank Steaks With Capers

Servings: 4
Cooking Time: 45 Minutes
Ingredients:
- 1 anchovy fillet, minced
- 1 clove of garlic, minced
- 1 cup pitted olives
- 1 tablespoon capers, minced
- 2 tablespoons fresh oregano
- 2 tablespoons garlic powder
- 2 tablespoons onion powder
- 2 tablespoons smoked paprika
- ⅓ cup extra-virgin olive oil
- 2 pounds flank steak, pounded
- Salt and pepper

Directions:
1. Season the anchovy fillet with salt and pepper.
2. Sprinkle the steaks with onion powder, oregano, paprika, and garlic powder.
3. Cook the steaks in your air fryer at 390 degrees F/ 200 degrees C for 45 minutes, flipping every 10 minutes.
4. Meanwhile, stir well the olive oil, capers, garlic, olives, and anchovy fillets.
5. When done, serve and enjoy.

Pork Sausage Bacon Rolls

Servings: 4
Cooking Time: 35 Minutes
Ingredients:
- 8 bacon strips
- 8 pork sausages
- Relish:
- 8 large tomatoes
- 1 garlic clove, peeled
- 1 small onion, peeled
- 3 tablespoons chopped parsley
- A pinch of salt
- A pinch of black pepper
- 2 tablespoons sugar
- 1 teaspoon smoked paprika
- 1 tablespoon white wine vinegar

Directions:
1. Start with the relish; add the tomatoes, garlic, and onion in a food processor.
2. Blitz them for almost 10 seconds until the mixture is pulpy.
3. Pour the pulp into a saucepan, add the vinegar, salt, black pepper, and place it over medium heat.
4. Bring to simmer for almost 10 minutes; add the paprika and sugar.
5. Stir with a spoon and simmer for almost 10 minutes until pulpy and thick.
6. Turn off the heat, transfer the relish to a bowl and chill it for an hour. In 30 minutes after putting the relish in the refrigerator, move on to the sausages.
7. Wrap each sausage with a bacon strip neatly and stick in a bamboo skewer at the end of the sausage to secure the bacon ends.
8. Open the air fryer, place in the wrapped sausages and cook for 12 minutes at 350 degrees F/ 175 degrees C.
9. Ensure that the bacon is golden and crispy before removing them.
10. Remove the relish from the refrigerator.
11. Serve the sausages and relish with turnip mash.

Tamari-seasoned Pork Strips

Servings: 4
Cooking Time: 40 Minutes
Ingredients:
- 3 tbsp olive oil
- 2 tbsp tamari
- 2 tsp red chili paste
- 2 tsp yellow mustard
- 2 tsp granulated sugar
- 1 lb pork shoulder strips
- 1 cup white rice, cooked
- 6 scallions, chopped
- ½ tsp garlic powder
- 1 tbsp lemon juice
- 1 tsp lemon zest
- ½ tsp salt

Directions:
1. Add 2 tbsp of olive oil, tamari, chili paste, mustard, and sugar to a bowl and whisk until everything is well mixed. Set aside half of the marinade. Toss pork strips in the remaining marinade and put in the fridge for 30 minutes.
2. Preheat air fryer to 350°F. Place the pork strips in the frying basket and Air Fry for 16-18 minutes, tossing once. Transfer cooked pork to the bowl along with the remaining marinade and toss to coat. Set aside. In a medium bowl, stir in the cooked rice, garlic, lemon juice, lemon zest, and salt and cover. Spread on a serving plate. Arrange the pork strips over and top with scallions. Serve.

Beef Cheeseburger Egg Rolls

Servings: 6
Cooking Time: 8 Minutes
Ingredients:
- 8 ounces (227 g) raw lean ground beef
- ½ cup chopped onion
- ½ cup chopped bell pepper
- ¼ teaspoon onion powder
- ¼ teaspoon garlic powder
- 3 tablespoons cream cheese
- 1 tablespoon yellow mustard
- 3 tablespoons shredded Cheddar cheese
- 6 chopped dill pickle chips
- 6 egg roll wrappers

Directions:
1. Preheat the air fryer to 392°F (200°C).
2. In a skillet, add the beef, onion, bell pepper, onion powder, and garlic powder. Stir and crumble beef until fully cooked, and vegetables are soft.
3. Take skillet off the heat and add cream cheese, mustard, and Cheddar cheese, stirring until melted.
4. Pour beef mixture into a bowl and fold in pickles.
5. Lay out egg wrappers and divide the beef mixture into each one. Moisten egg roll wrapper edges with water. Fold sides to the middle and seal with water.
6. Repeat with all other egg rolls.
7. Put rolls into air fryer, one batch at a time. Air fry for 8 minutes.
8. Serve immediately.

Kale And Beef Omelet

Servings: 4
Cooking Time: 16 Minutes
Ingredients:
- ½ pound (227 g) leftover beef, coarsely chopped
- 2 garlic cloves, pressed
- 1 cup kale, torn into pieces and wilted
- 1 tomato, chopped
- ¼ teaspoon sugar
- 4 eggs, beaten
- 4 tablespoons heavy cream
- ½ teaspoon turmeric powder
- Salt and ground black pepper, to taste
- ⅛ teaspoon ground allspice

- Cooking spray

Directions:
1. Preheat the air fryer to 360°F (182°C). Spritz four ramekins with cooking spray.
2. Put equal amounts of each of the ingredients into each ramekin and mix well.
3. Air fry for 16 minutes. Serve immediately.

Meatloaf With Tangy Tomato Glaze

Servings: 6
Cooking Time: 50 Minutes
Ingredients:
- 1 pound ground beef
- ½ pound ground pork
- ½ pound ground veal (or turkey)
- 1 medium onion, diced
- 1 small clove of garlic, minced
- 2 egg yolks, lightly beaten
- ½ cup tomato ketchup
- 1 tablespoon Worcestershire sauce
- ½ cup plain breadcrumbs*
- 2 teaspoons salt
- freshly ground black pepper
- ½ cup chopped fresh parsley, plus more for garnish
- 6 tablespoons ketchup
- 1 tablespoon balsamic vinegar
- 2 tablespoons brown sugar

Directions:
1. Combine the meats, onion, garlic, egg yolks, ketchup, Worcestershire sauce, breadcrumbs, salt, pepper and fresh parsley in a large bowl and mix well.
2. Preheat the air fryer to 350°F and pour a little water into the bottom of the air fryer drawer. (This will help prevent the grease that drips into the bottom drawer from burning and smoking.)
3. Transfer the meatloaf mixture to the air fryer basket, packing it down gently. Run a spatula around the meatloaf to create a space about ½-inch wide between the meat and the side of the air fryer basket.
4. Air-fry at 350°F for 20 minutes. Carefully invert the meatloaf onto a plate (remember to remove the basket from the air fryer drawer so you don't pour all the grease out) and slide it back into the air fryer basket to turn it over. Re-shape the meatloaf with a spatula if necessary. Air-fry for another 20 minutes at 350°F.
5. Combine the ketchup, balsamic vinegar and brown sugar in a bowl and spread the mixture over the meatloaf. Air-fry for another 10 minutes, until an instant read thermometer inserted into the center of the meatloaf registers 160°F.
6. Allow the meatloaf to rest for a few more minutes and then transfer it to a serving platter using a spatula. Slice the meatloaf, sprinkle a little chopped parsley on top if desired, and serve.

Cheeseburger Sliders With Pickle Sauce

Servings: 4
Cooking Time: 20 Minutes
Ingredients:
- 4 iceberg lettuce leaves, each halved lengthwise
- 2 red onion slices, rings separated
- ¼ cup shredded Swiss cheese
- 1 lb ground beef
- 1 tbsp Dijon mustard
- Salt and pepper to taste
- ¼ tsp shallot powder
- 2 tbsp mayonnaise
- 2 tsp ketchup
- ½ tsp mustard powder
- ½ tsp dill pickle juice
- ⅛ tsp onion powder
- ⅛ tsp garlic powder
- ⅛ tsp sweet paprika
- 8 tomato slices
- ½ cucumber, thinly sliced

Directions:
1. In a large bowl, use your hands to mix beef, Swiss cheese, mustard, salt, shallot, and black pepper. Do not overmix. Form 8 patties ½-inch thick. Mix together mayonnaise, ketchup, mustard powder, pickle juice, onion and garlic powder, and paprika in a medium bowl. Stir until smooth.
2. Preheat air fryer to 400°F. Place the sliders in the greased frying basket and Air Fry for about 8-10 minutes, flipping once until preferred doneness. Serve on top of lettuce halves with a slice of tomato, a slider, onion, a smear of special sauce, and cucumber.

Flavorsome Onion And Sausage Balls

Servings: 4
Cooking Time: 15 Minutes
Ingredients:
- Black pepper and salt to taste
- 1 cup onion, chopped
- 3 tablespoons breadcrumbs
- ½ teaspoon garlic puree
- 1 teaspoon sage

Directions:
1. At 340 degrees F/ 170 degrees C, preheat your air fryer.
2. In a suitable bowl, mix onions, sausage meat, sage, garlic puree, black pepper and salt.
3. Add breadcrumbs to a plate. Form balls using the mixture and roll them in breadcrumbs.
4. Add onion balls in your air fryer's cooking basket and cook for almost 15 minutes.
5. Serve and enjoy!

Honey-sriracha Pork Ribs

Servings: 4
Cooking Time: 25 Minutes
Ingredients:
- 3 pounds pork back ribs, white membrane removed
- 2 teaspoons salt
- 1 teaspoon ground black pepper

- ½ cup sriracha
- ⅓ cup honey
- 1 tablespoon lemon juice

Directions:
1. Preheat the air fryer to 400°F.
2. Place ribs on a work surface and cut the rack into two pieces to fit in the air fryer basket.
3. Sprinkle ribs with salt and pepper and place in the air fryer basket meat side down. Cook 15 minutes.
4. In a small bowl, combine the sriracha, honey, and lemon juice to make a sauce.
5. Remove ribs from the air fryer basket and pour sauce over both sides. Return them to the air fryer basket meat side up and cook an additional 10 minutes until brown and the internal temperature reaches at least 190°F. Serve warm.

Roast Beef With Herbs

Servings: 6 Servings
Cooking Time: 1 Hour 20 Minutes
Ingredients:
- 2 pounds of roast beef
- 2 teaspoons of onion powder
- 2 teaspoons of garlic powder
- 2 teaspoons of basil
- 2 teaspoons of parsley
- 2 teaspoons of thyme
- ½ tablespoons of salt
- 1 tablespoon of olive oil
- 1 teaspoon of black pepper

Directions:
1. Preheat your air fryer* to 390ºF. Spray the air fryer basket with some oil.
2. Add thyme, parsley, basil, pepper, salt, onion, and garlic powder in a small bow. Mix it until combined.
3. Grease the beef roast with olive oil, then rub it with the seasoning mixture.
4. Put the prepared roast beef in the preheated air fryer. Cook at 390ºF for 15 minutes. Flip it, reduce the temperature to 360ºF, and cook for another 60 minutes.
5. Serve warm** and enjoy your Roast Beef with Herbs!

Blackberry Bbq Glazed Country-style Ribs

Servings: 2
Cooking Time: 40 Minutes
Ingredients:
- ½ cup + 2 tablespoons sherry or Madeira wine, divided
- 1 pound boneless country-style pork ribs
- salt and freshly ground black pepper
- 1 tablespoon Chinese 5-spice powder
- ¼ cup blackberry preserves
- ¼ cup hoisin sauce*
- 1 clove garlic, minced
- 1 generous tablespoon grated fresh ginger
- 2 scallions, chopped
- 1 tablespoon sesame seeds, toasted

Directions:
1. Preheat the air fryer to 330°F and pour ½ cup of the sherry into the bottom of the air fryer drawer.
2. Season the ribs with salt, pepper and the 5-spice powder.
3. Air-fry the ribs at 330°F for 20 minutes, turning them over halfway through the cooking time.
4. While the ribs are cooking, make the sauce. Combine the remaining sherry, blackberry preserves, hoisin sauce, garlic and ginger in a small saucepan. Bring to a simmer on the stovetop for a few minutes, until the sauce thickens.
5. When the time is up on the air fryer, turn the ribs over, pour a little sauce on the ribs and air-fry for another 10 minutes at 330°F. Turn the ribs over again, pour on more of the sauce and air-fry at 330°F for a final 10 minutes.
6. Let the ribs rest for at least 5 minutes before serving them warm with a little more glaze brushed on and the scallions and sesame seeds sprinkled on top.

Balsamic Beef & Veggie Skewers

Servings: 4
Cooking Time: 25 Minutes
Ingredients:
- 2 tbsp balsamic vinegar
- 2 tsp olive oil
- ½ tsp dried oregano
- Salt and pepper to taste
- ¾ lb round steak, cubed
- 1 red bell pepper, sliced
- 1 yellow bell pepper, sliced
- 1 cup cherry tomatoes

Directions:
1. Preheat air fryer to 390°F. Put the balsamic vinegar, olive oil, oregano, salt, and black pepper in a bowl and stir. Toss the steak in and allow to marinate for 10 minutes. Poke 8 metal skewers through the beef, bell peppers, and cherry tomatoes, alternating ingredients as you go. Place the skewers in the air fryer and Air Fry for 5-7 minutes, turning once until the beef is golden and cooked through and the veggies are tender. Serve and enjoy!

Easy Tex-mex Chimichangas

Servings: 2
Cooking Time: 8 Minutes
Ingredients:
- ¼ pound Thinly sliced deli roast beef, chopped
- ½ cup (about 2 ounces) Shredded Cheddar cheese or shredded Tex-Mex cheese blend
- ¼ cup Jarred salsa verde or salsa rojo
- ½ teaspoon Ground cumin
- ½ teaspoon Dried oregano
- 2 Burrito-size (12-inch) flour tortilla(s), not corn tortillas (gluten-free, if a concern)
- ⅔ cup Canned refried beans

- Vegetable oil spray

Directions:
1. Preheat the air fryer to 375°F.
2. Stir the roast beef, cheese, salsa, cumin, and oregano in a bowl until well mixed.
3. Lay a tortilla on a clean, dry work surface. Spread ⅓ cup of the refried beans in the center lower third of the tortilla(s), leaving an inch on either side of the spread beans.
4. For one chimichanga, spread all of the roast beef mixture on top of the beans. For two, spread half of the roast beef mixture on each tortilla.
5. At either "end" of the filling mixture, fold the sides of the tortilla up and over the filling, partially covering it. Starting with the unfolded side of the tortilla just below the filling, roll the tortilla closed. Fold and roll the second filled tortilla, as necessary.
6. Coat the exterior of the tortilla(s) with vegetable oil spray. Set the chimichanga(s) seam side down in the basket, with at least ½ inch air space between them if you're working with two. Air-fry undisturbed for 8 minutes, or until the tortilla is lightly browned and crisp.
7. Use kitchen tongs to gently transfer the chimichanga(s) to a wire rack. Cool for at last 5 minutes or up to 20 minutes before serving.

Delicious Pork Shoulder With Molasses Sauce

Servings: 3
Cooking Time: 25 Minutes
Ingredients:
- 1 tablespoon molasses
- 1 tablespoon soy sauce
- 2-tablespoon Shaoxing wine
- 2 garlic cloves, minced
- 1 teaspoon fresh ginger, minced
- 1 tablespoon cilantro stems and leaves, finely chopped
- 1 lb. boneless pork shoulder
- 1 tablespoon sesame oil

Directions:
1. Thoroughly mix up the molasses, soy sauce, wine, garlic, ginger, and cilantro in a large bowl.
2. Put the pork shoulder in the spice mixture and allow it to refrigerate for 2 hours.
3. Oil the cooking basket with sesame oil, put the pork shoulder in it and reserve the marinade.
4. Cook the pork shoulder at 395 degrees F/ 200 degrees C for 14 to 17 minutes, turning them over and basting with the reserved marinade halfway through.
5. While cooking the pork should, heat a skillet and cook the marinade in it over medium heat, until thickened.
6. When the pork shoulder cooked, let it rest for 5 to 6 minutes before slicing and serving.
7. Brush the pork shoulder with the sauce and enjoy!

Tender Country Ribs

Servings: 4
Cooking Time: 20 To 25 Minutes
Ingredients:
- 12 country-style pork ribs, trimmed of excess fat
- 2 tablespoons cornstarch
- 2 tablespoons olive oil
- 1 teaspoon dry mustard
- ½ teaspoon thyme
- ½ teaspoon garlic powder
- 1 teaspoon dried marjoram
- Pinch salt
- Freshly ground black pepper

Directions:
1. Place the ribs on a clean work surface.
2. In a small bowl, combine the cornstarch, olive oil, mustard, thyme, garlic powder, marjoram, salt, and pepper, and rub into the ribs.
3. Place the ribs in the air fryer basket and roast for 10 minutes.
4. Carefully turn the ribs using tongs and roast for 10 to 15 minutes or until the ribs are crisp and register an internal temperature of at least 150°F.

Spiced Rib Eye Steak

Servings: 3
Cooking Time: 9 Minutes
Ingredients:
- 1 lb. rib eye steak
- ½-teaspoon chipotle powder
- ¼-teaspoon paprika
- ¼-teaspoon onion powder
- ½-teaspoon garlic powder
- ½ teaspoon chili powder
- ¼-teaspoon black pepper
- ⅛ teaspoon coffee powder
- ⅛-teaspoon cocoa powder
- ⅛-teaspoon coriander powder
- 1 ½-teaspoon sea salt

Directions:
1. In addition to the steak, mix the other ingredients well in a small bowl.
2. Rub the steak with the spice mixture and marinate the steak for 20 minutes.
3. Coat the cooking basket of your air fryer with cooking spray.
4. Cook the marinated steak on the basket in your air fryer at 390 degrees F/ 200 degrees C for 9 minutes.
5. Once done, serve and enjoy.

Parmesan Sausage Meatballs

Servings: 8
Cooking Time: 15 Minutes
Ingredients:
- 1 pound Italian sausage
- 1-pound ground beef
- ½ teaspoon Italian seasoning

The Ultimate Tower Air Fryer Cookbook

- ½ teaspoon red pepper flakes
- 1 ½ cups Parmesan cheese, grated
- 2 egg, lightly beaten
- 2 tablespoons parsley, chopped
- 2 garlic cloves, minced
- ¼ cup onion, minced
- Black pepper
- Salt

Directions:
1. Add all the recipe ingredients into the suitable mixing bowl and mix until well combined.
2. Grease its air fryer basket with cooking spray.
3. Make meatballs from bowl mixture and place into the air fryer basket.
4. Cook at almost 350 degrees F/ 175 degrees C for almost 15 minutes.
5. Serve and enjoy.

Better-than-chinese-take-out Sesame Beef

Servings: 4
Cooking Time: 14 Minutes
Ingredients:
- 1¼ pounds Beef flank steak
- 2½ tablespoons Regular or low-sodium soy sauce or gluten-free tamari sauce
- 2 tablespoons Toasted sesame oil
- 2½ teaspoons Cornstarch
- 1 pound 2 ounces (about 4½ cups) Frozen mixed vegetables for stir-fry, thawed, seasoning packet discarded
- 3 tablespoons Unseasoned rice vinegar (see here)
- 3 tablespoons Thai sweet chili sauce
- 2 tablespoons Light brown sugar
- 2 tablespoons White sesame seeds
- 2 teaspoons Water
- Vegetable oil spray
- 1½ tablespoons Minced peeled fresh ginger
- 1 tablespoon Minced garlic

Directions:
1. Set the flank steak on a cutting board and run your clean fingers across it to figure out which way the meat's fibers are running. (Usually, they run the long way from end to end, or perhaps slightly at an angle lengthwise along the cut.) Cut the flank steak into three pieces parallel to the meat's grain. Then cut each of these pieces into ½-inch-wide strips against the grain.
2. Put the meat strips in a large bowl. For a small batch, add 2 teaspoons of the soy or tamari sauce, 2 teaspoons of the sesame oil, and ½ teaspoon of the cornstarch; for a medium batch, add 1 tablespoon of the soy or tamari sauce, 1 tablespoon of the sesame oil, and 1 teaspoon of the cornstarch; and for a large batch, add 1½ tablespoons of the soy or tamari sauce, 1½ tablespoons of the sesame oil, and 1½ teaspoons of the cornstarch. Toss well until the meat is thoroughly coated in the marinade. Set aside at room temperature.
3. Preheat the air fryer to 400°F.
4. When the machine is at temperature, place the beef strips in the basket in as close to one layer as possible. The strips will overlap or even cover each other. Air-fry for 10 minutes, tossing and rearranging the strips three times so that the covered parts get exposed, until browned and even a little crisp. Pour the strips into a clean bowl.
5. Spread the vegetables in the basket and air-fry undisturbed for 4 minutes, just until they are heated through and somewhat softened. Pour these into the bowl with the meat strips. Turn off the air fryer.
6. Whisk the rice vinegar, sweet chili sauce, brown sugar, sesame seeds, the remaining soy sauce, and the remaining sesame oil in a small bowl until well combined. For a small batch, whisk the remaining 1 teaspoon cornstarch with the water in a second small bowl to make a smooth slurry; for medium batch, whisk the remaining 1½ teaspoons cornstarch with the water in a second small bowl to make a smooth slurry; and for a large batch, whisk the remaining 2 teaspoons cornstarch with the water in a second small bowl to make a smooth slurry.
7. Generously coat the inside of a large wok with vegetable oil spray, then set the wok over high heat for a few minutes. Add the ginger and garlic; stir-fry for 10 seconds or so, just until fragrant. Add the meat and vegetables; stir-fry for 1 minute to heat through.
8. Add the rice vinegar mixture and continue stir-frying until the sauce is bubbling, less than 1 minute. Add the cornstarch slurry and stir-fry until the sauce has thickened, just a few seconds. Remove the wok from the heat and serve hot.

Fried Spam

Servings: 2
Cooking Time: 12 Minutes
Ingredients:
- ½ cup All-purpose flour or gluten-free all-purpose flour
- 1 Large egg(s)
- 1 tablespoon Wasabi paste
- 1⅓ cups Plain panko bread crumbs (gluten-free, if a concern)
- 4 ½-inch-thick Spam slices
- Vegetable oil spray

Directions:
1. Preheat the air fryer to 400°F.
2. Set up and fill three shallow soup plates or small pie plates on your counter: one for the flour; one for the egg(s), whisked with the wasabi paste until uniform; and one for the bread crumbs.
3. Dip a slice of Spam in the flour, coating both sides. Slip it into the egg mixture and turn to coat on both sides, even along the edges. Let any excess egg mixture slip back into the rest, then set the slice in the bread crumbs. Turn it several times, pressing gently to make an even coating on both sides. Generously coat both sides of the

slice with vegetable oil spray. Set aside so you can dip, coat, and spray the remaining slice(s).
4. Set the slices in the basket in a single layer so that they don't touch. Air-fry undisturbed for 12 minutes, or until very brown and quite crunchy.
5. Use kitchen tongs to transfer the slices to a wire rack. Cool for a minute or two before serving.

Spicy Hoisin Bbq Pork Chops
Servings: 2
Cooking Time: 12 Minutes
Ingredients:
- 3 tablespoons hoisin sauce
- ¼ cup honey
- 1 tablespoon soy sauce
- 3 tablespoons rice vinegar
- 2 tablespoons brown sugar
- 1½ teaspoons grated fresh ginger
- 1 to 2 teaspoons Sriracha sauce, to taste
- 2 to 3 bone-in center cut pork chops, 1-inch thick (about 1¼ pounds)
- chopped scallions, for garnish

Directions:
1. Combine the hoisin sauce, honey, soy sauce, rice vinegar, brown sugar, ginger, and Sriracha sauce in a small saucepan. Whisk the ingredients together and bring the mixture to a boil over medium-high heat on the stovetop. Reduce the heat and simmer the sauce until it has reduced in volume and thickened slightly – about 10 minutes.
2. Preheat the air fryer to 400°F.
3. Place the pork chops into the air fryer basket and pour half the hoisin BBQ sauce over the top. Air-fry for 6 minutes. Then, flip the chops over, pour the remaining hoisin BBQ sauce on top and air-fry for 6 more minutes, depending on the thickness of the pork chops. The internal temperature of the pork chops should be 155°F when tested with an instant read thermometer.
4. Let the pork chops rest for 5 minutes before serving. You can spoon a little of the sauce from the bottom drawer of the air fryer over the top if desired. Sprinkle with chopped scallions and serve.

Greek-style Pork Stuffed Jalapeño Poppers
Servings:6
Cooking Time: 30 Minutes
Ingredients:
- 6 jalapeños, halved lengthwise
- 3 tbsp diced Kalamata olives
- 3 tbsp olive oil
- ¼ lb ground pork
- 2 tbsp feta cheese
- 1 oz cream cheese, softened
- ½ tsp dried mint
- ½ cup Greek yogurt

Directions:
1. Warm 2 tbsp of olive oil in a skillet over medium heat. Stir in ground pork and cook for 6 minutes until no longer pink. Preheat air fryer to 350°F. Mix the cooked pork, olives, feta cheese, and cream cheese in a bowl. Divide the pork mixture between the peppers. Place them in the frying basket and Air Fry for 6 minutes. Mix the Greek yogurt with the remaining olive oil and mint in a small bowl. Serve with the poppers.

Marinated Beef And Vegetable Stir Fry
Servings: 4
Cooking Time: 35 Minutes
Ingredients:
- 2 lbs. top round, cut into bite-sized strips
- 2 garlic cloves, sliced
- 1 teaspoon dried marjoram
- ¼ cup red wine
- 1 tablespoon tamari sauce
- Salt and black pepper, to taste
- ½ tablespoon olive oil
- 1 red onion, sliced
- 2 bell peppers, sliced
- 1 carrot, sliced

Directions:
1. In a suitable bowl, add the top round, marjoram, red wine, garlic, tamari sauce, salt, and pepper in a bowl; cover and marinate for 1 hour.
2. Oil the cooking tray of your air fryer.
3. Take the marinated beef out of the marinade and arrange to the tray.
4. Cook at 390 degrees F/200 degrees C for 15 minutes.
5. After that, add the garlic, onion, peppers and carrot, cook for 15 minutes more or until tender.
6. Open the Air Fryer every 5 minutes and baste the meat with the remaining marinade.
7. When done, serve and enjoy.

Horseradish Mustard Pork Chops
Servings:2
Cooking Time: 20 Minutes
Ingredients:
- ½ cup grated Pecorino cheese
- 1 egg white
- 1 tbsp horseradish mustard
- ¼ tsp black pepper
- 2 pork chops
- ¼ cup chopped cilantro

Directions:
1. Preheat air fryer to 350°F. Whisk egg white and horseradish mustard in a bowl. In another bowl, combine Pecorino cheese and black pepper. Dip pork chops in the mustard mixture, then dredge them in the Parmesan mixture. Place pork chops in the frying basket lightly greased with olive oil and Air Fry for 12-14 minutes until cooked through and tender, flipping twice. Transfer the chops to a cutting board and let sit for 5 minutes. Scatter with cilantro to serve.

The Ultimate Tower Air Fryer Cookbook

Pepperoni Pockets

Servings: 4
Cooking Time: 8 Minutes
Ingredients:
- 4 bread slices, 1-inch thick
- olive oil for misting
- 24 slices pepperoni
- 1 ounce roasted red peppers, drained and patted dry
- 1 ounce Pepper Jack cheese cut into 4 slices
- pizza sauce (optional)

Directions:
1. Spray both sides of bread slices with olive oil.
2. Stand slices upright and cut a deep slit in the top to create a pocket—almost to the bottom crust but not all the way through.
3. Stuff each bread pocket with 6 slices of pepperoni, a large strip of roasted red pepper, and a slice of cheese.
4. Place bread pockets in air fryer basket, standing up. Cook at 360°F for 8 minutes, until filling is heated through and bread is lightly browned. Serve while hot as is or with pizza sauce for dipping.

Lollipop Lamb Chops

Servings: 4
Cooking Time: 7 Minutes
Ingredients:
- ½ small clove garlic
- ¼ cup packed fresh parsley
- ¾ cup packed fresh mint
- ½ teaspoon lemon juice
- ¼ cup grated Parmesan cheese
- ⅓ cup shelled pistachios
- ¼ teaspoon salt
- ½ cup olive oil
- 8 lamb chops (1 rack)
- 2 tablespoons vegetable oil
- Salt and freshly ground black pepper, to taste
- 1 tablespoon dried rosemary, chopped
- 1 tablespoon dried thyme

Directions:
1. Make the pesto by combining the garlic, parsley and mint in a food processor and process until finely chopped. Add the lemon juice, Parmesan cheese, pistachios and salt. Process until all the ingredients have turned into a paste. With the processor running, slowly pour the olive oil in. Scrape the sides of the processor with a spatula and process for another 30 seconds.
2. Preheat the air fryer to 400ºF (204ºC).
3. Rub both sides of the lamb chops with vegetable oil and season with salt, pepper, rosemary and thyme, pressing the herbs into the meat gently with the fingers. Transfer the lamb chops to the air fryer basket.
4. Air fry the lamb chops for 5 minutes. Flip the chops over and air fry for an additional 2 minutes.
5. Serve the lamb chops with mint pesto drizzled on top.

Meat Loaves

Servings: 4
Cooking Time: 19 Minutes
Ingredients:
- Sauce
- ¼ cup white vinegar
- ¼ cup brown sugar
- 2 tablespoons Worcestershire sauce
- ½ cup ketchup
- Meat Loaves
- 1 pound very lean ground beef
- ⅔ cup dry bread (approx. 1 slice torn into small pieces)
- 1 egg
- ⅓ cup minced onion
- 1 teaspoon salt
- 2 tablespoons ketchup

Directions:
1. In a small saucepan, combine all sauce ingredients and bring to a boil. Remove from heat and stir to ensure that brown sugar dissolves completely.
2. In a large bowl, combine the beef, bread, egg, onion, salt, and ketchup. Mix well.
3. Divide meat mixture into 4 portions and shape each into a thick, round patty. Patties will be about 3 to 3½ inches in diameter, and all four should fit easily into the air fryer basket at once.
4. Cook at 360°F for 18 minutes, until meat is well done. Baste tops of mini loaves with a small amount of sauce, and cook 1 minute.
5. Serve hot with additional sauce on the side.

Marinated Flank Steak

Servings: 4
Cooking Time: 12 Minutes
Ingredients:
- 1 ½ pounds flank steak
- ½ cup red wine
- ½ cup apple cider vinegar
- 2 tablespoons soy sauce
- Salt, to taste
- ½ teaspoon black pepper
- ½ teaspoon red pepper flakes, crushed
- ½ teaspoon dried basil
- 1 teaspoon thyme

Directions:
1. Add all the recipe ingredients to a large ceramic bowl.
2. Cover and let it marinate for 3 hours in your refrigerator.
3. Transfer the flank steak to the Air Fryer basket that is previously greased with nonstick cooking oil.
4. Cook in the preheated Air Fryer at about 400 degrees F/ 205 degrees C for 12 minutes, flipping once halfway through cooking.
5. Serve and enjoy.

Roast Beef

Servings: 6
Cooking Time: 60 Minutes
Ingredients:
- 1 top round beef roast
- 1 teaspoon salt
- ½ teaspoon ground black pepper
- 1 teaspoon dried rosemary
- ½ teaspoon garlic powder
- 1 tablespoon coconut oil, melted

Directions:
1. Sprinkle all sides of roast with salt, pepper, rosemary, and garlic powder. Drizzle with coconut oil. Place roast into ungreased air fryer basket, fatty side down. Adjust the temperature to 375°F and set the timer for 60 minutes, turning the roast halfway through cooking. Roast will be done when no pink remains and internal temperature is at least 180°F. Serve warm.

Marinated Pork Tenderloin

Servings: 6
Cooking Time: 30 Minutes
Ingredients:
- ¼ cup olive oil
- ¼ cup soy sauce
- ¼ cup freshly squeezed lemon juice
- 1 garlic clove, minced
- 1 tablespoon Dijon mustard
- 1 teaspoon salt
- ½ teaspoon freshly ground black pepper
- 2 pounds (907 g) pork tenderloin

Directions:
1. In a large mixing bowl, make the marinade: Mix the olive oil, soy sauce, lemon juice, minced garlic, Dijon mustard, salt, and pepper. Reserve ¼ cup of the marinade.
2. Put the tenderloin in a large bowl and pour the remaining marinade over the meat. Cover and marinate in the refrigerator for about 1 hour.
3. Preheat the air fryer to 400ºF (204ºC).
4. Put the marinated pork tenderloin into the air fryer basket. Roast for 10 minutes. Flip the pork and baste it with half of the reserved marinade. Roast for 10 minutes more.
5. Flip the pork, then baste with the remaining marinade. Roast for another 10 minutes, for a total cooking time of 30 minutes.
6. Serve immediately.

Avocado Buttered Flank Steak

Servings: 1
Cooking Time: 12 Minutes
Ingredients:
- 1 flank steak
- Salt and ground black pepper, to taste
- 2 avocados
- 2 tablespoons butter, melted
- ½ cup chimichurri sauce

Directions:
1. Rub the flank steak with salt and pepper to taste and leave to sit for 20 minutes.
2. Preheat the air fryer to 400ºF (204ºC) and place a rack inside.
3. Halve the avocados and take out the pits. Spoon the flesh into a bowl and mash with a fork. Mix in the melted butter and chimichurri sauce, making sure everything is well combined.
4. Put the steak in the air fryer and air fry for 6 minutes. Flip over and allow to air fry for another 6 minutes.
5. Serve the steak with the avocado butter.

Mini Meatloaves With Pancetta

Servings: 4
Cooking Time: 40 Minutes
Ingredients:
- ¼ cup grated Parmesan
- 1/3 cup quick-cooking oats
- 2 tbsp milk
- 3 tbsp ketchup
- 3 tbsp Dijon mustard
- 1 egg
- 1 tsp dried oregano
- Salt and pepper to taste
- 1 lb lean ground beef
- 4 pancetta slices, uncooked

Directions:
1. Preheat the air fryer to 375°F. Combine the oats, milk, 1 tbsp of ketchup, 1 tbsp of mustard, the egg, oregano, Parmesan cheese, salt, and pepper, and mix. Add the beef and mix with your hands, then form 4 mini loaves. Wrap each mini loaf with pancetta, covering the meat.
2. Combine the remaining ketchup and mustard and set aside. Line the frying basket with foil and poke holes in it, then set the loaves in the basket. Brush with the ketchup/mustard mix. Bake for 17-22 minutes or until cooked and golden. Serve and enjoy!

Sage Pork With Potatoes

Servings: 4
Cooking Time: 30 Minutes
Ingredients:
- 2 cups potatoes
- 2 tsp olive oil
- 1 lb pork tenderloin, cubed
- 1 onion, chopped
- 1 red bell pepper, chopped
- 2 garlic cloves, minced
- ½ tsp dried sage
- ½ tsp fennel seeds, crushed
- 2 tbsp chicken broth

Directions:
1. Preheat air fryer to 370°F. Add the potatoes and olive oil to a bowl and toss to coat. Transfer them to the frying basket and Air Fry for 15 minutes. Remove the bowl. Add the pork, onion, red bell pepper, garlic, sage, and fennel seeds, to the potatoes, add chicken broth and stir gently. Return the bowl to the frying basket and cook for 10 minutes. Be sure to shake the basket at least once. The pork should be cooked through and the potatoes soft and crispy. Serve immediately.

Balsamic London Broil

Servings: 4
Cooking Time: 25 Minutes
Ingredients:
- 2 ½ lb top round London broil steak
- ¼ cup coconut aminos
- 1 tbsp balsamic vinegar
- 1 tbsp olive oil
- 1 tbsp mustard
- 2 tsp maple syrup
- 2 garlic cloves, minced
- 1 tsp dried oregano
- Salt and pepper to taste
- ¼ tsp smoked paprika
- 2 tbsp red onions, chopped

Directions:
1. Whisk coconut aminos, mustard, vinegar, olive oil, maple oregano, syrup, oregano garlic, red onions, salt, pepper, and paprika in a small bowl. Put the steak in a shallow container and pour the marinade over the steak. Cover and let sit for 20 minutes.
2. Preheat air fryer to 400°F. Transfer the steak to the frying basket and bake for 5 minutes. Flip the steak and bake for another 4 to 6 minutes. Allow sitting for 5 minutes before slicing. Serve warm and enjoy.

Hungarian Pork Burgers

Servings: 4
Cooking Time: 30 Minutes
Ingredients:
- 8 sandwich buns, halved
- ½ cup mayonnaise
- 2 tbsp mustard
- 1 tbsp lemon juice
- ¼ cup sliced red cabbage
- ¼ cup grated carrots
- 1 lb ground pork
- ½ tsp Hungarian paprika
- 1 cup lettuce, torn
- 2 tomatoes, sliced

Directions:
1. Mix the mayonnaise, 1 tbsp of mustard, lemon juice, cabbage, and carrots in a bowl. Refrigerate for 10 minutes.
2. Preheat air fryer to 400°F. Toss the pork, remaining mustard, and paprika in a bowl, mix, then make 8 patties. Place them in the air fryer and Air Fry for 7-9 minutes, flipping once until cooked through. Put some lettuce on one bottom bun, then top with a tomato slice, one burger, and some cabbage mix. Put another bun on top and serve. Repeat for all burgers. Serve and enjoy!

Beef Brazilian Empanadas

Servings: 6
Cooking Time: 40 Minutes
Ingredients:
- 1 cup shredded Pepper Jack cheese
- 1/3 minced green bell pepper
- 1 cup shredded mozzarella
- 2 garlic cloves, chopped
- 1/3 onion, chopped
- 8 oz ground beef
- 1 tsp allspice
- ½ tsp paprika
- ½ teaspoon chili powder
- Salt and pepper to taste
- 15 empanada wrappers
- 1 tbsp butter

Directions:
1. Spray a skillet with cooking oil. Over medium heat, stir-fry garlic, green pepper, and onion for 2 minutes or until aromatic. Add beef, allspice, chili, paprika, salt and pepper. Use a spoon to break up the beef. Cook until brown. Drain the excess fat. On a clean work surface, glaze each empanada wrapper edge with water using a basting brush to soften the crust. Mound 2-3 tbsp of meat onto each wrapper. Top with mozzarella and pepper Jack cheese. Fold one side of the wrapper to the opposite side. Press the edges with the back of a fork to seal.
2. Preheat air fryer to 400°F. Place the empanadas in the air fryer and spray with cooking oil. Bake for 8 minutes, then flip the empanadas. Cook for another 4 minutes. Melt butter in a microwave-safe bowl for 20 seconds. Brush melted butter over the top of each empanada. Serve warm.

Polish Beef Sausage With Worcestershire Sauce

Servings: 4
Cooking Time: 11 Minutes
Ingredients:
- 1 pound smoked Polish beef sausage, sliced
- 1 tablespoon mustard
- 1 tablespoon olive oil
- 2 tablespoons Worcestershire sauce
- 2 bell peppers, sliced
- 2 cups sourdough bread, cubed
- Salt and black pepper, to taste

Directions:
1. Toss the sausage with the mustard, olive, and Worcestershire sauce.
2. Thread sausage, black peppers, and bread onto skewers.
3. Sprinkle with black pepper and salt.
4. Cook in the preheated Air Fryer at about 360 degrees F/ 180 degrees C for 11 minutes.
5. Brush the skewers with the reserved marinade.
6. Serve

Best Damn Pork Chops

Servings: 2 Servings
Cooking Time: 20 Minutes
Ingredients:
- 2 bone-in 2-inch-thick pork chops
- 2 tablespoons of brown sugar
- 1 teaspoon of ground mustard

- ¼ teaspoon of garlic powder
- ½ teaspoon of onion powder
- 1 tablespoon of paprika
- 1 ½ teaspoons of black pepper
- 1 ½ teaspoons of salt
- 1–2 tablespoons olive oil

Directions:
1. Preheat your air fryer to 400ºF.
2. Rinse the pork chops and dry with a paper towel.
3. Add sugar, mustard, garlic and onion powder, paprika, salt, and black pepper in a bowl. Mix it well.
4. Grease the pork chops with olive oil and coat them with seasonings. Use almost all the rub mix.
5. Put the prepared pork chops in the preheated air fryer basket and cook at 400ºF for 12 minutes, flip them, and cook for extra 6 minutes.
6. Serve warm and enjoy your Best Damn Pork Chops!

Paprika Pork Chops

Servings: 6
Cooking Time: 12 Minutes
Ingredients:
- 1 ½ pounds pork chops, boneless
- 1 teaspoon paprika
- 1 teaspoon creole seasoning
- 1 teaspoon garlic powder
- ¼ cup parmesan cheese, grated
- ⅓ cup almond flour

Directions:
1. At 360 degrees F/ 180 degrees C, preheat your Air fryer.
2. Add all the recipe ingredients except pork chops in a zip-lock bag.
3. Add pork chops in the bag. Seal this bag and shake well to coat pork chops.
4. Remove pork chops from zip-lock bag and place in the air fryer basket.
5. Cook pork chops for almost 10-12 minutes.
6. Serve and enjoy.

Maple'n Soy Marinated Beef

Servings: 4
Cooking Time: 45 Minutes
Ingredients:
- 2 pounds sirloin flap steaks, pounded
- 3 tablespoons balsamic vinegar
- 3 tablespoons maple syrup
- 3 tablespoons soy sauce
- 4 cloves of garlic, minced

Directions:
1. Preheat the air fryer to 390ºF.
2. Place the grill pan accessory in the air fryer.
3. On a deep dish, place the flap steaks and season with soy sauce, balsamic vinegar, and maple syrup, and garlic.
4. Place on the grill pan and cook for 15 minutes in batches.

French-style Steak Salad

Servings: 4
Cooking Time: 25 Minutes
Ingredients:
- 1 cup sliced strawberries
- 4 tbsp crumbled blue cheese
- ¼ cup olive oil
- Salt and pepper to taste
- 1 flank steak
- ¼ cup balsamic vinaigrette
- 1 tbsp Dijon mustard
- 2 tbsp lemon juice
- 8 cups baby arugula
- ½ red onion, sliced
- 4 tbsp pecan pieces
- 4 tbsp sunflower seeds
- 1 sliced kiwi
- 1 sliced orange

Directions:
1. In a bowl, whisk olive oil, salt, lemon juice and pepper. Toss in flank steak and let marinate covered in the fridge for 30 minutes up to overnight. Preheat air fryer at 325ºF. Place flank steak in the greased frying basket and Bake for 18-20 minutes until rare, flipping once. Let rest for 5 minutes before slicing thinly against the grain.
2. In a salad bowl, whisk balsamic vinaigrette and mustard. Stir in arugula, salt, and pepper. Divide between 4 serving bowls. Top each salad with blue cheese, onion, pecan, sunflower seeds, strawberries, kiwi, orange and sliced steak. Serve immediately.

Homemade Steak

Servings: 6
Cooking Time: 20 Minutes
Ingredients:
- 3 pounds steak
- 1 cup chimichurri
- Salt and pepper

Directions:
1. To better marinate, mix up the beef steak with the remaining ingredients in a sealed zip-lock bag and refrigerate for at least 60 minutes.
2. When marinated, cook the steak in your air fryer at 390 degrees F/ 200 degrees C for 20 minutes in batches, flipping halfway through.
3. When done, serve and enjoy.

Pork Chops

Servings: 2
Cooking Time: 16 Minutes
Ingredients:
- 2 bone-in, centercut pork chops, 1-inch thick
- 2 teaspoons Worcestershire sauce
- salt and pepper
- cooking spray

Directions:

The Ultimate Tower Air Fryer Cookbook

1. Rub the Worcestershire sauce into both sides of pork chops.
2. Season with salt and pepper to taste.
3. Spray air fryer basket with cooking spray and place the chops in basket side by side.
4. Cook at 360°F for 16 minutes or until well done. Let rest for 5minutes before serving.

Garlic Lamb Rack

Servings: 6
Cooking Time: 30 Minutes
Ingredients:
- 1 egg, lightly beaten
- ½ tablespoon fresh thyme, chopped
- 1 ¾ lbs. rack of lamb
- ½ tablespoon fresh rosemary, chopped
- 1 tablespoon olive oil
- 2 garlic cloves, chopped
- Pepper
- Salt

Directions:
1. Mix up the oil and garlic, then brush the lamb rack with the mixture.
2. Season the lamb rack with pepper and salt.
3. After mix the thyme and rosemary well, coat the lamb rack with the egg and the herb mixture.
4. Place lamb rack in the air fryer basket and cook for at 390 degrees F/ 200 degrees C for 30 minutes.
5. After 25 minutes of cooking time, turn the lamb rack and cook for 5 minutes more.
6. Serve and enjoy.

Classic Salisbury Steak Burgers

Servings: 4
Cooking Time: 35 Minutes
Ingredients:
- ¼ cup bread crumbs
- 2 tbsp beef broth
- 1 tbsp cooking sherry
- 1 tbsp ketchup
- 1tbsp Dijon mustard
- 2 tsp Worcestershire sauce
- ½ tsp onion powder
- ½ tsp garlic powder
- 1 lb ground beef
- 1 cup sliced mushrooms
- 1 tbsp butter
- 4 buns, split and toasted

Directions:
1. Preheat the air fryer to 375°F. Combine the bread crumbs, broth, cooking sherry, ketchup, mustard, Worcestershire sauce, garlic and onion powder and mix well. Add the beef and mix with hands, then form into 4 patties and refrigerate while preparing the mushrooms. Mix the mushrooms and butter in a 6-inch pan. Place the pan in the air fryer and Bake for 8-10 minutes, stirring once until the mushrooms are brown and tender. Remove and set aside. Line the frying basket with round parchment paper and punch holes in it. Lay the burgers in a single layer and cook for 11-14 minutes or until cooked through. Put the burgers on the bun bottoms, top with the mushrooms, then the bun tops.

Tonkatsu

Servings: 3
Cooking Time: 10 Minutes
Ingredients:
- ½ cup All-purpose flour or tapioca flour
- 1 Large egg white(s), well beaten
- ¾ cup Plain panko bread crumbs (gluten-free, if a concern)
- 3 4-ounce center-cut boneless pork loin chops (about ½ inch thick)
- Vegetable oil spray

Directions:
1. Preheat the air fryer to 375°F .
2. Set up and fill three shallow soup plates or small pie plates on your counter: one for the flour, one for the beaten egg white(s), and one for the bread crumbs.
3. Set a chop in the flour and roll it to coat all sides, even the ends. Gently shake off any excess flour and set it in the egg white(s). Gently roll and turn it to coat all sides. Let any excess egg white slip back into the rest, then set the chop in the bread crumbs. Turn it several times, pressing gently to get an even coating on all sides and the ends. Generously coat the breaded chop with vegetable oil spray, then set it aside so you can dredge, coat, and spray the remaining chop(s).
4. Set the chops in the basket with as much air space between them as possible. Air-fry undisturbed for 10 minutes, or until golden brown and crisp.
5. Use kitchen tongs to transfer the chops to a wire rack and cool for a couple of minutes before serving.

Stuffed Cabbage Rolls

Servings: 4
Cooking Time: 50 Minutes
Ingredients:
- ½ cup long-grain brown rice
- 12 green cabbage leaves
- 1 lb ground beef
- 4 garlic cloves, minced
- Salt and pepper to taste
- 1 tsp ground cinnamon
- ½ tsp ground cumin
- 2 tbsp chopped mint
- 1 lemon, juiced and zested
- ½ cup beef broth
- 1 tbsp olive oil
- 2 tbsp parsley, chopped

Directions:
1. Place a large pot of salted water over medium heat and bring to a boil. Add the cabbage leaves and boil them for 3 minutes. Remove from the water and set aside. Combine the ground beef, rice, garlic, salt, pepper, cinnamon, cumin, mint, lemon juice and zest in a bowl.

2. Preheat air fryer to 360°F. Divide the beef mixture between the cabbage leaves and roll them up. Place the finished rolls into a greased baking dish. Pour the beef broth over the cabbage rolls and then brush the tops with olive oil. Put the casserole dish into the frying basket and Bake for 30 minutes. Top with parsley and enjoy!

Pepperoni And Bell Pepper Pockets

Servings:4
Cooking Time: 8 Minutes
Ingredients:
- 4 bread slices, 1-inch thick
- Olive oil, for misting
- 24 slices pepperoni
- 1 ounce (28 g) roasted red peppers, drained and patted dry
- 1 ounce (28 g) Pepper Jack cheese, cut into 4 slices

Directions:
1. Preheat the air fryer to 360°F (182°C).
2. Spray both sides of bread slices with olive oil.
3. Stand slices upright and cut a deep slit in the top to create a pocket (almost to the bottom crust, but not all the way through).
4. Stuff each bread pocket with 6 slices of pepperoni, a large strip of roasted red pepper, and a slice of cheese.
5. Put bread pockets in air fryer basket, standing up. Air fry for 8 minutes, until filling is heated through and bread is lightly browned.
6. Serve hot.

Cheese Ground Pork

Servings: 4
Cooking Time: 40 Minutes
Ingredients:
- 1 tablespoon olive oil
- 1 ½ pounds pork, ground
- Salt and black pepper, to taste
- 1 medium-sized leek, sliced
- 1 teaspoon fresh garlic, minced
- 2 carrots, trimmed and sliced
- 1 (2-ounce) jar pimiento, drained and chopped
- 1 can (10 ¾-ounces) condensed cream of mushroom soup
- 1 cup water
- ½ cup ale
- 1 cup cream cheese
- ½ cup soft fresh breadcrumbs
- 1 tablespoon fresh cilantro, chopped

Directions:
1. At 320 degrees F/ 160 degrees C, preheat your Air Fryer.
2. Spread the olive oil in a suitable baking dish and heat for 1 to 2 minutes.
3. Add the pork, salt, black pepper and cook for 6 minutes, crumbling with a fork.
4. Then stir in the leeks and cook for 4 to 5 minutes, with occasional stirring.
5. Add the garlic, carrots, pimiento, mushroom soup, water, ale, and cream cheese.
6. Gently stir to combine.
7. Turn the temperature to 370 degrees F/ 185 degrees C.
8. Top with the breadcrumbs.
9. Place the stuffed baking dish in the cooking basket and cook approximately 30 minutes or until everything is thoroughly cooked.
10. Serve garnished with fresh cilantro.

Carne Asada Tacos

Servings:4
Cooking Time: 14 Minutes
Ingredients:
- ⅓ cup olive oil
- 1½ pounds (680 g) flank steak
- Salt and freshly ground black pepper, to taste
- ⅓ cup freshly squeezed lime juice
- ½ cup chopped fresh cilantro
- 4 teaspoons minced garlic
- 1 teaspoon ground cumin
- 1 teaspoon chili powder

Directions:
1. Brush the air fryer basket with olive oil.
2. Put the flank steak in a large mixing bowl. Season with salt and pepper.
3. Add the lime juice, cilantro, garlic, cumin, and chili powder and toss to coat the steak.
4. For the best flavor, let the steak marinate in the refrigerator for about 1 hour.
5. Preheat the air fryer to 400°F (204°C)
6. Put the steak in the air fryer basket. Air fry for 7 minutes. Flip the steak. Air fry for 7 minutes more or until an internal temperature reaches at least 145°F (63°C).
7. Let the steak rest for about 5 minutes, then cut into strips to serve.

Chapter 8: Vegetarians Recipes

Pizza Eggplant Rounds

Servings: 4
Cooking Time: 25 Minutes
Ingredients:
- 3 tsp olive oil
- ¼ cup diced onion
- ½ tsp garlic powder
- ½ tsp dried oregano
- ½ cup diced mushrooms
- ½ cup marinara sauce
- 1 eggplant, sliced
- 1 tsp salt
- 1 cup shredded mozzarella
- 2 tbsp Parmesan cheese
- ¼ cup chopped basil

Directions:
1. Warm 2 tsp of olive oil in a skillet over medium heat. Add in onion and mushrooms and cook for 5 minutes until the onions are translucent. Stir in marinara sauce, then add oregano and garlic powder. Turn the heat off.
2. Preheat air fryer at 375ºF. Rub the remaining olive oil over both sides of the eggplant circles. Lay circles on a large plate and sprinkle with salt and black pepper. Top each circle with the marinara sauce mixture and shredded mozzarella and Parmesan cheese. Place eggplant circles in the frying basket and Bake for 5 minutes. Scatter with the basil and serve.

Caramelized Brussels Sprout

Servings: 4
Cooking Time: 35 Minutes
Ingredients:
- 1 pound Brussels sprouts, trimmed and halved
- 4 teaspoons butter, melted
- Salt and black pepper, to taste

Directions:
1. Preheat the Air fryer to 400°F and grease an Air fryer basket.
2. Mix all the ingredients in a bowl and toss to coat well.
3. Arrange the Brussels sprouts in the Air fryer basket and cook for about 35 minutes.
4. Dish out and serve warm.

Chili Tofu & Quinoa Bowls

Servings: 2
Cooking Time: 30 Minutes
Ingredients:
- 1 cup diced peeled sweet potatoes
- ¼ cup chopped mixed bell peppers
- 1/8 cup sprouted green lentils
- ½ onion, sliced
- 1 tsp avocado oil
- 1/8 cup chopped carrots
- 8 oz extra-firm tofu, cubed
- ½ tsp smoked paprika
- ½ tsp chili powder
- ¼ tsp salt
- 2 tsp lime zest
- 1 cup cooked quinoa
- 2 lime wedges

Directions:
1. Preheat air fryer at 350ºF. Combine the onion, carrots, bell peppers, green lentils, sweet potato, and avocado oil in a bowl. In another bowl, mix the tofu, paprika, chili powder, and salt. Add veggie mixture to the frying basket and Air Fry for 8 minutes. Stir in tofu mixture and cook for 8 more minutes. Combine lime zest and quinoa. Divide into 2 serving bowls. Top each with the tofu mixture and squeeze a lime wedge over. Serve warm.

Tropical Salsa

Servings: 4
Cooking Time: 15 Minutes
Ingredients:
- 1 cup pineapple cubes
- ½ apple, cubed
- Salt to taste
- ¼ tsp olive oil
- 2 tomatoes, diced
- 1 avocado, diced
- 3-4 strawberries, diced
- ¼ cup diced red onion
- 1 tbsp chopped cilantro
- 1 tbsp chopped parsley
- 2 cloves garlic, minced
- ½ tsp granulated sugar
- ½ lime, juiced

Directions:
1. Preheat air fryer at 400ºF. Combine pineapple cubes, apples, olive oil, and salt in a bowl. Place pineapple in the greased frying basket, and Air Fry for 8 minutes, shaking once. Transfer it to a bowl. Toss in tomatoes, avocado, strawberries, onion, cilantro, parsley, garlic, sugar, lime juice, and salt. Let chill in the fridge before using.

Pizza Margherita With Spinach

Servings: 4
Cooking Time: 50 Minutes
Ingredients:
- ½ cup pizza sauce
- 1 tsp dried oregano
- 1 tsp garlic powder
- 1 pizza dough
- 1 cup baby spinach
- ½ cup mozzarella cheese

Directions:
1. Preheat air fryer to 400°F. Whisk pizza sauce, oregano, and garlic in a bowl. Set aside. Form 4 balls with the pizza dough and roll out each into a 6-inch round pizza.
2. Lay one crust in the basket, spread ¼ of the sauce, then scatter with ¼ of spinach, and finally top with mozzarella cheese. Grill for 8 minutes until golden brown and the crust is crispy. Repeat the process with the remaining crusts. Serve immediately.

Easy Zucchini Lasagna Roll-ups
Servings: 2
Cooking Time: 40 Minutes
Ingredients:
- 2 medium zucchini
- 2 tbsp lemon juice
- 1 ½ cups ricotta cheese
- 1 tbsp allspice
- 2 cups marinara sauce
- 1/3 cup mozzarella cheese

Directions:
1. Preheat air fryer to 400°F. Cut the ends of each zucchini, then slice into 1/4-inch thick pieces and drizzle with lemon juice. Roast for 5 minutes until slightly tender. Let cool slightly. Combine ricotta cheese and allspice in a bowl; set aside. Spread 2 tbsp of marinara sauce on the bottom of a baking pan. Spoon 1-2 tbsp of the ricotta mixture onto each slice, roll up each slice and place them spiral-side up in the pan. Scatter with the remaining ricotta mixture and drizzle with marinara sauce. Top with mozzarella cheese and Bake at 360°F for 20 minutes until the cheese is bubbly and golden brown. Serve warm.

Cauliflower Steaks Gratin
Servings: 2
Cooking Time: 13 Minutes
Ingredients:
- 1 head cauliflower
- 1 tablespoon olive oil
- salt and freshly ground black pepper
- ½ teaspoon chopped fresh thyme leaves
- 3 tablespoons grated Parmigiano-Reggiano cheese
- 2 tablespoons panko breadcrumbs

Directions:
1. Preheat the air-fryer to 370°F.
2. Cut two steaks out of the center of the cauliflower. To do this, cut the cauliflower in half and then cut one slice about 1-inch thick off each half. The rest of the cauliflower will fall apart into florets, which you can roast on their own or save for another meal.
3. Brush both sides of the cauliflower steaks with olive oil and season with salt, freshly ground black pepper and fresh thyme. Place the cauliflower steaks into the air fryer basket and air-fry for 6 minutes. Turn the steaks over and air-fry for another 4 minutes. Combine the Parmesan cheese and panko breadcrumbs and sprinkle the mixture over the tops of both steaks and air-fry for another 3 minutes until the cheese has melted and the breadcrumbs have browned. Serve this with some sautéed bitter greens and air-fried blistered tomatoes.

General Tso's Cauliflower
Servings: 4
Cooking Time: 15 Minutes
Ingredients:
- 1 head cauliflower cut into florets
- ¾ cup all-purpose flour, divided*
- 3 eggs, lightly beaten
- 1 cup panko breadcrumbs*
- canola or peanut oil, in a spray bottle
- 2 tablespoons oyster sauce
- ¼ cup soy sauce
- 2 teaspoons chili paste
- 2 tablespoons rice wine vinegar
- 2 tablespoons sugar
- ¼ cup water
- white or brown rice for serving
- steamed broccoli

Directions:
1. Set up dredging station using three bowls. Place the cauliflower in a large bowl and sprinkle ¼ cup of the flour over the top. Place the eggs in a second bowl and combine the panko breadcrumbs and remaining ½ cup flour in a third bowl. Toss the cauliflower in the flour to coat all the florets thoroughly. Dip the cauliflower florets in the eggs and finally toss them in the breadcrumbs to coat on all sides. Place the coated cauliflower florets on a baking sheet and spray generously with canola or peanut oil.
2. Preheat the air fryer to 400°F.
3. Air-fry the cauliflower at 400°F for 15 minutes, flipping the florets over for the last 3 minutes of the cooking process and spraying again with oil.
4. While the cauliflower is air-frying, make the General Tso Sauce. Combine the oyster sauce, soy sauce, chili paste, rice wine vinegar, sugar and water in a saucepan and bring the mixture to a boil on the stove top. Lower the heat and let it simmer for 10 minutes, stirring occasionally.
5. When the timer is up on the air fryer, transfer the cauliflower to a large bowl, pour the sauce over it all and toss to coat. Serve with white or brown rice and some steamed broccoli.

Vegan Buddha Bowls(2)
Servings:4
Cooking Time: 20 Minutes
Ingredients:
- 1 carrot, peeled and julienned
- ½ onion, sliced into half-moons
- ¼ cup apple cider vinegar
- ½ tsp ground ginger
- ⅛ tsp cayenne pepper
- 1 parsnip, diced
- 1 tsp avocado oil
- 4 oz extra-firm tofu, cubed
- ½ tsp five-spice powder
- ½ tsp chili powder
- 2 tsp fresh lime zest
- 1 cup fresh arugula
- ½ cup cooked quinoa
- 2 tbsp canned kidney beans
- 2 tbsp canned sweetcorn
- 1 avocado, diced
- 2 tbsp pine nuts

Directions:
1. Preheat air fryer to 350°F. Combine carrot, vinegar, ginger, and cayenne in a bowl. In another bowl, combine

onion, parsnip, and avocado oil. In a third bowl, mix the tofu, five-spice powder, and chili powder.
2. Place the onion mixture in the greased basket. Air Fry for 6 minutes. Stir in tofu mixture and cook for 8 more minutes. Mix in lime zest. Divide arugula, cooked quinoa, kidney beans, sweetcorn, drained carrots, avocado, pine nuts, and tofu mixture between 2 bowls. Serve.

Cauliflower Rice-stuffed Peppers

Servings: 4
Cooking Time: 15 Minutes
Ingredients:
- 2 cups uncooked cauliflower rice
- ¾ cup drained canned petite diced tomatoes
- 2 tablespoons olive oil
- 1 cup shredded mozzarella cheese
- ¼ teaspoon salt
- ¼ teaspoon ground black pepper
- 4 medium green bell peppers, tops removed, seeded

Directions:
1. In a large bowl, mix all ingredients except bell peppers. Scoop mixture evenly into peppers.
2. Place peppers into ungreased air fryer basket. Adjust the temperature to 350°F and set the timer for 15 minutes. Peppers will be tender and cheese will be melted when done. Serve warm.

Cheese Ravioli

Servings: 4
Cooking Time: 9 Minutes
Ingredients:
- 1 egg
- ¼ cup milk
- 1 cup breadcrumbs
- 2 teaspoons Italian seasoning
- ⅛ teaspoon ground rosemary
- ¼ teaspoon basil
- ¼ teaspoon parsley
- 9-ounce package uncooked cheese ravioli
- ¼ cup flour
- oil for misting or cooking spray

Directions:
1. Preheat air fryer to 390°F.
2. In a medium bowl, beat together egg and milk.
3. In a large plastic bag, mix together the breadcrumbs, Italian seasoning, rosemary, basil, and parsley.
4. Place all the ravioli and the flour in a bag or a bowl with a lid and shake to coat.
5. Working with a handful at a time, drop floured ravioli into egg wash. Remove ravioli, letting excess drip off, and place in bag with breadcrumbs.
6. When all ravioli are in the breadcrumbs' bag, shake well to coat all pieces.
7. Dump enough ravioli into air fryer basket to form one layer. Mist with oil or cooking spray. Dump the remaining ravioli on top of the first layer and mist with oil.
8. Cook for 5 minutes. Shake well and spray with oil. Break apart any ravioli stuck together and spray any spots you missed the first time.
9. Cook 4 minutes longer, until ravioli puff up and are crispy golden brown.

Asparagus, Mushroom And Cheese Soufflés

Servings: 3
Cooking Time: 21 Minutes
Ingredients:
- butter
- grated Parmesan cheese
- 3 button mushrooms, thinly sliced
- 8 spears asparagus, sliced ½-inch long
- 1 teaspoon olive oil
- 1 tablespoon butter
- 4½ teaspoons flour
- pinch paprika
- pinch ground nutmeg
- salt and freshly ground black pepper
- ½ cup milk
- ½ cup grated Gruyère cheese or other Swiss cheese (about 2 ounces)
- 2 eggs, separated

Directions:
1. Butter three 6-ounce ramekins and dust with grated Parmesan cheese. (Butter the ramekins and then coat the butter with Parmesan by shaking it around in the ramekin and dumping out any excess.)
2. Preheat the air fryer to 400°F.
3. Toss the mushrooms and asparagus in a bowl with the olive oil. Transfer the vegetables to the air fryer and air-fry for 7 minutes, shaking the basket once or twice to redistribute the Ingredients while they cook.
4. While the vegetables are cooking, make the soufflé base. Melt the butter in a saucepan on the stovetop over medium heat. Add the flour, stir and cook for a minute or two. Add the paprika, nutmeg, salt and pepper. Whisk in the milk and bring the mixture to a simmer to thicken. Remove the pan from the heat and add the cheese, stirring to melt. Let the mixture cool for just a few minutes and then whisk the egg yolks in, one at a time. Stir in the cooked mushrooms and asparagus. Let this soufflé base cool.
5. In a separate bowl, whisk the egg whites to soft peak stage (the point at which the whites can almost stand up on the end of your whisk). Fold the whipped egg whites into the soufflé base, adding a little at a time.
6. Preheat the air fryer to 330°F.
7. Transfer the batter carefully to the buttered ramekins, leaving about ½-inch at the top. Place the ramekins into the air fryer basket and air-fry for 14 minutes. The soufflés should have risen nicely and be brown on top. Serve immediately.

Thyme Lentil Patties

Servings: 2
Cooking Time: 35 Minutes
Ingredients:

- ½ cup grated American cheese
- 1 cup cooked lentils
- ¼ tsp dried thyme
- 2 eggs, beaten
- Salt and pepper to taste
- 1 cup bread crumbs

Directions:
1. Preheat air fryer to 350°F. Put the eggs, lentils, and cheese in a bowl and mix to combine. Stir in half the bread crumbs, thyme, salt, and pepper. Form the mixture into 2 patties and coat them in the remaining bread crumbs. Transfer to the greased frying basket. Air Fry for 14-16 minutes until brown, flipping once. Serve.

Garlic Okra Chips

Servings: 4
Cooking Time: 20 Minutes
Ingredients:
- 2 cups okra, cut into rounds
- 1 ½ tbsp. melted butter
- 1 garlic clove, minced
- 1 tsp powdered paprika
- Salt and pepper to taste

Directions:
1. Preheat air fryer to 350°F. Toss okra, melted butter, paprika, garlic, salt and pepper in a medium bowl until okra is coated. Place okra in the frying basket and Air Fry for 5 minutes. Shake the basket and Air Fry for another 5 minutes. Shake one more time and Air Fry for 2 minutes until crispy. Serve warm and enjoy.

Powerful Jackfruit Fritters

Servings:4
Cooking Time: 30 Minutes
Ingredients:
- 1 can jackfruit, chopped
- 1 egg, beaten
- 1 tbsp Dijon mustard
- 1 tbsp mayonnaise
- 1 tbsp prepared horseradish
- 2 tbsp grated yellow onion
- 2 tbsp chopped parsley
- 2 tbsp chopped nori
- 2 tbsp flour
- 1 tbsp Cajun seasoning
- ¼ tsp garlic powder
- ¼ tsp salt
- 2 lemon wedges

Directions:
1. In a bowl, combine jackfruit, egg, mustard, mayonnaise, horseradish, onion, parsley, nori, flour, Cajun seasoning, garlic, and salt. Let chill in the fridge for 15 minutes. Preheat air fryer to 350°F. Divide the mixture into 12 balls. Place them in the frying basket and Air Fry for 10 minutes. Serve with lemon wedges.

Stuffed Mushrooms

Servings:4
Cooking Time: 10 Minutes
Ingredients:

- 12 baby bella mushrooms, stems removed
- 4 ounces full-fat cream cheese, softened
- ¼ cup grated vegetarian Parmesan cheese
- ¼ cup Italian bread crumbs
- 1 teaspoon crushed red pepper flakes

Directions:
1. Preheat the air fryer to 400°F.
2. Use a spoon to hollow out mushroom caps.
3. In a medium bowl, combine cream cheese, Parmesan, bread crumbs, and red pepper flakes. Scoop approximately 1 tablespoon mixture into each mushroom cap.
4. Place stuffed mushrooms in the air fryer basket and cook 10 minutes until stuffing is brown. Let cool 5 minutes before serving.

Skewered Corn In Air Fryer

Servings:2
Cooking Time: 25 Minutes
Ingredients:
- 1-pound apricot, halved
- 2 ears of corn
- 2 medium green peppers, cut into large chunks
- 2 teaspoons prepared mustard
- Salt and pepper to taste

Directions:
1. Preheat the air fryer to 330°F.
2. Place the grill pan accessory in the air fryer.
3. On the double layer rack with the skewer accessories, skewer the corn, green peppers, and apricot. Season with salt and pepper to taste.
4. Place skewered corn on the double layer rack and cook for 25 minutes.
5. Once cooked, brush with prepared mustard.

Vegetarian Eggplant "pizzas"

Servings:4
Cooking Time: 25 Minutes
Ingredients:
- ½ cup diced baby bella mushrooms
- 3 tbsp olive oil
- ¼ cup diced onions
- ½ cup pizza sauce
- 1 eggplant, sliced
- 1 tsp salt
- 1 cup shredded mozzarella
- ¼ cup chopped oregano

Directions:
1. Warm 2 tsp of olive oil in a skillet over medium heat. Add in onion and mushrooms and stir-fry for 4 minutes until tender. Stir in pizza sauce. Turn the heat off.
2. Preheat air fryer to 375ºF. Brush the eggplant slices with the remaining olive oil on both sides. Lay out slices on a large plate and season with salt. Then, top with the sauce mixture and shredded mozzarella. Place the eggplant pizzas in the frying basket and Air Fry for 5 minutes. Garnish with oregano to serve.

Italian Stuffed Bell Peppers

Servings: 4
Cooking Time: 75 Minutes
Ingredients:
- 4 green and red bell peppers, tops and insides discarded
- 2 russet potatoes, scrubbed and perforated with a fork
- 2 tsp olive oil
- 2 Italian sausages, cubed
- 2 tbsp milk
- 2 tbsp yogurt
- 1 tsp olive oil
- 1 tbsp Italian seasoning
- Salt and pepper to taste
- ¼ cup canned corn kernels
- ½ cup mozzarella shreds
- 2 tsp chopped parsley
- 1 cup bechamel sauce

Directions:
1. Preheat air fryer at 400ºF. Rub olive oil over both potatoes and sprinkle with salt and pepper. Place them in the frying basket and Bake for 45 minutes, flipping at 30 minutes mark. Let cool onto a cutting board for 5 minutes until cool enough to handle. Scoop out cooled potato into a bowl. Discard skins.
2. Place Italian sausages in the frying basket and Air Fry for 2 minutes. Using the back of a fork, mash cooked potatoes, yogurt, milk, olive oil, Italian seasoning, salt, and pepper until smooth. Toss in cooked sausages, corn, and mozzarella cheese. Stuff bell peppers with the potato mixture. Place bell peppers in the frying basket and Bake for 10 minutes. Serve immediately sprinkled with parsley and bechamel sauce on side.

Roasted Green Beans

Servings: 6 Servings
Cooking Time: 15 Minutes
Ingredients:
- 1 pound of fresh green beans
- ½ pound of sliced mushrooms
- 1 sliced small red onion
- 1 teaspoon of Italian seasonings
- ¼ teaspoon of salt
- 1/8 teaspoon of black pepper
- 2 tablespoons of olive oil

Directions:
1. Preheat your air fryer to 350ºF. Spray some oil inside the air fryer basket.
2. Mix all the ingredients in a bowl, toss them until fully coated.
3. Transfer the prepared mixture in the preheated air fryer basket. Cook at 350ºF for 8–10 minutes until tender or 10–12 minutes until browned.
4. Serve warm and enjoy your Roasted Green Beans!

Roasted Vegetable, Brown Rice And Black Bean Burrito

Servings: 2
Cooking Time: 20 Minutes
Ingredients:
- ½ zucchini, sliced ¼-inch thick
- ½ red onion, sliced
- 1 yellow bell pepper, sliced
- 2 teaspoons olive oil
- salt and freshly ground black pepper
- 2 burrito size flour tortillas
- 1 cup grated pepper jack cheese
- ½ cup cooked brown rice
- ½ cup canned black beans, drained and rinsed
- ¼ teaspoon ground cumin
- 1 tablespoon chopped fresh cilantro
- fresh salsa, guacamole and sour cream, for serving

Directions:
1. Preheat the air fryer to 400°F.
2. Toss the vegetables in a bowl with the olive oil, salt and freshly ground black pepper. Air-fry at 400°F for 12 to 15 minutes, shaking the basket a few times during the cooking process. The vegetables are done when they are cooked to your liking.
3. In the meantime, start building the burritos. Lay the tortillas out on the counter. Sprinkle half of the cheese in the center of the tortillas. Combine the rice, beans, cumin and cilantro in a bowl, season to taste with salt and freshly ground black pepper and then divide the mixture between the two tortillas. When the vegetables have finished cooking, transfer them to the two tortillas, placing the vegetables on top of the rice and beans. Sprinkle the remaining cheese on top and then roll the burritos up, tucking in the sides of the tortillas as you roll. Brush or spray the outside of the burritos with olive oil and transfer them to the air fryer.
4. Air-fry at 360°F for 8 minutes, turning them over when there are about 2 minutes left. The burritos will have slightly brown spots, but will still be pliable.
5. Serve with some fresh salsa, guacamole and sour cream.

Crustless Spinach And Cheese Frittata

Servings:4
Cooking Time: 20 Minutes
Ingredients:
- 6 large eggs
- ½ cup heavy whipping cream
- 1 cup frozen chopped spinach, drained
- 1 cup shredded sharp Cheddar cheese
- ¼ cup peeled and diced yellow onion
- ½ teaspoon salt
- ¼ teaspoon ground black pepper

Directions:
1. In a large bowl, whisk eggs and cream together. Whisk in spinach, Cheddar, onion, salt, and pepper.
2. Pour mixture into an ungreased 6" round nonstick baking dish. Place dish into air fryer basket. Adjust the temperature to 320°F and set the timer for 20 minutes. Eggs will be firm and slightly browned when done. Serve immediately.

Home-style Cinnamon Rolls

Servings: 4
Cooking Time: 40 Minutes

Ingredients:
- ½ pizza dough
- 1/3 cup dark brown sugar
- ¼ cup butter, softened
- ½ tsp ground cinnamon

Directions:
1. Preheat air fryer to 360°F. Roll out the dough into a rectangle. Using a knife, spread the brown sugar and butter, covering all the edges, and sprinkle with cinnamon. Fold the long side of the dough into a log, then cut it into 8 equal pieces, avoiding compression. Place the rolls, spiral-side up, onto a parchment-lined sheet. Let rise for 20 minutes. Grease the rolls with cooking spray and Bake for 8 minutes until golden brown. Serve right away.

Chive Potato Pierogi

Servings: 4
Cooking Time: 55 Minutes

Ingredients:
- 2 boiled potatoes, mashed
- Salt and pepper to taste
- 1 tsp cumin powder
- 2 tbsp sour cream
- ¼ cup grated Parmesan
- 2 tbsp chopped chives
- 1 tbsp chopped parsley
- 1 ¼ cups flour
- ¼ tsp garlic powder
- ¾ cup Greek yogurt
- 1 egg

Directions:
1. Combine the mashed potatoes along with sour cream, cumin, parsley, chives, pepper, and salt and stir until slightly chunky. Mix the flour, salt, and garlic powder in a large bowl. Stir in yogurt until it comes together as a sticky dough. Knead in the bowl for about 2-3 minutes to make it smooth. Whisk the egg and 1 teaspoon of water in a small bowl. Roll out the dough on a lightly floured work surface to ¼-inch thickness. Cut out 12 circles with a cookie cutter.
2. Preheat air fryer to 350°F. Divide the potato mixture and Parmesan cheese between the dough circles. Brush the edges of them with the egg wash and fold the dough over the filling into half-moon shapes. Crimp the edges with a fork to seal. Arrange the on the greased frying basket and Air Fry for 8-10 minutes, turning the pierogies once, until the outside is golden. Serve warm.

Spaghetti Squash And Kale Fritters With Pomodoro Sauce

Servings: 3
Cooking Time: 45 Minutes

Ingredients:
- 1½-pound spaghetti squash (about half a large or a whole small squash)
- olive oil
- ½ onion, diced
- ½ red bell pepper, diced
- 2 cloves garlic, minced
- 4 cups coarsely chopped kale
- salt and freshly ground black pepper
- 1 egg
- ⅓ cup breadcrumbs, divided*
- ⅓ cup grated Parmesan cheese
- ½ teaspoon dried rubbed sage
- pinch nutmeg
- Pomodoro Sauce:
- 2 tablespoons olive oil
- ½ onion, chopped
- 1 to 2 cloves garlic, minced
- 1 (28-ounce) can peeled tomatoes
- ¼ cup red wine
- 1 teaspoon Italian seasoning
- 2 tablespoons chopped fresh basil, plus more for garnish
- salt and freshly ground black pepper
- ½ teaspoon sugar (optional)

Directions:
1. Preheat the air fryer to 370°F.
2. Cut the spaghetti squash in half lengthwise and remove the seeds. Rub the inside of the squash with olive oil and season with salt and pepper. Place the squash, cut side up, into the air fryer basket and air-fry for 30 minutes, flipping the squash over halfway through the cooking process.
3. While the squash is cooking, Preheat a large sauté pan over medium heat on the stovetop. Add a little olive oil and sauté the onions for 3 minutes, until they start to soften. Add the red pepper and garlic and continue to sauté for an additional 4 minutes. Add the kale and season with salt and pepper. Cook for 2 more minutes, or until the kale is soft. Transfer the mixture to a large bowl and let it cool.
4. While the squash continues to cook, make the Pomodoro sauce. Preheat the large sauté pan again over medium heat on the stovetop. Add the olive oil and sauté the onion and garlic for 2 to 3 minutes, until the onion begins to soften. Crush the canned tomatoes with your hands and add them to the pan along with the red wine and Italian seasoning and simmer for 20 minutes. Add the basil and season to taste with salt, pepper and sugar (if using).
5. When the spaghetti squash has finished cooking, use a fork to scrape the inside flesh of the squash onto a sheet pan. Spread the squash out and let it cool.
6. Once cool, add the spaghetti squash to the kale mixture, along with the egg, breadcrumbs, Parmesan cheese, sage, nutmeg, salt and freshly ground black pepper. Stir to combine well and then divide the mixture into 6 thick portions. You can shape the portions into patties, but I prefer to keep them a little random and unique in shape. Spray or brush the fritters with olive oil.
7. Preheat the air fryer to 370°F.
8. Brush the air fryer basket with a little olive oil and transfer the fritters to the basket. Air-fry the squash and kale fritters at 370°F for 15 minutes, flipping them over halfway through the cooking process.
9. Serve the fritters warm with the Pomodoro sauce spooned over the top or pooled on your plate. Garnish with the fresh basil leaves.

Chapter 9: Vegetable Side Dishes Recipes

Saltine Wax Beans

Servings: 4
Cooking Time: 7 Minutes
Ingredients:
- ½ cup flour
- 1 teaspoon smoky chipotle powder
- ½ teaspoon ground black pepper
- 1 teaspoon sea salt flakes
- 2 eggs, beaten
- ½ cup crushed saltines
- 10 ounces (283 g) wax beans
- Cooking spray

Directions:
1. Preheat the air fryer to 360ºF (182ºC).
2. Combine the flour, chipotle powder, black pepper, and salt in a bowl. Put the eggs in a second bowl. Put the crushed saltines in a third bowl.
3. Wash the beans with cold water and discard any tough strings.
4. Coat the beans with the flour mixture, before dipping them into the beaten egg. Cover them with the crushed saltines.
5. Spritz the beans with cooking spray.
6. Air fry for 4 minutes. Give the air fryer basket a good shake and continue to air fry for 3 minutes. Serve hot.

Beef Stuffed Bell Peppers

Servings: 4
Cooking Time: 30 Minutes
Ingredients:
- 1 pound (454 g) ground beef
- 1 tablespoon taco seasoning mix
- 1 can diced tomatoes and green chilis
- 4 green bell peppers
- 1 cup shredded Monterey jack cheese, divided

Directions:
1. Preheat the air fryer to 350ºF (177ºC).
2. Set a skillet over a high heat and cook the ground beef for 8 minutes. Make sure it is cooked through and browned all over. Drain the fat.
3. Stir in the taco seasoning mix, and the diced tomatoes and green chilis. Allow the mixture to cook for a further 4 minutes.
4. In the meantime, slice the tops off the green peppers and remove the seeds and membranes.
5. When the meat mixture is fully cooked, spoon equal amounts of it into the peppers and top with the Monterey jack cheese. Then place the peppers into the air fryer. Air fry for 15 minutes.
6. The peppers are ready when they are soft, and the cheese is bubbling and brown. Serve warm.

Roasted Lemony Broccoli

Servings: 6
Cooking Time: 15 Minutes
Ingredients:
- 2 heads broccoli, cut into florets
- 2 teaspoons extra-virgin olive oil, plus more for coating
- 1 teaspoon salt
- ½ teaspoon black pepper
- 1 clove garlic, minced
- ½ teaspoon lemon juice

Directions:
1. Cover the air fryer basket with aluminum foil and coat with a light brushing of oil.
2. Preheat the air fryer to 375ºF (191ºC).
3. In a bowl, combine all ingredients, save for the lemon juice, and transfer to the air fryer basket. Roast for 15 minutes.
4. Serve with the lemon juice.

Beef Stuffed Bell Pepper

Servings: 4
Cooking Time: 15 Minutes
Ingredients:
- 2 garlic cloves, minced
- 1 small onion, chopped
- Cooking spray
- 1 pound (454 g) ground beef
- 1 teaspoon dried basil
- ½ teaspoon chili powder
- 1 teaspoon black pepper
- 1 teaspoon garlic salt
- ⅔ cup shredded cheese, divided
- ½ cup cooked rice
- 2 teaspoons Worcestershire sauce
- 8 ounces (227 g) tomato sauce
- 4 bell peppers, tops removed

Directions:
1. Grease a frying pan with cooking spray and fry the onion and garlic over a medium heat.
2. Stir in the beef, basil, chili powder, black pepper, and garlic salt, combining everything well. Air fry until the beef is nicely browned, before taking the pan off the heat.
3. Add half of the cheese, the rice, Worcestershire sauce, and tomato sauce and stir to combine.
4. Spoon equal amounts of the beef mixture into the four bell peppers, filling them entirely.
5. Preheat the air fryer to 400ºF (204ºC).
6. Spritz the air fryer basket with cooking spray.
7. Put the stuffed bell peppers in the basket and air fry for 11 minutes.
8. Add the remaining cheese on top of each bell pepper and air fry for a further 2 minutes. When the cheese is melted and the bell peppers are piping hot, serve immediately.

Crispy Tofu With Soy Sauce

Servings: 4
Cooking Time: 35 Minutes
Ingredients:
- 1 block firm tofu, pressed and diced
- 1 tablespoon arrowroot flour

- 2 teaspoon sesame oil
- 1 teaspoon vinegar
- 2 tablespoon soy sauce

Directions:
1. In a suitable bowl, toss tofu with oil, vinegar, and soy sauce and let sit for almost 15 minutes.
2. Toss marinated tofu with arrowroot flour.
3. Grease its air fryer basket with cooking spray.
4. Add tofu in air fryer basket and cook for 20 minutes at 370 degrees F/ 185 degrees C. Shake basket halfway through.
5. Serve and enjoy.

Gorgonzola Mushrooms With Horseradish Mayo

Servings: 5
Cooking Time: 10 Minutes
Ingredients:
- ½ cup bread crumbs
- 2 cloves garlic, pressed
- 2 tablespoons chopped fresh coriander
- ⅓ teaspoon kosher salt
- ½ teaspoon crushed red pepper flakes
- 1½ tablespoons olive oil
- 20 medium mushrooms, stems removed
- ½ cup grated Gorgonzola cheese
- ¼ cup low-fat mayonnaise
- 1 teaspoon prepared horseradish, well-drained
- 1 tablespoon finely chopped fresh parsley

Directions:
1. Preheat the air fryer to 380°F (193°C).
2. Combine the bread crumbs together with the garlic, coriander, salt, red pepper, and olive oil.
3. Take equal-sized amounts of the breadcrumb mixture and use them to stuff the mushroom caps. Add the grated Gorgonzola on top of each.
4. Put the mushrooms in the air fryer baking pan and transfer to the air fryer.
5. Air fry for 10 minutes, ensuring the stuffing is warm throughout.
6. In the meantime, prepare the horseradish mayo. Mix the mayonnaise, horseradish and parsley.
7. When the mushrooms are ready, serve with the mayo.

Chili Fingerling Potatoes

Servings: 4
Cooking Time: 16 Minutes
Ingredients:
- 1 pound (454 g) fingerling potatoes, rinsed and cut into wedges
- 1 teaspoon olive oil
- 1 teaspoon salt
- 1 teaspoon black pepper
- 1 teaspoon cayenne pepper
- 1 teaspoon nutritional yeast
- ½ teaspoon garlic powder

Directions:
1. Preheat the air fryer to 400°F (204°C).
2. Coat the potatoes with the rest of the ingredients.
3. Transfer to the air fryer basket and air fry for 16 minutes, shaking the basket at the halfway point.
4. Serve immediately.

Balsamic Stuffed Mushrooms

Servings: 4
Cooking Time: 30 Minutes
Ingredients:
- ¼ cup chopped roasted red peppers
- 12 portobello mushroom caps
- 2 tsp grated Parmesan cheese
- 10 oz spinach, chopped
- 3 scallions, chopped
- ¼ cup chickpea flour
- 1 tsp garlic powder
- 1 tbsp balsamic vinegar
- ½ lemon

Directions:
1. Preheat air fryer to 360°F. In a bowl, squeeze any excess water from the spinach; discard the water. Stir in scallions, red pepper, chickpea flour, Parmesan cheese, garlic, and balsamic vinegar until well combined. Fill each mushroom cap with spinach mixture until covering the tops, pressing down slightly. Bake for 12 minutes until crispy. Drizzle with lemon juice before serving.

Rutabaga Fries

Servings: 4
Cooking Time: 20 Minutes
Ingredients:
- 15 ounces rutabaga, cut into fries
- 4 tablespoons olive oil
- ½ teaspoon chili powder
- A pinch of salt and black pepper

Directions:
1. Mix the rutabaga, olive oil, chili powder, salt, and black pepper in a bowl.
2. Transfer into your air fryer basket.
3. Cook the seasoned rutabaga in your air fryer at 400 degrees F/ 205 degrees C for 20 minutes.
4. Serve on plates as a side dish.

Simple Green Bake

Servings: 4
Cooking Time: 15 Minutes
Ingredients:
- 1 cup asparagus, chopped
- 2 cups broccoli florets
- 1 tbsp olive oil
- 1 tbsp lemon juice
- 1 cup green peas
- 2 tbsp honey mustard
- Salt and pepper to taste

Directions:
1. Preheat air fryer to 330°F. Add asparagus and broccoli to the frying basket. Drizzle with olive oil and

lemon juice and toss. Bake for 6 minutes. Remove the basket and add peas. Steam for another 3 minutes or until the vegetables are hot and tender. Pour the vegetables into a serving dish. Drizzle with honey mustard and season with salt and pepper. Toss and serve warm.

Cauliflower Fried Rice

Servings: 5
Cooking Time: 20 Minutes
Ingredients:
- 2½ cups riced cauliflower (1 head cauliflower if making your own)
- 2 teaspoons sesame oil, divided
- 1 medium green bell pepper, chopped
- 1 cup peas
- 1 cup diced carrots
- ½ cup chopped onion
- Salt
- Pepper
- 1 tablespoon soy sauce
- 2 medium eggs, scrambled

Directions:
1. If you choose to make your own riced cauliflower, grate the head of cauliflower using the medium-size holes of a cheese grater. Or you can cut the head of cauliflower into florets and pulse in a food processor until it has the appearance of rice.
2. Coat the bottom of a barrel pan with 1 teaspoon of sesame oil.
3. In a large bowl, combine the riced cauliflower, green bell pepper, peas, carrots, and onion. Drizzle the remaining 1 teaspoon of sesame oil over the vegetables and stir. Add salt and pepper to taste.
4. Transfer the mixture to the barrel pan. Cook for 10 minutes.
5. Remove the barrel pan. Drizzle the soy sauce all over and add the scrambled eggs. Stir to combine.
6. Serve warm.

Cheesy Cauliflower Tots

Servings:4
Cooking Time: 12 Minutes Per Batch
Ingredients:
- 1 steamer bag riced cauliflower
- ⅓ cup Italian bread crumbs
- ¼ cup all-purpose flour
- 1 large egg
- ¾ cup shredded sharp Cheddar cheese
- ½ teaspoon salt
- ¼ teaspoon ground black pepper

Directions:
1. Cook cauliflower according to the package directions. Let cool, then squeeze in a cheesecloth or kitchen towel to drain excess water.
2. Preheat the air fryer to 400°F. Cut parchment paper to fit the air fryer basket.
3. In a large bowl, mix drained cauliflower, bread crumbs, flour, egg, and Cheddar. Sprinkle in salt and pepper, then mix until well combined.
4. Roll 2 tablespoons of mixture into a tot shape. Repeat to use all of the mixture.
5. Place tots on parchment in the air fryer basket, working in batches as necessary. Spritz with cooking spray. Cook 12 minutes, turning tots halfway through cooking time, until golden brown. Serve warm.

Basmati Risotto

Servings:2
Cooking Time: 30 Minutes
Ingredients:
- 1 onion, diced
- 1 small carrot, diced
- 2 cups vegetable broth, boiling
- ½ cup grated Cheddar cheese
- 1 clove garlic, minced
- ¾ cup long-grain basmati rice
- 1 tablespoon olive oil
- 1 tablespoon unsalted butter

Directions:
1. Preheat the air fryer to 390°F (199°C).
2. Grease a baking tin with oil and stir in the butter, garlic, carrot, and onion.
3. Put the tin in the air fryer and bake for 4 minutes.
4. Pour in the rice and bake for a further 4 minutes, stirring three times throughout the baking time.
5. Turn the temperature down to 320°F (160°C).
6. Add the vegetable broth and give the dish a gentle stir. Bake for 22 minutes, leaving the air fryer uncovered.
7. Pour in the cheese, stir once more and serve.

Green Beans

Servings: 4
Cooking Time: 12 Minutes
Ingredients:
- 1 pound fresh green beans
- 2 tablespoons Italian salad dressing
- salt and pepper

Directions:
1. Wash beans and snap off stem ends.
2. In a large bowl, toss beans with Italian dressing.
3. Cook at 330°F for 5minutes. Shake basket or stir and cook 5minutes longer. Shake basket again and, if needed, continue cooking for 2 minutes, until as tender as you like. Beans should shrivel slightly and brown in places.
4. Sprinkle with salt and pepper to taste.

Sweet Potato Curly Fries

Servings: 4
Cooking Time: 10 Minutes
Ingredients:
- 2 medium sweet potatoes, washed
- 2 tablespoons avocado oil
- ¾ teaspoon salt, divided
- 1 medium avocado

- ½ teaspoon garlic powder
- ½ teaspoon paprika
- ¼ teaspoon black pepper
- ½ juice lime
- 3 tablespoons fresh cilantro

Directions:
1. Preheat the air fryer to 400°F.
2. Using a spiralizer, create curly spirals with the sweet potatoes. Keep the pieces about 1½ inches long. Continue until all the potatoes are used.
3. In a large bowl, toss the curly sweet potatoes with the avocado oil and ½ teaspoon of the salt.
4. Place the potatoes in the air fryer basket and cook for 5 minutes; shake and cook another 5 minutes.
5. While cooking, add the avocado, garlic, paprika, pepper, the remaining ¼ teaspoon of salt, lime juice, and cilantro to a blender and process until smooth. Set aside.
6. When cooking completes, remove the fries and serve warm with the lime avocado sauce.

Truffle Vegetable Croquettes

Servings: 4
Cooking Time: 40 Minutes
Ingredients:
- 2 cooked potatoes, mashed
- 1 cooked carrot, mashed
- 1 tbsp onion, minced
- 2 eggs, beaten
- 2 tbsp melted butter
- 1 tbsp truffle oil
- ½ tbsp flour
- Salt and pepper to taste

Directions:
1. Preheat air fryer to 350°F. Sift the flour, salt, and pepper in a bowl and stir to combine. Add the potatoes, carrot, onion, butter, and truffle oil to a separate bowl and mix well. Shape the potato mixture into small bite-sized patties. Dip the potato patties into the beaten eggs, coating thoroughly, then roll in the flour mixture to cover all sides. Arrange the croquettes in the greased frying basket and Air Fry for 14-16 minutes. Halfway through cooking, shake the basket. The croquettes should be crispy and golden. Serve hot and enjoy!

Fried Green Tomatoes With Sriracha Mayo

Servings: 4
Cooking Time: 12 Minutes
Ingredients:
- 3 green tomatoes
- salt and freshly ground black pepper
- ⅓ cup all-purpose flour*
- 2 eggs
- ½ cup buttermilk
- 1 cup panko breadcrumbs*
- 1 cup cornmeal
- olive oil, in a spray bottle
- fresh thyme sprigs or chopped fresh chives
- Sriracha Mayo
- ½ cup mayonnaise
- 1 to 2 tablespoons sriracha hot sauce
- 1 tablespoon milk

Directions:
1. Cut the tomatoes in ¼-inch slices. Pat them dry with a clean kitchen towel and season generously with salt and pepper.
2. Set up a dredging station using three shallow dishes. Place the flour in the first shallow dish, whisk the eggs and buttermilk together in the second dish, and combine the panko breadcrumbs and cornmeal in the third dish.
3. Preheat the air fryer to 400°F.
4. Dredge the tomato slices in flour to coat on all sides. Then dip them into the egg mixture and finally press them into the breadcrumbs to coat all sides of the tomato.
5. Spray or brush the air-fryer basket with olive oil. Transfer 3 to 4 tomato slices into the basket and spray the top with olive oil. Air-fry the tomatoes at 400°F for 8 minutes. Flip them over, spray the other side with oil and air-fry for an additional 4 minutes until golden brown.
6. While the tomatoes are cooking, make the sriracha mayo. Combine the mayonnaise, 1 tablespoon of the sriracha hot sauce and milk in a small bowl. Stir well until the mixture is smooth. Add more sriracha sauce to taste.
7. When the tomatoes are done, transfer them to a cooling rack or a platter lined with paper towels so the bottom does not get soggy. Before serving, carefully stack the all the tomatoes into air fryer and air-fry at 350°F for 1 to 2 minutes to heat them back up.
8. Serve the fried green tomatoes hot with the sriracha mayo on the side. Season one last time with salt and freshly ground black pepper and garnish with sprigs of fresh thyme or chopped fresh chives.

Cheese Broccoli With Basil

Servings: 4
Cooking Time: 7 Minutes
Ingredients:
- 1 cup broccoli, chopped, boiled
- 1 teaspoon nut oil
- 1 teaspoon salt
- 1 teaspoon dried basil
- ½ cup Cheddar cheese, shredded
- ½ cup of coconut milk
- ½ teaspoon butter, softened

Directions:
1. In the air fryer basket, place the broccoli, nut oil, dried dill, and salt.
2. Stir together the mixture and then pour in the coconut milk.
3. Drizzle butter and Cheddar cheese on the top of the meal.
4. Before cooking, heat your air fryer to 400 degrees F/ 205 degrees C.
5. Cook the mixture inside the preheated air fryer for 7 minutes.

The Ultimate Tower Air Fryer Cookbook 87

Broccoli With Paprika

Servings: 4
Cooking Time: 15 Minutes
Ingredients:
- 1 broccoli head, florets separated
- Black pepper and salt to the taste
- ½ cup keto tomato sauce
- 1 tablespoon sweet paprika
- ¼ cup scallions, chopped
- 1 tablespoon olive oil

Directions:
1. In a pan that fits the air fryer, combine the broccoli with the rest of the ingredients, toss, put the pan in the air fryer and cook at almost 380 degrees F/ 195 degrees C for almost 15 minutes.
2. Divide between plates and serve.

Cheesy Cauliflower Tart

Servings: 4
Cooking Time: 40 Minutes
Ingredients:
- ½ cup cooked cauliflower, chopped
- ¼ cup grated Swiss cheese
- ¼ cup shredded cheddar
- 1 pie crust
- 2 eggs
- ¼ cup milk
- 6 black olives, chopped
- Salt and pepper to taste

Directions:
1. Preheat air fryer to 360°F. Grease and line a tart tin with the pie crust. Trim the edges and prick lightly with a fork. Whisk the eggs in a bowl until fluffy. Add the milk, cauliflower, salt, pepper, black olives, and half the cheddar and Swiss cheeses; stir to combine. Carefully spoon the mixture into the pie crust and spread it level. Bake in the air fryer for 15 minutes. Slide the basket out and sprinkle the rest of the cheeses on top. Cook for another 5 minutes or until golden on the top and cooked through. Leave to cool before serving.

Smashed Fried Baby Potatoes

Servings: 3
Cooking Time: 18 Minutes
Ingredients:
- 1½ pounds baby red or baby Yukon gold potatoes
- ¼ cup butter, melted
- 1 teaspoon olive oil
- ½ teaspoon paprika
- 1 teaspoon dried parsley
- salt and freshly ground black pepper
- 2 scallions, finely chopped

Directions:
1. Bring a large pot of salted water to a boil. Add the potatoes and boil for 18 minutes or until the potatoes are fork-tender.
2. Drain the potatoes and transfer them to a cutting board to cool slightly. Spray or brush the bottom of a drinking glass with a little oil. Smash or flatten the potatoes by pressing the glass down on each potato slowly. Try not to completely flatten the potato or smash it so hard that it breaks apart.
3. Combine the melted butter, olive oil, paprika, and parsley together.
4. Preheat the air fryer to 400°F.
5. Spray the bottom of the air fryer basket with oil and transfer one layer of the smashed potatoes into the basket. Brush with some of the butter mixture and season generously with salt and freshly ground black pepper.
6. Air-fry at 400°F for 10 minutes. Carefully flip the potatoes over and air-fry for an additional 8 minutes until crispy and lightly browned.
7. Keep the potatoes warm in a 170°F oven or tent with aluminum foil while you cook the second batch. Sprinkle minced scallions over the potatoes and serve warm.

Potato And Broccoli With Tofu Scramble

Servings: 3
Cooking Time: 30 Minutes
Ingredients:
- 2½ cups chopped red potato
- 2 tablespoons olive oil, divided
- 1 block tofu, chopped finely
- 2 tablespoons tamari
- 1 teaspoon turmeric powder
- ½ teaspoon onion powder
- ½ teaspoon garlic powder
- ½ cup chopped onion
- 4 cups broccoli florets

Directions:
1. Preheat the air fryer to 400ºF (204ºC).
2. Toss together the potatoes and 1 tablespoon of the olive oil.
3. Air fry the potatoes in a baking dish for 15 minutes, shaking once during the cooking time to ensure they fry evenly.
4. Combine the tofu, the remaining 1 tablespoon of the olive oil, turmeric, onion powder, tamari, and garlic powder together, stirring in the onions, followed by the broccoli.
5. Top the potatoes with the tofu mixture and air fry for an additional 15 minutes. Serve warm.

Garlic Asparagus With Provolone

Servings: 3
Cooking Time: 6 Minutes
Ingredients:
- 9 ounces Asparagus
- ¼ teaspoon chili powder
- ¼ teaspoon garlic powder
- 1 teaspoon olive oil
- 4 Provolone cheese slices

Directions:
1. Trim the asparagus and sprinkle with chili powder and garlic powder.

2. At 400 degrees F/ 205 degrees C, preheat your air fryer.
3. Spread the asparagus in the air fryer basket and sprinkle with olive oil.
4. Cook the vegetables for 3 minutes. Then top the asparagus with Provolone cheese and cook for 3 minutes more.
5. Serve.

Fried Green Tomatoes

Servings: 4
Cooking Time: 6 To 8 Minutes
Ingredients:
- 4 medium green tomatoes
- ⅓ cup all purpose flour
- 2 egg whites
- ¼ cup almond milk
- 1 cup ground almonds
- ½ cup panko bread crumbs
- 2 teaspoons olive oil
- 1 teaspoon paprika
- 1 clove garlic, minced

Directions:
1. Rinse the tomatoes and pat dry. Cut the tomatoes into ½-inch slices, discarding the thinner ends.
2. Put the flour on a plate. In a shallow bowl, beat the egg whites with the almond milk until frothy. And on another plate, combine the almonds, bread crumbs, olive oil, paprika, and garlic and mix well.
3. Dip the tomato slices into the flour, then into the egg white mixture, then into the almond mixture to coat.
4. Place four of the coated tomato slices in the air fryer basket. Air fry for 6 to 8 minutes or until the tomato coating is crisp and golden brown. Repeat with remaining tomato slices and serve immediately.

Turmeric Tofu Cubes

Servings: 2
Cooking Time: 9 Minutes
Ingredients:
- 6 ounces tofu, cubed
- 1 teaspoon avocado oil
- 1 teaspoon apple cider vinegar
- 1 garlic clove, diced
- ¼ teaspoon ground turmeric
- ¼ teaspoon ground paprika
- ½ teaspoon dried cilantro
- ¼ teaspoon lemon zest, grated

Directions:
1. Before cooking, firstly heat your air fryer to 400 degrees F/ 205 degrees C.
2. Mix together apple cider vinegar, ground turmeric, diced garlic, paprika, avocado oil, lime zest, and cilantro in a bowl.
3. Coat the tofu cubes with the oil mixture.
4. Transfer the tofu cubes in the air fryer basket and cook in your air fryer for 9 minutes.
5. During cooking shake the basket from time to time.

Chili-oiled Brussels Sprouts

Servings: 4
Cooking Time: 30 Minutes
Ingredients:
- 1 cup Brussels sprouts, quartered
- 1 tsp olive oil
- 1 tsp chili oil
- Salt and pepper to taste

Directions:
1. Preheat air fryer to 350°F. Coat the Brussels sprouts with olive oil, chili oil, salt, and black pepper in a bowl. Transfer to the frying basket. Bake for 20 minutes, shaking the basket several times throughout cooking until the sprouts are crispy, browned on the outside, and juicy inside. Serve and enjoy!

Citrusy Brussels Sprouts

Servings: 4
Cooking Time: 15 Minutes
Ingredients:
- 1 lb Brussels sprouts, quartered
- 1 clementine, cut into rings
- 2 garlic cloves, minced
- 1 tbsp olive oil
- 1 tbsp butter, melted
- ½ tsp salt

Directions:
1. Preheat air fryer to 360°F. Add the quartered Brussels sprouts with the garlic, olive oil, butter and salt in a bowl and toss until well coated. Pour the Brussels sprouts into the air fryer, top with the clementine slices, and Roast for 10 minutes. Remove from the air fryer and set the clementines aside. Toss the Brussels sprouts and serve.

Mexican-style Roasted Corn

Servings: 3
Cooking Time: 14 Minutes
Ingredients:
- 3 tablespoons Butter, melted and cooled
- 2 teaspoons Minced garlic
- ¾ teaspoon Ground cumin
- Up to ¾ teaspoon Red pepper flakes
- ¼ teaspoon Table salt
- 3 Cold 4-inch lengths husked and de-silked corn on the cob
- Minced fresh cilantro leaves
- Crumbled queso fresco

Directions:
1. Preheat the air fryer to 400°F.
2. Mix the melted butter, garlic, cumin, red pepper flakes, and salt in a large zip-closed plastic bag. Add the cold corn pieces, seal the bag, and massage the butter mixture into the surface of the corn.
3. When the machine is at temperature, take the pieces of corn out of the plastic bag and put them in the basket with as much air space between the pieces as possible.

Air-fry undisturbed for 14 minutes, until golden brown and maybe even charred in a few small spots.
4. Use kitchen tongs to gently transfer the pieces of corn to a serving platter. Sprinkle each piece with the cilantro and queso fresco. Serve warm.

Roasted Yellow Squash And Onions
Servings: 3
Cooking Time: 20 Minutes
Ingredients:
- 1 medium squash Yellow or summer crookneck squash, cut into ½-inch-thick rounds
- 1½ cups Yellow or white onion, roughly chopped
- ¾ teaspoon Table salt
- ¼ teaspoon Ground cumin (optional)
- Olive oil spray
- 1½ tablespoons Lemon or lime juice

Directions:
1. Preheat the air fryer to 375°F.
2. Toss the squash rounds, onion, salt, and cumin in a large bowl. Lightly coat the vegetables with olive oil spray, toss again, spray again, and keep at it until the vegetables are evenly coated.
3. When the machine is at temperature, scrape the contents of the bowl into the basket, spreading the vegetables out into as close to one layer as you can. Air-fry for 20 minutes, tossing once very gently, until the squash and onions are soft, even a little browned at the edges.
4. Pour the contents of the basket into a serving bowl, add the lemon or lime juice, and toss gently but well to coat. Serve warm or at room temperature.

Tomato Salad
Servings: 4
Cooking Time: 15 Minutes
Ingredients:
- 10 cherry tomatoes, halved
- ½ pound kale leaves, torn
- Salt and black pepper to the taste
- ¼ cup veggie stock
- 2 tablespoons keto tomato sauce

Directions:
1. In a pan that fits your air fryer, mix tomatoes with the remaining ingredients, toss, put the pan in the fryer and cook at 360°F for 15 minutes. Divide between plates and serve right away.

Creamy And Cheesy Spinach
Servings:4
Cooking Time: 15 Minutes
Ingredients:
- Vegetable oil spray
- 1 (10-ounce / 283-g) package frozen spinach, thawed and squeezed dry
- ½ cup chopped onion
- 2 cloves garlic, minced
- 4 ounces (113 g) cream cheese, diced
- ½ teaspoon ground nutmeg
- 1 teaspoon kosher salt
- 1 teaspoon black pepper
- ½ cup grated Parmesan cheese

Directions:
1. Preheat the air fryer to 350°F (177°C). Spray a heatproof pan with vegetable oil spray.
2. In a medium bowl, combine the spinach, onion, garlic, cream cheese, nutmeg, salt, and pepper. Transfer to the prepared pan.
3. Put the pan in the air fryer basket. Bake for 10 minutes. Open and stir to thoroughly combine the cream cheese and spinach.
4. Sprinkle the Parmesan cheese on top. Bake for 5 minutes, or until the cheese has melted and browned.
5. Serve hot.

Kale And Brussels Sprouts
Servings: 8
Cooking Time: 15 Minutes
Ingredients:
- 1 pound Brussels sprouts, trimmed
- 2 cups kale, torn
- 1 tablespoon olive oil
- Black pepper and salt to the taste
- 3 ounces. mozzarella, shredded

Directions:
1. In a pan that fits the air fryer, combine all the recipe ingredients except the mozzarella and toss.
2. Put the pan in the preheated Air Fryer and Cook at almost 380 degrees F/ 195 degrees C for almost 15 minutes.
3. Divide between plates, sprinkle the cheese on top and serve.

Awesome Mushroom Tots
Servings: 2
Cooking Time: 6 Minutes
Ingredients:
- 1 cup white mushrooms, grinded
- 1 teaspoon onion powder
- 1 egg yolk
- 3 teaspoons flax meal
- ½ teaspoon ground black pepper
- 1 teaspoon avocado oil
- 1 tablespoon coconut flour

Directions:
1. Add the onion powder, flax meal, ground black pepper, coconut flour, and grinded white mushrooms in a mixing bowl. Mix until smooth and homogenous.
2. Then make the mushroom tots from the mixture.
3. Before cooking, heat your air fryer to 400 degrees F/ 205 degrees C.
4. Brush the coconut oil over the inside of the air fryer basket.
5. Arrange evenly the mushroom tots on the air fryer basket.
6. Cook in your air fryer for 3 minutes.
7. Then flip the tots to the other side and continue cooking for 2to 3 minutes or until they are lightly brown.

Polenta

Servings: 4
Cooking Time: 15 Minutes
Ingredients:
- 1 pound polenta
- ¼ cup flour
- oil for misting or cooking spray

Directions:
1. Cut polenta into ½-inch slices.
2. Dip slices in flour to coat well. Spray both sides with oil or cooking spray.
3. Cook at 390°F for 5minutes. Turn polenta and spray both sides again with oil.
4. Cook 10 more minutes or until brown and crispy.

Stuffed Avocados

Servings: 4
Cooking Time: 8 Minutes
Ingredients:
- 1 cup frozen shoepeg corn, thawed
- 1 cup cooked black beans
- ¼ cup diced onion
- ½ teaspoon cumin
- 2 teaspoons lime juice, plus extra for serving
- salt and pepper
- 2 large avocados, split in half, pit removed

Directions:
1. Mix together the corn, beans, onion, cumin, and lime juice. Season to taste with salt and pepper.
2. Scoop out some of the flesh from center of each avocado and set aside. Divide corn mixture evenly between the cavities.
3. Set avocado halves in air fryer basket and cook at 360°F for 8 minutes, until corn mixture is hot.
4. Season the avocado flesh that you scooped out with a squirt of lime juice, salt, and pepper. Spoon it over the cooked halves.

Quick Air Fried Potatoes

Servings: 3
Cooking Time: 55 Minutes
Ingredients:
- 3 whole potatoes
- 2 tsp olive oil
- 1 tbsp salt
- 1 tbsp minced garlic
- 1 tsp parsley, chopped
- 4 oz grated Swiss cheese

Directions:
1. Preheat air fryer to 390°F. Prick the potatoes all over using a fork. Drizzle with olive oil all over the skins and rub them with minced garlic, salt, and parsley. Place the potatoes in the frying basket and Bake for 20-25 minutes or until tender. Remove the potatoes from the basket and serve them along with grated Swiss cheese. Serve.

Vegetable Fried Rice

Servings: 5
Cooking Time: 20 Minutes
Ingredients:
- 2 (9-ounce) packages precooked, microwavable rice
- 2 teaspoons sesame oil, divided
- 1 medium green bell pepper, seeded and chopped
- 1 cup peas
- 2 medium carrots, diced (about 1 cup)
- ½ cup chopped onion
- Salt
- Pepper
- 1 tablespoon soy sauce
- 2 medium eggs, scrambled

Directions:
1. Cook the rice in the microwave according to the package instructions and place in the refrigerator. The rice will need to cool for 15 to 20 minutes. You can also place it in the freezer until cold.
2. Add 1 teaspoon of sesame oil to the bottom of the barrel pan.
3. In a large bowl, combine the cold rice, green bell pepper, peas, carrots, and onion. Drizzle with the remaining 1 teaspoon of sesame oil and stir. Add salt and pepper to taste.
4. Transfer the mixture to the barrel pan. Cook for 15 minutes.
5. Remove the barrel pan. Drizzle the soy sauce all over and add the scrambled eggs. Stir to combine.
6. Serve warm.

Zucchini Tots With Mozzarella

Servings: 4
Cooking Time: 6 Minutes
Ingredients:
- 1 zucchini, grated
- ½ cup Mozzarella, shredded
- 1 egg, beaten
- 2 tablespoons. almond flour
- ½ teaspoon black pepper
- 1 teaspoon coconut oil, melted

Directions:
1. Mix up grated zucchini, shredded Mozzarella, egg, almond flour, and black pepper.
2. Then make the small zucchini tots with the help of the fingertips.
3. At 385 degrees F/ 195 degrees C, preheat your air fryer.
4. Place the zucchini tots in the air fryer basket and cook for 3 minutes from each side or until the zucchini tots are golden brown.
5. Serve.

Brussels Sprouts

Servings: 3
Cooking Time: 5 Minutes
Ingredients:
- 1 10-ounce package frozen brussels sprouts, thawed and halved
- 2 teaspoons olive oil
- salt and pepper

Directions:

The Ultimate Tower Air Fryer Cookbook

1. Toss the brussels sprouts and olive oil together.
2. Place them in the air fryer basket and season to taste with salt and pepper.
3. Cook at 360°F for approximately 5minutes, until the edges begin to brown.

Creole Seasoned Okra
Servings:4
Cooking Time: 25 Minutes
Ingredients:
- 1 teaspoon olive oil, plus more for spraying
- 12 ounces frozen sliced okra
- 1 to 2 teaspoons Creole seasoning

Directions:
1. Spray a fryer basket lightly with olive oil.
2. In a medium bowl, toss the frozen okra with 1 teaspoon of olive oil and the Creole seasoning.
3. Place the okra into the fryer basket. You may need to cook them in batches.
4. Air fry until the okra is browned and crispy, 20 to 25 minutes, making sure to shake the basket and lightly spray with olive oil every 5 minutes.

Creamy Corn Casserole
Servings:4
Cooking Time: 15 Minutes
Ingredients:
- Nonstick baking spray with flour
- 2 cups frozen yellow corn
- 3 tablespoons flour
- 1 egg, beaten
- ¼ cup milk
- ½ cup light cream
- ½ cup grated Swiss or Havarti cheese
- Pinch salt
- Freshly ground black pepper
- 2 tablespoons butter, cut in cubes

Directions:
1. Spray a 6-by-6-by-2-inch baking pan with nonstick spray.
2. In a medium bowl, combine the corn, flour, egg, milk, and light cream, and mix until combined. Stir in the cheese, salt, and pepper.
3. Pour this mixture into the prepared baking pan. Dot with the butter.
4. Bake for 15 minutes.

Famous Potato Au Gratin
Servings: 4
Cooking Time: 35 Minutes
Ingredients:
- 2 russet potatoes, sliced
- ½ cup grated Gruyère cheese
- 2 tbsp Parmesan cheese
- ½ cup half-and-half
- 2 eggs
- 1 tbsp flour
- 1 garlic clove minced
- Salt and pepper to taste
- 1 tsp smoked paprika
- 1 cup diced cooked ham
- 1 tbsp butter, melted
- 1 tbsp bread crumbs
- 1 tbsp cilantro, chopped

Directions:
1. Combine the half-and-half, eggs, flour, salt, garlic, pepper, and paprika in a bowl Toss in potatoes until all sides of potato slices are coated. Preheat air fryer at 375°F. Add half of the potato slices to a greased baking pan and pour half of the egg mixture. Top with ham and Gruyère cheese; then repeat the process with the remaining ingredients. Whisk the butter, Parmesan cheese, breadcrumbs, and cilantro in a bowl. Pour over casserole and cover with aluminum foil. Place baking pan in the fryer. Bake for 15 minutes. Uncover and cook for 5 more minutes. Let rest for 10 minutes before serving.

Chinese Cabbage With Bacon
Servings: 2
Cooking Time: 12 Minutes
Ingredients:
- 8 ounces Chinese cabbage, roughly chopped
- 2 ounces bacon, chopped
- 1 tablespoon sunflower oil
- ½ teaspoon onion powder
- ½ teaspoon salt

Directions:
1. In your air fryer, add the chopped bacon and cook at 400 degrees F/ 205 degrees C for 10 minutes. During cooking, stir from time to time.
2. Sprinkle the cooked bacon with salt and onion powder.
3. Then add Chinese cabbage and shake to mix well.
4. Cook for 2 minutes.
5. Before serving, add sunflower oil and stir.
6. Serve on plates.

Healthy Caprese Salad
Servings: 2
Cooking Time: 20 Minutes
Ingredients:
- 1 ball mozzarella cheese, sliced
- 16 grape tomatoes
- 2 tsp olive oil
- Salt and pepper to taste
- 1 tbsp balsamic vinegar
- 1 tsp mix of seeds
- 1 tbsp chopped basil

Directions:
1. Preheat air fryer at 350°F. Toss tomatoes with 1 tsp of olive oil and salt in a bowl. Place them in the frying basket and Air Fry for 15 minutes, shaking twice. Divide mozzarella slices between 2 serving plates, top with blistered tomatoes, and drizzle with balsamic vinegar and the remaining olive oil. Sprinkle with basil, black pepper and the mixed seeds and serve.

Panzanella Salad With Crispy Croutons

Servings: 4
Cooking Time: 3 Minutes
Ingredients:
- ½ French baguette, sliced in half lengthwise
- 2 large cloves garlic
- 2 large ripe tomatoes, divided
- 2 small Persian cucumbers, quartered and diced
- ¼ cup Kalamata olives
- 1 tablespoon chopped, fresh oregano or 1 teaspoon dried oregano
- ¼ cup chopped fresh basil
- ¼ cup chopped fresh parsley
- ½ cup sliced red onion
- 2 tablespoons red wine vinegar
- ¼ cup extra-virgin olive oil
- Salt and pepper, to taste

Directions:
1. Preheat the air fryer to 380°F.
2. Place the baguette into the air fryer and toast for 3 to 5 minutes or until lightly golden brown.
3. Remove the bread from air fryer and immediately rub 1 raw garlic clove firmly onto the inside portion of each piece of bread, scraping the garlic onto the bread.
4. Slice 1 of the tomatoes in half and rub the cut edge of one half of the tomato onto the toasted bread. Season the rubbed bread with sea salt to taste.
5. Cut the bread into cubes and place in a large bowl. Cube the remaining 1½ tomatoes and add to the bowl. Add the cucumbers, olives, oregano, basil, parsley, and onion; stir to mix. Drizzle the red wine vinegar into the bowl, and stir. Drizzle the olive oil over the top, stir, and adjust the seasonings with salt and pepper.
6. Serve immediately or allow to sit at room temperature up to 1 hour before serving.

Marinara Pepperoni Mushroom Pizza

Servings: 4
Cooking Time: 18 Minutes
Ingredients:
- 4 large portobello mushrooms, stems removed
- 4 teaspoons olive oil
- 1 cup marinara sauce
- 1 cup shredded Mozzarella cheese
- 10 slices sugar-free pepperoni

Directions:
1. Preheat the air fryer to 375°F (191°C).
2. Brush each mushroom cap with the olive oil, one teaspoon for each cap.
3. Put on a baking sheet and bake, stem-side down, for 8 minutes.
4. Take out of the air fryer and divide the marinara sauce, Mozzarella cheese and pepperoni evenly among the caps.
5. Air fry for another 10 minutes until browned.
6. Serve hot.

Breadcrumb Crusted Agnolotti

Servings: 6
Cooking Time: 14 Minutes
Ingredients:
- 1 cup flour
- Black pepper and salt
- 4 eggs, beaten
- 2 cups breadcrumbs
- Cooking spray

Directions:
1. Mix flour with black pepper and salt.
2. Dip pasta into the flour, then into the egg, and finally in the breadcrumbs.
3. Spray with oil and arrange in the preheated air fryer in an even layer.
4. Set its temperature to 400 degrees F/ 205 degrees C and cook for 14 minutes, turning once halfway through cooking.
5. Cook until nice and golden.
6. Serve with goat cheese.

Air Fried Bell Peppers With Onion

Servings: 3
Cooking Time: 15 Minutes
Ingredients:
- 6 bell pepper, sliced
- 1 tablespoon Italian seasoning
- 1 tablespoon olive oil
- 1 onion, sliced

Directions:
1. Add all the recipe ingredients into the suitable mixing bowl and toss well.
2. At 320 degrees F/ 160 degrees C, preheat your air fryer.
3. Transfer bell pepper and onion mixture into the air fryer basket and cook for almost 15 minutes.
4. Toss well and cook for almost 10 minutes more.
5. Serve and enjoy.

Pork Tenderloin Salad

Servings: 4
Cooking Time: 25 Minutes
Ingredients:
- Pork Tenderloin
- ½ teaspoon smoked paprika
- ¼ teaspoon salt
- ¼ teaspoon garlic powder
- ½ teaspoon onion powder
- ⅛ teaspoon ginger
- 1 teaspoon extra-light olive oil
- ¾ pound pork tenderloin
- Dressing
- 3 tablespoons extra-light olive oil
- 2 tablespoons red wine vinegar
- 2 tablespoons Dijon mustard
- 1 tablespoon honey
- Salad

- ¼ sweet red bell pepper
- 1 large Granny Smith apple
- 8 cups shredded Napa cabbage

Directions:
1. Mix the tenderloin seasonings together with oil and rub all over surface of meat.
2. Place pork tenderloin in the air fryer basket and cook at 390°F for 25minutes, until meat registers 130°F on a meat thermometer.
3. Allow meat to rest while preparing salad and dressing.
4. In a jar, shake all dressing ingredients together until well mixed.
5. Cut the bell pepper into slivers, then core, quarter, and slice the apple crosswise.
6. In a large bowl, toss together the cabbage, bell pepper, apple, and dressing.
7. Divide salad mixture among 4 plates.
8. Slice pork tenderloin into ½-inch slices and divide among the 4 salads.
9. Serve with sweet potato or other vegetable chips.

Cheese & Bacon Pasta Bake

Servings: 4
Cooking Time: 35 Minutes
Ingredients:
- ½ cup shredded sharp cheddar cheese
- ½ cup shredded mozzarella cheese
- 4 oz cooked bacon, crumbled
- 3 tbsp butter, divided
- 1 tbsp flour
- 1 tsp black pepper
- 2 oz crushed feta cheese
- ¼ cup heavy cream
- ½ lb cooked rotini
- ¼ cup bread crumbs

Directions:
1. Melt 2 tbsp of butter in a skillet over medium heat. Stir in flour until the sauce thickens. Stir in all cheeses, black pepper and heavy cream and cook for 2 minutes until creamy. Toss in rotini and bacon until well coated. Spoon rotini mixture into a greased cake pan.
2. Preheat air fryer at 370°F. Microwave the remaining butter in 10-seconds intervals until melted. Then stir in breadcrumbs. Scatter over pasta mixture. Place cake pan in the frying basket and Bake for 15 minutes. Let sit for 10 minutes before serving.

Provence French Fries

Servings: 4
Cooking Time: 25 Minutes
Ingredients:
- 2 russet potatoes
- 1 tbsp olive oil
- 1 tbsp herbs de Provence

Directions:
1. Preheat air fryer to 400°F. Slice the potatoes lengthwise into ½-inch thick strips. In a bowl, whisk the olive oil and herbs de Provence. Toss in the potatoes to coat. Arrange them in a single and Air Fry for 18-20 minutes, shaking once, until crispy. Serve warm.

Fried Pickles With Mayo Sauce

Servings: 2
Cooking Time: 10 Minutes
Ingredients:
- 1 egg, whisked
- 2 tablespoons buttermilk
- ½ cup fresh breadcrumbs
- ¼ cup Romano cheese, grated
- ½ teaspoon onion powder
- ½ teaspoon garlic powder
- 1 ½ cups dill pickle chips
- Mayo Sauce:
- ¼ cup mayonnaise
- ½ tablespoon mustard
- ½ teaspoon molasses
- 1 tablespoon ketchup
- ¼ teaspoon black pepper

Directions:
1. In a suitable shallow bowl, whisk the egg with buttermilk.
2. In another bowl, mix the breadcrumbs, cheese, onion powder, and garlic powder.
3. Dredge the pickle chips in the egg mixture, then, in the breadcrumb/cheese mixture.
4. Cook the mixture in the preheated air fryer at about 400 degrees F/ 205 degrees C for 5 minutes; shake the basket and cook for 5 minutes more.
5. Meanwhile, mix all the sauce ingredients until well combined. Serve the fried pickles with the mayo sauce for dipping.

Tamari Green Beans

Servings: 2
Cooking Time: 10 Minutes
Ingredients:
- 8 ounces green beans, trimmed
- 1 teaspoon sesame oil
- 1 tablespoon tamari

Directions:
1. Add all the recipe ingredients into the suitable mixing bowl and toss well.
2. Grease its air fryer basket with cooking spray.
3. Transfer green beans in air fryer basket and cook at almost 400 degrees F/ 205 degrees C for almost 10 minutes. Toss halfway through.
4. Serve and enjoy.

Home Fries

Servings: 4
Cooking Time: 20 Minutes
Ingredients:
- 3 pounds potatoes, cut into 1-inch cubes
- ½ teaspoon oil
- salt and pepper

Directions:
1. In a large bowl, mix the potatoes and oil thoroughly.
2. Cook at 390°F for 10minutes and shake the basket to redistribute potatoes.
3. Cook for an additional 10 minutes, until brown and crisp.
4. Season with salt and pepper to taste.

Southwest-style Corn Cobs

Servings: 6
Cooking Time: 15 Minutes
Ingredients:
- ½ cup sour cream
- 1 ½ teaspoons chili powder
- Juice and zest of 1 medium lime
- ¼ teaspoon salt
- 6 mini corn cobs
- ½ cup crumbled cotija cheese

Directions:
1. Preheat the air fryer to 350°F.
2. In a medium bowl, mix sour cream, chili powder, lime zest and juice, and salt.
3. Brush mixture all over corn cobs and place them in the air fryer basket. Cook 15 minutes until corn is tender.
4. Sprinkle with cotija and serve.

Chapter 10: Desserts And Sweets Recipes

Nutty Fudge Muffins

Servings: 10
Cooking Time: 10 Minutes
Ingredients:
- 1 package fudge brownie mix
- 1 egg
- 2 teaspoons water
- ¼ cup walnuts, chopped
- 1/3 cup vegetable oil

Directions:
1. Preheat the Air fryer to 300°F and grease 10 muffin tins lightly.
2. Mix brownie mix, egg, oil and water in a bowl.
3. Fold in the walnuts and pour the mixture in the muffin cups.
4. Transfer the muffin tins in the Air fryer basket and cook for about 10 minutes.
5. Dish out and serve immediately.

Fudgy Brownie Cake

Servings: 6
Cooking Time: 25-35 Minutes
Ingredients:
- 6½ tablespoons All-purpose flour
- ¼ cup plus 1 teaspoon Unsweetened cocoa powder
- ½ teaspoon Baking powder
- ¼ teaspoon Table salt
- 6½ tablespoons Butter, at room temperature
- 9½ tablespoons Granulated white sugar
- 1 egg plus 1 large egg white Large egg(s)
- ¾ teaspoon Vanilla extract
- Baking spray (see here)

Directions:
1. Preheat the air fryer to 325°F (or 330°F, if that's the closest setting).
2. Mix the flour, cocoa powder, baking powder, and salt in a small bowl until well combined.
3. Using an electric hand mixer at medium speed, beat the butter and sugar in a medium bowl until creamy and smooth, about 3 minutes, occasionally scraping down the inside of the bowl.
4. Beat in the egg(s) and the white or yolk (as necessary), as well as the vanilla, until smooth. Turn off the beaters and add the flour mixture. Beat at low speed until thick and smooth.
5. Use the baking spray to generously coat the inside of a 6-inch round cake pan for a small batch, a 7-inch round cake pan for a medium batch, or an 8-inch round cake pan for a large batch. Scrape and spread the batter into the pan, smoothing the batter out to an even layer.
6. Set the pan in the basket and air-fry for 25 minutes for a 6-inch layer, 30 minutes for a 7-inch layer, or 35 minutes for an 8-inch layer, or until the cake is set but soft to the touch. Start checking it at the 20-minute mark to know where you are.
7. Use hot pads or silicone baking mitts to transfer the cake pan to a wire rack. Cool for at least 1 hour or up to 4 hours. Using a nonstick-safe knife, slice the cake into wedges right in the pan and lift them out one by one.

Black Forest Pies

Servings: 6
Cooking Time: 15 Minutes
Ingredients:
- 3 tablespoons milk or dark chocolate chips
- 2 tablespoons thick, hot fudge sauce
- 2 tablespoons chopped dried cherries
- 1 (10-by-15-inch) sheet frozen puff pastry, thawed
- 1 egg white, beaten
- 2 tablespoons sugar
- ½ teaspoon cinnamon

Directions:
1. Preheat the air fryer to 350°F (177°C).
2. In a small bowl, combine the chocolate chips, fudge sauce, and dried cherries.
3. Roll out the puff pastry on a floured surface. Cut into 6 squares with a sharp knife.
4. Divide the chocolate chip mixture into the center of each puff pastry square. Fold the squares in half to make triangles. Firmly press the edges with the tines of a fork to seal.
5. Brush the triangles on all sides sparingly with the beaten egg white. Sprinkle the tops with sugar and cinnamon.
6. Put in the air fryer basket and bake for 15 minutes or until the triangles are golden brown. The filling will be hot, so cool for at least 20 minutes before serving.

Chocolate Rum Brownies

Servings: 6
Cooking Time: 30 Minutes + Cooling Time
Ingredients:
- ½ cup butter, melted
- 1 cup white sugar
- 1 tsp dark rum
- 2 eggs
- ½ cup flour
- 1/3 cup cocoa powder
- ¼ tsp baking powder
- Pinch of salt

Directions:
1. Preheat air fryer to 350°F. Whisk the melted butter, eggs, and dark rum in a mixing bowl until slightly fluffy and all ingredients are thoroughly combined. Place the flour, sugar, cocoa, salt, and baking powder in a separate bowl and stir to combine. Gradually pour the dry ingredients into the wet ingredients, stirring continuously until thoroughly blended and there are no lumps in the batter. Spoon the batter into a greased cake pan. Put the pan in the frying basket and Bake for 20 minutes until a toothpick comes out dry and clean. Let cool for several minutes. Cut and serve. Enjoy!

Vanilla Banana Puffs

Servings: 8
Cooking Time: 10 Min.
Ingredients:
- 4 ounces instant vanilla pudding
- 4 ounces cream cheese, softened
- 1 package (8-ounce) crescent dinner rolls, refrigerated
- 1 cup milk
- 2 bananas, sliced
- 1 egg, lightly beaten

Directions:
1. On a flat kitchen surface, plug your air fryer and turn it on.
2. Before cooking, heat your air fryer to 355 degrees F/ 180 degrees C for about 4 to 5 minutes.
3. Make 8 squares from the crescent dinner rolls.
4. Mix thoroughly the milk and pudding in a medium sized bowl. Then whisk the cream cheese in the mixture.
5. Divide the mixture onto the squares. Add the banana slices on the top.
6. Fold the rolls over and press the edges to seal the filling inside. Brush the whisked egg over each pastry puff.
7. Transfer to the air fryer basket.
8. Cook the banana puffs in the preheated air fryer for 10 minutes.
9. When the cooking time runs out, remove from the air fryer and serve warm.
10. Enjoy!

Fluffy Orange Cake

Servings: 6
Cooking Time: 30 Minutes
Ingredients:
- 1/3 cup cornmeal
- 1 ¼ cups flour
- ¾ cup white sugar
- 1 tsp baking soda
- ¼ cup safflower oil
- 1 ¼ cups orange juice
- 1 tsp orange zest
- ¼ cup powdered sugar

Directions:
1. Preheat air fryer to 340°F. Mix cornmeal, flour, sugar, baking soda, safflower oil, 1 cup of orange juice, and orange zest in a medium bowl. Mix until combined.
2. Pour the batter into a greased baking pan and set into the air fryer. Bake until a toothpick in the center of the cake comes out clean. Remove the cake and place it on a cooling rack. Use the toothpick to make 20 holes in the cake. Meanwhile, combine the rest of the juice with the powdered sugar in a small bowl. Drizzle the glaze over the hot cake and allow it to absorb. Leave to cool completely, then cut into pieces. Serve and enjoy!

Banana Chips With Chocolate Glaze

Servings: 2
Cooking Time: 20 Minutes
Ingredients:
- 2 banana, cut into slices
- 1/4 teaspoon lemon zest
- 1 tablespoon agave syrup
- 1 tablespoon cocoa powder
- 1 tablespoon coconut oil, melted

Directions:
1. Toss the bananas with the lemon zest and agave syrup. Transfer your bananas to the parchment-lined cooking basket.
2. Bake in the preheated Air Fryer at 370°F for 12 minutes, turning them over halfway through the cooking time.
3. In the meantime, melt the coconut oil in your microwave; add the cocoa powder and whisk to combine well.
4. Serve the baked banana chips. Enjoy!

Creamy Pudding

Servings: 6
Cooking Time: 25 Minutes
Ingredients:
- 2 cups fresh cream
- 6 egg yolks, whisked
- 6 tablespoons white sugar
- Zest of 1 orange

Directions:
1. Combine all ingredients in a bowl and whisk well.
2. Divide the mixture between 6 small ramekins.
3. Place the ramekins in your air fryer and cook at 340°F for 25 minutes.
4. Place in the fridge for 1 hour before serving.

Donuts With Cardamom

Servings: 4
Cooking Time: 6 Minutes
Ingredients:
- 1 teaspoon ground cardamom
- ½ teaspoon ground cinnamon
- ½ teaspoon baking powder
- ½ cup coconut flour
- 1 tablespoon Erythritol
- 1 egg, beaten
- 1 tablespoon butter, softened
- ¼ teaspoon salt
- Cooking spray

Directions:
1. Thoroughly mix up the Erythritol, ground cinnamon and ground cardamom in a suitable bowl.
2. In another bowl, mix up the coconut flour, baking powder, egg, salt, and butter. Knead the non-sticky dough.
3. Roll up the dough and use the donut cutter to form 4 donuts.
4. Coat every donut with the cardamom mixture, then place the donuts in a warm place to let it rest for 10 minutes.

5. Spray the cooking basket of your air fryer with cooking spray and transfer the donuts on it.
6. Cook the donuts at 355 degrees F/ 180 degrees C for 6 minutes or until they are golden brown.
7. Sprinkle the remaining cardamom mixture on the hot donuts.
8. Enjoy!

Thumbprint Sugar Cookies

Servings: 10
Cooking Time: 8 Minutes
Ingredients:
- 2½ tablespoons butter
- ⅓ cup cane sugar
- 1 teaspoon pure vanilla extract
- 1 large egg
- 1 cup all-purpose flour
- ½ teaspoon baking soda
- ¼ teaspoon salt
- 10 chocolate kisses

Directions:
1. Preheat the air fryer to 350°F.
2. In a large bowl, cream the butter with the sugar and vanilla. Whisk in the egg and set aside.
3. In a separate bowl, mix the flour, baking soda, and salt. Then gently mix the dry ingredients into the wet. Portion the dough into 10 balls; then press down on each with the bottom of a cup to create a flat cookie.
4. Liberally spray the metal trivet of an air fryer basket with olive oil mist.
5. Place the cookies in the air fryer basket on the trivet and cook for 8 minutes or until the tops begin to lightly brown.
6. Remove and immediately press the chocolate kisses into the tops of the cookies while still warm.
7. Let cool 5 minutes and then enjoy.

Brownies For Two

Servings:2
Cooking Time: 15 Minutes
Ingredients:
- ½ cup blanched finely ground almond flour
- 3 tablespoons granular erythritol
- 3 tablespoons unsweetened cocoa powder
- ½ teaspoon baking powder
- 1 teaspoon vanilla extract
- 2 large eggs, whisked
- 2 tablespoons salted butter, melted

Directions:
1. In a medium bowl, combine flour, erythritol, cocoa powder, and baking powder.
2. Add in vanilla, eggs, and butter, and stir until a thick batter forms.
3. Pour batter into two 4" ramekins greased with cooking spray and place ramekins into air fryer basket. Adjust the temperature to 325°F and set the timer for 15 minutes. Centers will be firm when done. Let ramekins cool 5 minutes before serving.

Pumpkin Almond Flour Muffins

Servings: 10
Cooking Time: 20 Minutes
Ingredients:
- 4 large eggs
- ½ cup pumpkin puree
- 1 tbsp. pumpkin pie spice
- 1 tbsp. baking powder, gluten-free
- ⅔ cup erythritol
- 1 tsp. vanilla
- ⅓ cup coconut oil, melted
- ½ cup almond flour
- ½ cup coconut flour
- ½ tsp sea salt

Directions:
1. Before cooking, heat your air fryer to 325 degrees F/ 160 degrees C.
2. Add pumpkin pie spice, erythritol, sea salt, almond flour, and coconut flour in a large bowl and stir until well combined.
3. Then combine the mixture with the whisked eggs, pumpkin puree, and coconut oil.
4. Divide the batter into the silicone muffin molds.
5. Cook in batches in your air fryer for 20 minutes.
6. Serve and enjoy!

Merengues

Servings: 6
Cooking Time: 65 Minutes
Ingredients:
- 2 egg whites
- 1 teaspoon lime zest, grated
- 1 teaspoon lime juice
- 4 tablespoons Erythritol

Directions:
1. Whisk the egg whites until soft peaks. Then add Erythritol and lime juice and whisk the egg whites until you get strong peaks. After this, add lime zest and carefully stir the egg white mixture. Preheat the air fryer to 275°F. Line the air fryer basket with baking paper. With the help of the spoon make the small merengues and put them in the air fryer in one layer. Cook the dessert for 65 minutes.

Apple-cinnamon Hand Pies

Servings:8
Cooking Time: 20 Minutes
Ingredients:
- 2 apples, cored and diced
- ¼ cup honey
- 1 teaspoon cinnamon
- 1 teaspoon vanilla extract
- ⅛ teaspoon nutmeg
- 2 teaspoons cornstarch
- 1 teaspoon water
- 4 frozen piecrusts, thawed if frozen hard
- Cooking oil

Directions:

1. Place a saucepan over medium-high heat. Add the apples, honey, cinnamon, vanilla, and nutmeg. Stir and cook for 2 to 3 minutes, until the apples are soft.
2. In a small bowl, mix the cornstarch and water. Add to the pan and stir. Cook for 30 seconds.
3. Cut each piecrust into two 4-inch circles. You should have 8 circles of crust total.
4. Lay the piecrusts on a flat work surface. Mound ⅓ cup of apple filling on the center of each.
5. Fold each piecrust over so that the top layer of crust is about an inch short of the bottom layer. (The edges should not meet.)
6. Using your fingers, tap along the edges of the top layer to seal. Use the back of a fork to press lines into the edges.
7. Place the hand pies in the air fryer. I do not recommend stacking the hand pies. They will stick together if stacked. You may need to prepare them in two batches. Cook for 10 minutes.
8. Allow the hand pies to cool fully before removing from the air fryer.

Banana Bread Cake

Servings: 6
Cooking Time: 18-22 Minutes
Ingredients:
- ¾ cup plus 2 tablespoons All-purpose flour
- ½ teaspoon Baking powder
- ¼ teaspoon Baking soda
- ¼ teaspoon Table salt
- 4 tablespoons (¼ cup/½ stick) Butter, at room temperature
- ½ cup Granulated white sugar
- 2 Small ripe bananas, peeled
- 5 tablespoons Pasteurized egg substitute, such as Egg Beaters
- ¼ cup Buttermilk
- ¾ teaspoon Vanilla extract
- Baking spray (see here)

Directions:
1. Preheat the air fryer to 325°F (or 330°F, if that's the closest setting).
2. Mix the flour, baking powder, baking soda, and salt in a small bowl until well combined.
3. Using an electric hand mixer at medium speed, beat the butter and sugar in a medium bowl until creamy and smooth, about 3 minutes, occasionally scraping down the inside of the bowl.
4. Beat in the bananas until smooth. Then beat in egg substitute or egg, buttermilk, and vanilla until uniform. (The batter may look curdled at this stage. The flour mixture will smooth it out.) Add the flour mixture and beat at low speed until smooth and creamy.
5. Use the baking spray to generously coat the inside of a 6-inch round cake pan for a small batch, a 7-inch round cake pan for a medium batch, or an 8-inch round cake pan for a large batch. Scrape and spread the batter into the pan, smoothing the batter out to an even layer.
6. Set the pan in the basket and air-fry for 18 minutes for a 6-inch layer, 20 minutes for a 7-inch layer, or 22 minutes for an 8-inch layer, or until the cake is well browned and set even if there's a little soft give right at the center. Start checking it at the 16-minute mark to know where you are.
7. Use hot pads or silicone baking mitts to transfer the cake pan to a wire rack. To unmold, set a cutting board over the baking pan and invert both the board and the pan. Lift the still-warm pan off the cake layer. Set the wire rack on top of that layer and invert all of it with the cutting board so that the cake layer is now right side up on the wire rack. Remove the cutting board and continue cooling the cake for at least 10 minutes or to room temperature, about 40 minutes, before slicing into wedges.

Keto Butter Balls

Servings: 4
Cooking Time: 10 Minutes
Ingredients:
- 1 tablespoon butter, softened1 tablespoon Erythritol
- ½ teaspoon ground cinnamon
- 1 tablespoon coconut flour
- 1 teaspoon coconut flakes
- Cooking spray

Directions:
1. Put the butter, Erythritol, ground cinnamon, coconut flour, and coconut flakes. Then stir the mixture with the help of the fork until homogenous. Make 4 balls. Preheat the air fryer to 375°F. Spray the air fryer basket with cooking spray and place the balls inside. Cook the dessert for 10 minutes.

Enticing Cappuccino Muffins

Servings: 12
Cooking Time: 20 Minutes
Ingredients:
- 4 eggs
- 2 cups almond flour
- ½ teaspoon vanilla
- 1 teaspoon espresso powder
- ½ cup sour cream
- 1 teaspoon cinnamon
- 2 teaspoons baking powder
- ¼ cup coconut flour
- ½ cup Swerve
- ¼ teaspoon salt

Directions:
1. Before cooking, heat your air fryer to 325 degrees F/ 160 degrees C.
2. In a blender, mix together vanilla, espresso powder, eggs, and sour cream until smooth.
3. Then blend again with cinnamon, coconut flour, baking powder, salt, and sweetener until smooth.
4. Divide the batter into the silicone muffin molds.
5. Cook in batches in the preheated air fryer for 20 minutes.
6. Serve and enjoy!

Vanilla Cookies

Servings: 12
Cooking Time: 15 Minutes
Ingredients:
- 2 cups almond flour 1 cup swerve
- ¼ cup butter, melted 1 egg
- 2 teaspoons ginger, grated
- ¼ teaspoon nutmeg, ground
- ¼ teaspoon cinnamon powder
- 1 teaspoon vanilla extract

Directions:
1. Thoroughly mix up all of the ingredients in a bowl.
2. Form small balls from the mixture with a spoon, then arrange them to the cooking pan lined with parchment patter and flatten them.
3. Cook the balls in your air fryer at 360 degrees F/ 180 degrees C for 15 minutes.
4. Before serving, cool them.

Coconut Cheese Muffins

Servings: 8
Cooking Time: 10 Minutes
Ingredients:
- 1 egg
- 1 teaspoon baking soda
- 1 cup almond flour
- 2 tablespoons coconut flakes
- 2 teaspoons erythritol
- 1 teaspoon vinegar
- 1 cup cream cheese
- Pinch of salt

Directions:
1. Beat cream cheese and egg in a suitable bowl until well combined.
2. Add almond flour, vinegar, baking soda, coconut flakes, sweetener, and salt and beat until well combined.
3. At 360 degrees F/ 180 degrees C, preheat your air fryer.
4. Pour batter into silicone muffin molds and place into the air fryer.
5. Cook for almost 10 minutes.
6. Serve and enjoy.

Brownies With White Chocolate

Servings: 6
Cooking Time: 30 Minutes
Ingredients:
- ¼ cup white chocolate chips
- ¼ cup muscovado sugar
- 1 egg
- 2 tbsp white sugar
- 2 tbsp canola oil
- 1 tsp vanilla
- ¼ cup cocoa powder
- 1/3 cup flour

Directions:
1. Preheat air fryer to 340°F. Beat the egg with muscovado sugar and white sugar in a bowl. Mix in the canola oil and vanilla. Next, stir in cocoa powder and flour until just combined. Gently fold in white chocolate chips. Spoon the batter into a lightly pan. Bake until the brownies are set when lightly touched on top, about 20 minutes. Let to cool completely before slicing.

Peanut Cookies

Servings: 4
Cooking Time: 5 Minutes
Ingredients:
- 4 tablespoons peanut butter
- 4 teaspoons Erythritol
- 1 egg, beaten
- ¼ teaspoon vanilla extract

Directions:
1. In the mixing bowl mix up peanut butter, Erythritol, egg, and vanilla extract. Stir the mixture with the help of the fork. Then make 4 cookies. Preheat the air fryer to 355°F. Place the cookies in the air fryer and cook them for 5 minutes.

Air-fried Beignets

Servings: 24
Cooking Time: 5 Minutes
Ingredients:
- ¾ cup lukewarm water (about 90°F)
- ¼ cup sugar
- 1 generous teaspoon active dry yeast (½ envelope)
- 3½ to 4 cups all-purpose flour
- ½ teaspoon salt
- 2 tablespoons unsalted butter, room temperature and cut into small pieces
- 1 egg, lightly beaten
- ½ cup evaporated milk
- ¼ cup melted butter
- 1 cup confectioners' sugar
- chocolate sauce or raspberry sauce, to dip

Directions:
1. Combine the lukewarm water, a pinch of the sugar and the yeast in a bowl and let it proof for 5 minutes. It should froth a little. If it doesn't froth, your yeast is not active and you should start again with new yeast.
2. Combine 3½ cups of the flour, salt, 2 tablespoons of butter and the remaining sugar in a large bowl, or in the bowl of a stand mixer. Add the egg, evaporated milk and yeast mixture to the bowl and mix with a wooden spoon (or the paddle attachment of the stand mixer) until the dough comes together in a sticky ball. Add a little more flour if necessary to get the dough to form. Transfer the dough to an oiled bowl, cover with plastic wrap or a clean kitchen towel and let it rise in a warm place for at least 2 hours or until it has doubled in size. Longer is better for flavor development and you can even let the dough rest in the refrigerator overnight (just remember to bring it to room temperature before proceeding with the recipe).
3. Roll the dough out to ½-inch thickness. Cut the dough into rectangular or diamond-shaped pieces. You can make the beignets any size you like, but this recipe will give you 24 (2-inch x 3-inch) rectangles.
4. Preheat the air fryer to 350°F.

5. Brush the beignets on both sides with some of the melted butter and air-fry in batches at 350°F for 5 minutes, turning them over halfway through if desired. (They will brown on all sides without being flipped, but flipping them will brown them more evenly.)
6. As soon as the beignets are finished, transfer them to a plate or baking sheet and dust with the confectioners' sugar. Serve warm with a chocolate or raspberry sauce.

Chocolate Bars

Servings: 4
Cooking Time: 30 Minutes
Ingredients:
- 2 tbsp chocolate toffee chips
- ¼ cup chopped pecans
- 2 tbsp raisins
- 1 tbsp dried blueberries
- 2 tbsp maple syrup
- ¼ cup light brown sugar
- 1/3 cup peanut butter
- 2 tbsp chocolate chips
- 2 tbsp butter, melted
- ½ tsp vanilla extract
- Salt to taste

Directions:
1. Preheat air fryer at 350°F. In a bowl, combine the pecans, maple syrup, sugar, peanut butter, toffee chips, raisins, dried blueberries, chocolate chips, butter, vanilla extract, and salt. Press mixture into a lightly greased cake pan and cover it with aluminum foil. Place cake pan in the frying basket and Bake for 15 minutes. Remove the foil and cook for 5 more minutes. Let cool completely for 15 minutes. Turn over on a place and cut into 6 bars. Enjoy!

Spiced Fruit Skewers

Servings: 4
Cooking Time: 15 Minutes
Ingredients:
- 2 peeled peaches, thickly sliced
- 3 plums, halved and pitted
- 3 peeled kiwi, quartered
- 1 tbsp honey
- ½ tsp ground cinnamon
- ¼ tsp ground allspice
- ¼ tsp cayenne pepper

Directions:
1. Preheat air fryer to 400°F. Combine the honey, cinnamon, allspice, and cayenne and set aside. Alternate fruits on 8 bamboo skewers, then brush the fruit with the honey mix. Lay the skewers in the air fryer and Air Fry for 3-5 minutes. Allow to chill for 5 minutes before serving.

Puff Pastry Apples

Servings: 4
Cooking Time: 10 Minutes
Ingredients:
- 3 Rome or Gala apples, peeled
- 2 tablespoons sugar
- 1 teaspoon all-purpose flour
- 1 teaspoon ground cinnamon
- ⅛ teaspoon ground ginger
- pinch ground nutmeg
- 1 sheet puff pastry
- 1 tablespoon butter, cut into 4 pieces
- 1 egg, beaten
- vegetable oil
- vanilla ice cream (optional)
- caramel sauce (optional)

Directions:
1. Remove the core from the apple by cutting the four sides off the apple around the core. Slice the pieces of apple into thin half-moons, about ¼-inch thick. Combine the sugar, flour, cinnamon, ginger, and nutmeg in a large bowl. Add the apples to the bowl and gently toss until the apples are evenly coated with the spice mixture. Set aside.
2. Cut the puff pastry sheet into a 12-inch by 12-inch square. Then quarter the sheet into four 6-inch squares. Save any remaining pastry for decorating the apples at the end.
3. Divide the spiced apples between the four puff pastry squares, stacking the apples in the center of each square and placing them flat on top of each other in a circle. Top the apples with a piece of the butter.
4. Brush the four edges of the pastry with the egg wash. Bring the four corners of the pastry together, wrapping them around the apple slices and pinching them together at the top in the style of a "beggars purse" appetizer. Fold the ends of the pastry corners down onto the apple making them look like leaves. Brush the entire apple with the egg wash.
5. Using the leftover dough, make leaves to decorate the apples. Cut out 8 leaf shapes, about 1½-inches long, "drawing" the leaf veins on the pastry leaves with a paring knife. Place 2 leaves on the top of each apple, tucking the ends of the leaves under the pastry in the center of the apples. Brush the top of the leaves with additional egg wash. Sprinkle the entire apple with some granulated sugar.
6. Preheat the air fryer to 350°F.
7. Spray or brush the inside of the air fryer basket with oil. Place the apples in the basket and air-fry for 6 minutes. Carefully turn the apples over – it's easiest to remove one apple, then flip the others over and finally return the last apple to the air fryer. Air-fry for an additional 4 minutes.
8. Serve the puff pastry apples warm with vanilla ice cream and drizzle with some caramel sauce.

Applesauce And Chocolate Brownies

Servings: 8
Cooking Time: 15 Minutes
Ingredients:
- ¼ cup unsweetened cocoa powder
- ¼ cup all-purpose flour
- ¼ teaspoon kosher salt
- ½ teaspoons baking powder
- 3 tablespoons unsalted butter, melted

- ½ cup granulated sugar
- 1 large egg
- 3 tablespoons unsweetened applesauce
- ¼ cup miniature semisweet chocolate chips
- Coarse sea salt, to taste

Directions:
1. Preheat the air fryer to 300°F (149°C).
2. In a large bowl, whisk together the cocoa powder, all-purpose flour, kosher salt, and baking powder.
3. In a separate large bowl, combine the butter, granulated sugar, egg, and applesauce, then use a spatula to fold in the cocoa powder mixture and the chocolate chips until well combined.
4. Spray a baking pan with nonstick cooking spray, then pour the mixture into the pan. Place the pan in the air fryer and bake for 15 minutes or until a toothpick comes out clean when inserted in the middle.
5. Remove the brownies from the air fryer, sprinkle some coarse sea salt on top, and allow to cool in the pan on a wire rack for 20 minutes before cutting and serving.

Banana-lemon Bars

Servings: 6
Cooking Time: 40 Minutes
Ingredients:
- ¾ cup flour
- 2 tbsp powdered sugar
- ¼ cup coconut oil, melted
- ½ cup brown sugar
- 1 tbsp lemon zest
- ¼ cup lemon juice
- ⅛ tsp salt
- ¼ cup mashed bananas
- 1¾ tsp cornstarch
- ¾ tsp baking powder

Directions:
1. Combine the flour, powdered sugar, and coconut oil in a bowl. Place in the fridge. Mix the brown sugar, lemon zest and juice, salt, bananas, cornstarch, and baking powder in a bowl. Stir well. Preheat air fryer to 350°F. Spray a baking pan with oil. Remove the crust from the fridge and press it into the bottom of the pan to form a crust. Place in the air fryer and Bake for 5 minutes or until firm. Remove and spread the lemon filling over the crust. Bake for 18-20 minutes or until the top is golden. Cool for an hour in the fridge. Once firm and cooled, cut into pieces and serve.

Oatmeal And Carrot Cookie Cups

Servings:16
Cooking Time: 8 Minutes
Ingredients:
- 3 tablespoons unsalted butter, at room temperature
- ¼ cup packed brown sugar
- 1 tablespoon honey
- 1 egg white
- ½ teaspoon vanilla extract
- ⅓ cup finely grated carrot
- ½ cup quick-cooking oatmeal
- ⅓ cup whole-wheat pastry flour
- ½ teaspoon baking soda
- ¼ cup dried cherries

Directions:
1. Preheat the air fryer to 350°F (177°C)
2. In a medium bowl, beat the butter, brown sugar, and honey until well combined.
3. Add the egg white, vanilla, and carrot. Beat to combine.
4. Stir in the oatmeal, pastry flour, and baking soda.
5. Stir in the dried cherries.
6. Double up 32 mini muffin foil cups to make 16 cups. Fill each with about 4 teaspoons of dough. Bake the cookie cups, 8 at a time, for 8 minutes, or until light golden brown and just set. Serve warm.

Cauliflower Rice Plum Pudding

Servings: 4
Cooking Time: 25 Minutes
Ingredients:
- 1 ½ cups cauliflower rice
- 2 cups coconut milk
- 3 tablespoons stevia
- 2 tablespoons ghee, melted
- 4 plums, pitted and chopped

Directions:
1. In a suitable bowl, mix all the recipe ingredients, toss, divide into ramekins, put them in the air fryer, and cook at almost 340 degrees F/ 170 degrees C for 25 minutes.
2. Cool down and serve.

Cinnamon And Pecan Pie

Servings:4
Cooking Time: 25 Minutes
Ingredients:
- 1 pie dough
- ½ teaspoons cinnamon
- ¾ teaspoon vanilla extract
- 2 eggs
- ¾ cup maple syrup
- ⅛ teaspoon nutmeg
- 3 tablespoons melted butter, divided
- 2 tablespoons sugar
- ½ cup chopped pecans

Directions:
1. Preheat the air fryer to 370°F (188°C).
2. In a small bowl, coat the pecans in 1 tablespoon of melted butter.
3. Transfer the pecans to the air fryer and air fry for about 10 minutes.
4. Put the pie dough in a greased pie pan and add the pecans on top.
5. In a bowl, mix the rest of the ingredients. Pour this over the pecans.
6. Put the pan in the air fryer and bake for 25 minutes.
7. Serve immediately.

Recipes Index

A

Air Fried Bell Peppers With Onion	93
Air Fried Calamari	39
Air Fried Pork With Fennel	29
Air Fried Pot Stickers	21
Air Fry Bacon	31
Air-fried Beignets	101
Almond Topped Trout	41
Almond-crusted Fish	37
Antipasto-stuffed Cherry Tomatoes	30
Apple-cinnamon Hand Pies	99
Apple-cinnamon-walnut Muffins	13
Applesauce And Chocolate Brownies	102
Apricot-cheese Mini Pies	13
Asparagus, Mushroom And Cheese Soufflés	79
Autenthic Greek Fish Pitas	42
Avocado Buttered Flank Steak	71
Avocado Egg Rolls	30
Avocado Quesadillas	19
Awesome Everything Bagels	13
Awesome Mushroom Tots	90

B

Bacon Puff Pastry Pinwheels	15
Bacon-wrapped Goat Cheese Poppers	26
Bacon-wrapped Jalapeño Poppers	25
Bacon-wrapped Onion Rings	23
Baked Eggs With Bacon-tomato Sauce	15
Baked Ricotta	22
Balsamic Beef & Veggie Skewers	66
Balsamic London Broil	72
Balsamic Stuffed Mushrooms	85
Baltimore Crab Cakes	44
Banana Bread Cake	100
Banana Chips With Chocolate Glaze	98
Banana-lemon Bars	103
Banana-pecan French Toast	11
Banana-strawberry Cakecups	17
Bang Bang Shrimp	35
Basil Crab Cakes With Fresh Salad	45
Basmati Risotto	86
Bbq Cocktail Sausage	23
Bean Burritos With Cheddar Cheese	38
Beef Brazilian Empanadas	72
Beef Cheeseburger Egg Rolls	64
Beef Stuffed Bell Pepper	84
Beef Stuffed Bell Peppers	84
Best Damn Pork Chops	72
Better-than-chinese-take-out Sesame Beef	68
Betty's Baked Chicken	54
Black Forest Pies	97
Blackberry Bbq Glazed Country-style Ribs	66

Blueberry Pannenkoek (dutch Pancake)	16
Breadcrumb Crusted Agnolotti	93
Broccoli With Paprika	88
Brownies For Two	99
Brownies With White Chocolate	101
Brussels Sprouts	91
Buffalo Cauliflower Snacks	31
Buffalo Chicken Meatballs	59
Buffalo Egg Rolls	47
Buffalo French Fries	29
Buttery Scallops	14

C

Cajun Breakfast Potatoes	11
Cajun Chicken Drumsticks	57
Cajun Fish Cakes	44
Cajun Lobster Tails	36
Caramelized Brussels Sprout	77
Carne Asada Tacos	75
Catfish Fillets With Tortilla Chips	43
Cauliflower Fried Rice	86
Cauliflower Rice Plum Pudding	103
Cauliflower Rice–stuffed Peppers	79
Cauliflower Steaks Gratin	78
Cauliflower Wings With Buffalo Sauce	30
Cheddar Chicken Stuffed Mushrooms	47
Cheddar Tater Tot With Sausage	15
Cheese & Bacon Pasta Bake	94
Cheese Broccoli With Basil	87
Cheese Ground Pork	75
Cheese Ravioli	79
Cheeseburger Sliders With Pickle Sauce	65
Cheesy Cauliflower Tart	88
Cheesy Cauliflower Tots	86
Cheesy Green Dip	28
Cheesy Jalapeño Poppers	24
Cheesy Tortellini Bites	24
Chicago-style Turkey Meatballs	56
Chicken Breast Burgers	47
Chicken Burgers With Blue Cheese Sauce	60
Chicken Burgers With Ham And Cheese	50
Chicken Cordon Bleu	51
Chicken Pesto Pizzas	48
Chicken Saltimbocca Sandwiches	11
Chicken Tenderloins With Parmesan Cheese	49
Chili Fingerling Potatoes	85
Chili Tofu & Quinoa Bowls	77
Chili-lime Shrimp	34
Chili-oiled Brussels Sprouts	89
Chinese Cabbage With Bacon	92
Chinese Firecracker Shrimp	36
Chinese-style Potstickers	22
Chipotle Drumsticks	50

Chive Potato Pierogi 82
Chives Meatballs 31
Chocolate Bars 102
Chocolate Rum Brownies 97
Chorizo Sausage & Cheese Balls 14
Cilantro Sea Bass 34
Cinnamon And Pecan Pie 103
Cinnamon Rolls 17
Citrusy Brussels Sprouts 89
Classic Chicken Wings 29
Classic Cinnamon Rolls 11
Classic Salisbury Steak Burgers 74
Coconut Cheese Muffins 101
Coconut Shrimp 40
Coriander Cod And Green Beans 35
Corn With Coriander And Parmesan Cheese 28
Cornmeal Shrimp Po'boy 36
Country Shrimp "boil" 45
Crab Cakes On A Budget 40
Crab-stuffed Mushrooms 23
Cranberry Beignets 12
Cream Cheese Danish 17
Creamy And Cheesy Spinach 90
Creamy Cinnamon Rolls 15
Creamy Corn Casserole 92
Creamy Pudding 98
Creole Seasoned Okra 92
Crispy Bacon Strips 28
Crispy Cordon Bleu 55
Crispy Fish Sticks 18
Crispy Fish Tacos 42
Crispy Old Bay Chicken Wings 24
Crispy Tofu With Soy Sauce 84
Crunchy Spicy Chickpeas 24
Crunchy Zucchini Fries With Parmesan 26
Crustless Spinach And Cheese Frittata 81

D

Daadi Chicken Salad 58
Delicious Grouper Filets 40
Delicious Pork Shoulder With Molasses Sauce 67
Deviled Eggs With Ricotta 27
Donuts With Cardamom 98

E

Easy Crispy Prawns 27
Easy Tex-mex Chimichangas 66
Easy Turkey Meatballs 50
Easy Zucchini Lasagna Roll-ups 78
Egg & Bacon Pockets 17
Egg & Bacon Toasts 17
Enticing Cappuccino Muffins 100

F

Family Chicken Fingers 59
Famous Potato Au Gratin 92
Fiesta Chicken Plate 54
Fish-in-chips 43

Five Spice Red Snapper With Green Onions And Orange Salsa 44
Flank Steaks With Capers 63
Flavor Moroccan Harissa Shrimp 41
Flavorful Chicken With Bacon 53
Flavorful Spiced Chicken Pieces 57
Flavorsome Onion And Sausage Balls 65
Fluffy Orange Cake 98
French Grouper Nicoise 34
French Mustard Chicken Thighs 55
French-style Steak Salad 73
Fried Catfish Fillets 42
Fried Cheese Ravioli With Marinara Sauce 31
Fried Green Tomatoes With Sriracha Mayo 87
Fried Green Tomatoes 89
Fried Pickles With Mayo Sauce 94
Fried Spam 68
Fudgy Brownie Cake 97

G

Garlic Asparagus With Provolone 88
Garlic Edamame 27
Garlic Lamb Rack 74
Garlic Mushroom Bites 21
Garlic Okra Chips 80
Garlic Parmesan Kale Chips 32
Garlic Salmon Patties 38
Garlic-lemon Scallops 39
Garlic-roasted Chicken With Creamer Potatoes 52
General Tso's Cauliflower 78
Ginger Turmeric Chicken Thighs 54
Glazed Chicken Thighs 56
Gluten-free Nutty Chicken Fingers 52
Gorgonzola Mushrooms With Horseradish Mayo 85
Greek Street Tacos 32
Greek-style Pork Stuffed Jalapeño Poppers 69
Green Beans 86
Green Onion Pancakes 19
Grilled Cheese Sandwich Deluxe 30
Grilled Chicken Legs With Coconut Cream 55

H

Halibut Soy Treat With Rice 35
Ham And Cheese Stuffed Chicken Burgers 52
Healthy Caprese Salad 92
Healthy Chicken With Veggies 50
Herb-buttermilk Chicken Breast 49
Herbs Chicken Drumsticks With Tamari Sauce 54
Home Fries 94
Homemade Chicken Sliders 57
Homemade Steak 73
Home-style Cinnamon Rolls 81
Home-style Taro Chips 22
Honey Pecan Shrimp 38
Honey-mustard Chicken Wings 24
Honey-sriracha Pork Ribs 65
Horseradish Mustard Pork Chops 69
Horseradish-crusted Salmon Fillets 34

Hungarian Pork Burgers 72

I

Israeli Chicken Schnitzel 53
Italian Stuffed Bell Peppers 81

J

Jalapeño Cheese Balls 26
Jerk Chicken Kebabs 51
Jerk Turkey Meatballs 59

K

Kale And Beef Omelet 64
Kale And Brussels Sprouts 90
Keto Butter Balls 100
Kid´s Flounder Fingers 37
King Prawns Al Ajillo 38
Korean-style Fried Calamari 41

L

Lemon Herb Whole Cornish Hen 52
Lemon Jumbo Scallops 43
Lollipop Lamb Chops 70

M

Maewoon Chicken Legs 48
Maple Balsamic Glazed Salmon 45
Maple'n Soy Marinated Beef 73
Marinara Pepperoni Mushroom Pizza 93
Marinated Beef And Vegetable Stir Fry 69
Marinated Flank Steak 70
Marinated Pork Tenderloin 71
Marjoram Butter Chicken 47
Mashed Potato Taquitos With Hot Sauce 13
Meat Loaves 70
Meatloaf With Tangy Tomato Glaze 65
Mediterranean Fried Chicken 55
Merengues 99
Mexican-style Roasted Corn 89
Mini Meatloaves With Pancetta 71
Mojo Sea Bass 39
Mozzarella-stuffed Meatloaf 62
Mumbai Chicken Nuggets 58
Mushroom And Asparagus Frittata 19
Mustard Pork Tenderloin With Ground Walnuts ... 63

N

Nacho Chicken Fries 53
Nutty Fudge Muffins 97

O

Oatmeal And Carrot Cookie Cups 103
Oyster Shrimp With Fried Rice 36

P

Panko-breaded Onion Rings 22
Panzanella Salad With Crispy Croutons 93

Paprika Chicken Drumettes 57
Paprika Pork Chops 73
Parmesan Breaded Zucchini Chips 27
Parmesan Cabbage Chips 22
Parmesan Chicken Fingers 56
Parmesan Sausage Meatballs 67
Parsley Egg Scramble With Cottage Cheese 12
Pasta Shrimp 37
Peanut Cookies 101
Pecan-crusted Tilapia 43
Pepperoni And Bell Pepper Pockets 75
Pepperoni Pockets 70
Peppery Tilapia Roulade 34
Pesto Bruschetta 29
Pizza Eggplant Rounds 77
Pizza Margherita With Spinach 77
Plantain Chips 21
Polenta 91
Polish Beef Sausage With Worcestershire Sauce ... 72
Popcorn Chicken Tenders With Vegetables 49
Pork & Beef Egg Rolls 63
Pork And Pinto Bean Gorditas 62
Pork Chops 73
Pork Sausage Bacon Rolls 64
Pork Tenderloin Salad 93
Potato And Broccoli With Tofu Scramble 88
Potato Skin Bites 28
Powerful Jackfruit Fritters 80
Provence French Fries 94
Puff Pastry Apples 102
Pumpkin Almond Flour Muffins 99

Q

Quick Air Fried Potatoes 91
Rice And Meatball Stuffed Bell Peppers 62
Roast Beef With Herbs 66
Roast Beef 71
Roasted Green Beans 81
Roasted Lemony Broccoli 84
Roasted Nut Mixture 23
Roasted Pork Tenderloin 63
Roasted Red Salsa 25
Roasted Vegetable, Brown Rice
And Black Bean Burrito 81
Roasted Yellow Squash And Onions 90
Root Vegetable Crisps 21
Rosemary Chicken With Sweet Potatoes 59
Rosemary Partridge 48
Rumaki 27
Rutabaga Fries 85

S

Sage Pork With Potatoes 71
Salmon And Brown Rice Frittata 12
Salmon On Bed Of Fennel And Carrot 37
Saltine Wax Beans 84
Savory Eggplant Fries 31
Seasoned Chicken Thighs With Italian Herbs ... 54

Shakshuka-style Pepper Cups	12
Shrimp Al Pesto	38
Simple & Delicious Chicken Wings	51
Simple Green Bake	85
Simple Grilled Chicken	49
Simple Salmon	41
Skewered Corn In Air Fryer	80
Smashed Fried Baby Potatoes	88
Smoked Fried Tofu	14
Snapper Fillets With Thai Sauce	35
Snapper Scampi	44
Snow Crab Legs	39
Soufflé	14
Southwest Cornbread	18
Southwestern Prawns With Asparagus	45
Southwest-style Corn Cobs	95
Spaghetti Squash And Kale Fritters With Pomodoro Sauce	82
Speedy Shrimp Paella	40
Spiced Fruit Skewers	102
Spiced Rib Eye Steak	67
Spicy Chickpeas With Paprika	29
Spicy Hoisin Bbq Pork Chops	69
Spicy Turkey Meatballs	29
Spinach And Feta Stuffed Chicken Breasts	48
Stevia Cod	35
Strawberry Pastry	18
String Bean Fries	25
Stuffed Avocados	91
Stuffed Cabbage Rolls	74
Stuffed Mushrooms With Bacon	23
Stuffed Mushrooms	80
Sweet Marinated Chicken Wings	51
Sweet Potato & Mushroom Hash	12
Sweet Potato Curly Fries	86
Sweet-hot Pepperoni Pizza	16

T

Tamari Green Beans	94
Tamari-seasoned Pork Strips	64
Tandoori Chicken	56
Tender Country Ribs	67
The Ultimate Chicken Bulgogi	58
Thumbprint Sugar Cookies	99
Thyme Lentil Patties	79
Tomato & Halloumi Bruschetta	26
Tomato Salad	90
Tonkatsu	74
Tortilla Chips	21
Trimmed Mackerel With Spring Onions	41
Tropical Salsa	77
Truffle Vegetable Croquettes	87
Turkey And Cranberry Quesadillas	49
Turkey Stuffed Bell Peppers	58
Turmeric Tofu Cubes	89

V

Vanilla Banana Puffs	98
Vanilla Cookies	101
Vegan Buddha Bowls(2)	78
Vegetable Fried Rice	91
Vegetarian Eggplant "pizzas"	80
Veggie Chips	25
Veggie Salmon Nachos	25
Very Easy Lime-garlic Shrimps	34
Viking Toast	16

W

Windsor´s Chicken Salad	56

Y

Yummy Salmon Burgers With Salsa Rosa	39

Z

Zesty Garlic Scallops	37
Zesty Mahi Mahi	42
Zucchini Tots With Mozzarella	91

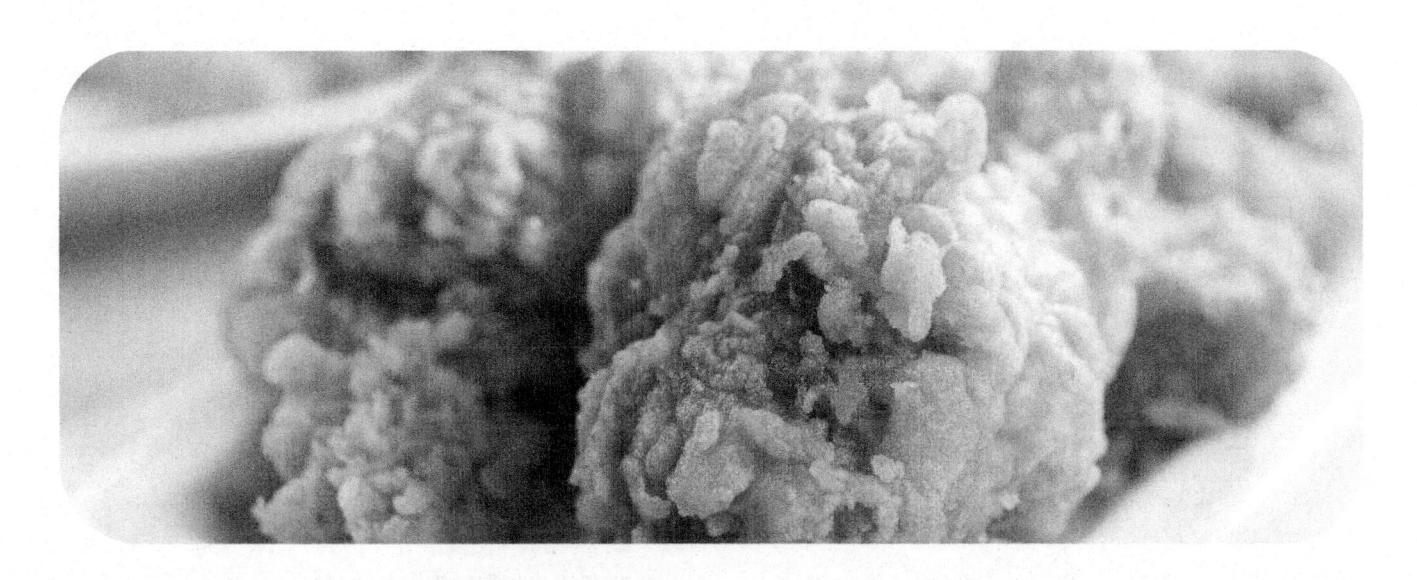

Printed in Great Britain
by Amazon